Seven Plays of Mystery & Suspense

with Writing Manual

Sylvia Z. Brodkin   Elizabeth J. Pearson

Globe Book Company
New York   Chicago   Cleveland

SYLVIA Z. BRODKIN received her B.A. from Brooklyn College and her M.A. from New York University. Ms. Brodkin served for fifteen years as Head of the English Department of the West Hempstead school system (Long Island, New York), where she supervised the English, reading, speech and drama programs in the middle and senior high schools. As a supervisor and teacher of teachers, she has formulated curriculum in the study of literature and in written and oral English, grades 7 through 12, and has contributed monographs on reading skills and on writing about literature. With Elizabeth Pearson, Ms. Brodkin is co-author of Globe's *Modern American Essays* and *Native Voices*.

ELIZABETH J. PEARSON holds a B.A. from Barnard College and an M.A. from New York University. Ms. Pearson has taught high school English for twenty-five years. She initiated a creative writing course at West Hempstead (New York) High School and, in conjunction with this course, served for many years as faculty advisor to that school's literary magazine. Ms. Pearson has co-authored five anthologies for high school use and has contributed chapters to standard high school texts.

Project Editor: Howard N. Portnoy
Illustrations: Susan Fischer and Peter Friedrich
Cover Design: Susan Fischer
Editorial, Design and Production Assistance: Allen Wayne Communications, Inc.

Acknowledgments for works reprinted herein appear on page iv.

ISBN: 0-87065-318-0

PRINTED IN THE UNITED STATES OF AMERICA

0 9 8 7 6 5 4

Contents

Acknowledgments

Introduction

EVERYONE THRILLS to stories of life-and-death struggles, to tales of the supernatural, to fearful glimpses into the unknown. From ghost stories whispered around a campfire to horror movies like "Frankenstein" and "Dracula," the appeal is the same. In the past, radio serials with provocative titles like *Escape*, *Suspense*, and *The Witch's Tale* helped satisfy this appetite for adventure. Later, TV presented its own science fiction, fantasy and horror in shows like *Alfred Hitchcock Presents* and Rod Serling's *The Twilight Zone*. And always, there are stage plays, both one-acters and full-length dramas, that focus on suspense.

The plays in this book include four one-act stage plays, two longer TV plays and one full-length drama. They were all chosen for their sense of mystery, adventure or horror. In subject, they range from the quiet investigation of a strange death to desperate struggles for survival and fearful encounters with a supernatural power. In style, they share one vital ingredient—suspense.

How to Read a Play

Everyone enjoys seeing exciting plays. But reading them can be just as pleasurable. All it requires is the active use of your imagination. Like a novel, short story or narrative poem, a play has a tale to tell, but its story is not so much *told* as *shown*. Learn to visualize and you have learned how to read a play.

Imagine people sitting in a theater blindfolded. Think how much they would miss! They would never see the stage settings, nor would they see the actors. The costumes, the gestures, the expressions on actors' faces, any important pantomime—all would be lost.

Don't be blindfolded when you read these plays. Keep your eyes and ears open to all that is presented. Even when you read silently you can train yourself to see and hear in your imagination. These are the things an alert audience looks for.

1. STAGE SET: The curtain goes up and you have a stage set before you. Probably it is the interior of a room. It may be carefully furnished, with an emphasis on realistic detail, or it may be sparsely furnished, more suggestive than explicit. Whatever its style, you look at this stage set and you register impressions, much as you do when you visit any place for the first time. From these impressions you draw certain conclusions about the kind of people who live in this room or the kind of action that might take place there.

"Trifles" opens with the following stage directions:

> The scene is the kitchen in the farmhouse of John Wright, a gloomy kitchen, abandoned without having been put in order—the walls covered with a faded wall paper. . . . Running along the Left wall from the shed door is an old iron sink and sink shelf, in which is set a hand pump and an uncurtained window. Near the window is an old wooden rocker. Centerstage is an unpainted wooden kitchen table with straight chairs on either side.

At the very beginning you are presented with a hard-working, practical, cheerless approach to living. You might guess that the people who use this kitchen have no time for lightness and laughter.

Now look at the stage set for "The Monkey's Paw." In part, it reads:

> In the Center a round table. Against the Upstage wall, an old-fashioned piano. A comfortable armchair each side of the fireplace. On the mantelpiece a clock, old china figures, etc. An air of comfort pervades the room.

Here are people who enjoy music, who like their comfort, and who decorate their mantel with pretty things.

These stage sets do more than introduce characters. They also arouse definite feelings in the audience, establishing in this way the dominant mood of the play. Note how the descriptive details at the beginning of "Heat Lightning" arouse uneasiness and foreboding:

> *The drab interior of a bus station along a deserted highway somewhere in the midwest. . . . The sound of heavy RAIN can be heard outside. LIGHTNING flashes outside followed by large bursts of THUNDER. With each flash of lightning the light in the room dims almost to the point of going out, but somehow feebly struggles back to its full strength.*

It is easier, of course, to respond to a stage set in the theater than to one on the printed page. With practice, however, you can visualize what the author has in mind. Don't let the stage directions confuse you. Simply remember that these directions are always given from the actor's right and left, not the audience's. Here is the stage with its various areas indicated.

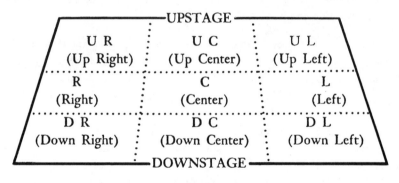

UPSTAGE		
U R (Up Right)	U C (Up Center)	U L (Up Left)
R (Right)	C (Center)	L (Left)
D R (Down Right)	D C (Down Center)	D L (Down Left)
DOWNSTAGE		

AUDIENCE

2. EXPOSITION AND PANTOMIME: A play places special demands on the audience. In the first few minutes, a group of characters is presented in a specific setting and situation. Questions occur immediately. Who are these people? Where are they? What is their relationship to one another? What are the problems they seem to be struggling with? How did they get these problems? What do they plan to do about them?

Generally, these questions are answered by the initial dialogue and action of the play. This opening dialogue is called *exposition*. The audience must be particularly alert at this time or it will miss some of the answers. Reading exposition is a little bit like arriving late at a party. Some of the guests are strangers to you and the conversation is already in full swing. It will take several minutes of looking and listening before you can orient yourself. But meanwhile the party doesn't stop; you must catch up on the past while you keep up with the present. Like the party, the exposition is never static. The playwright raises new questions while he is answering old ones. He also reveals characters and advances plot.

Read the beginning of each play carefully. With practice you will come to recognize the exposition and to appreciate the playwright's skill in handling it.

Sometimes the play begins with an extended bit of wordless action called *pantomime*. Pantomime is particularly effective for establishing mood. Notice how the beginning of "Heat Lightning" plunges the audience into the midst of violent action. No dialogue is needed.

> *The door up Center suddenly bursts open and a Girl of about twenty-three rushes into the room. She is sobbing and out of breath. She throws the bolt into place and turns slowly....The Girl's clothes are wet and muddy. Her hair is disheveled.*

Once the characters speak, the exposition of the play begins. "The Monkey's Paw" provides an excellent example of exposition in the initial dialogue. Look at this exposition to see how skillfully the playwright presents a warm family relationship, emphasizes an isolated setting and reveals details about the mortgage on the house and the nature of the son's work.

3. CHARACTERS: Your first impression of the characters in a play often comes from what you *see*, not what you *hear*. The clothes a character wears or the way he or she walks may tell you something important before even a single word is spoken. Read the description of Van Helsing given at his entrance in "Dracula."

> *Maid shows in Abraham Van Helsing, who enters briskly. Man of medium height, in his early fifties, with clean-shaven, astute face, shaggy gray eyebrows and a mass of gray hair which is brushed backward showing a high forehead. Dark, piercing eyes set far apart; nervous, alert manner; an air of resolution, clearly a man of resourceful action.*

Van Helsing soon engages in a conversation with Dr. Seward, but you do not have to wait for this conversation to come to certain conclusions about Van Helsing. What he says and how he says it reinforce the impression made by his appearance.

As the play progresses, the characters interact with one another, each playing a part in the unfolding story. A character may represent a particular quality, attitude or approach to life. Sometimes the key to such a character comes in a single speech; sometimes one character is defined through contrast to another. In "I Shot an Arrow," for example, the values Donlin expresses through his actions are in direct contrast to those of Corey.

An excellent way to understand a character is to concentrate on his or her needs and goals. In "The Dogs of War," a young wife fears that she has failed her husband. What is uppermost in her mind when she confronts her husband's deadly enemy? What is of major concern to the Nun who observes the interaction of these three characters? Answering questions like these will help to explain why a character behaves in a given way.

To repeat, you can appreciate the characters more fully if you are alert to the speeches that define them, the contrasts that help to present them more clearly and the goals and needs that make their actions understandable.

Sometimes an important character never appears on stage at all, but, rather, is known only through the other characters and their conversations. In "Trifles," for example, the audience never sees Mr. or Mrs. Wright, the two characters who hold the answer to the mystery of the play. They are a constant presence, however, through the dialogue of the other characters.

The most important character in any play becomes the focus of the audience's attention. It is this person's struggle and conflict that give movement to the plot. This person is called the *protagonist*. The protagonist may be opposed by another character, an *antagonist*, or by forces that go beyond a single individual. The protagonist's behavior is most important in the development of the plot. His or her actions determine the outcome of the play.

4. PLOT. Just as the dialogue in a play is not random conversation, neither is the plot a random sequence of events. In a one-act play in particular, the plot is carefully structured: a conflict is introduced, complication is added to complication until the climax is reached and then, with the resolution of the conflict, the play ends.

It is the conflict that motivates all action in the play. There are many types of conflict: between two people, within an individual, or between an individual and some force of nature or society. A play may emphasize an inner conflict between a principle and a material goal. Often there are both outer and inner conflicts that are interrelated. In "Dracula," for example, Lucy's inner struggle against the power of evil coincides with the outer conflict between Van Helsing and the Count. The resolution of this inner conflict shortly precedes the final resolution of the play.

When you read the plays in this book, keep conflict in mind. Ask yourself certain questions as the action unfolds. What are the characters struggling against? What are they struggling for? Is the protagonist fighting for a material goal, for an ideal, or for life itself?

The conflict builds through complication. The tension mounts as characters take action to solve their problems and succeed only in further entangling themselves. Inevitably, a point of crisis is reached. This is the *climax*, the turning point of the play. Here the protagonist faces a crucial choice, makes a decision, takes decisive action and pushes the play onward to its conclusion. It is at this point of crisis that the ending of the play is determined; once the climax is passed, the play can end in only one way. In a short drama the plot rushes to its conclusion after the climax. There is no slow unwinding or quiet recapitulation at the end. Instead, the effect is often sudden and stunning.

See if you can find the climax in each of the plays that you read in this book. Look for the choice that the protagonist faces and the point at which he or she makes a decision. In some cases this will be easy; in others, more difficult. In "Heat Lightning," the climax is evident: a frightened girl, facing two strangers, decides which one is a potential enemy and which one is a friend. The crisis is less clear, perhaps, in "The Dogs of War," and yet here too a young girl makes a fateful decision. Your ability to identify the protagonist and to recognize a moment of crisis will enhance your appreciation not only of these plays but of all drama.

About the Plays in This Book

The plays in this book are exciting human dramas, effective to act out and interesting to read. They are about men and women in crucial moments of their lives, being tested, making vital choices and conveying, through their actions and their fates, certain basic ideas about life and about people.

Although they vary in theme, the plays are alike in theatrical vitality. Each has a mystery to present, whether it is an unsolved murder or a supernatural menace. Each moves suspensefully to a thrilling climax.

Careful study of these plays can lead to a deeper understanding of drama and, in turn, of life. But it is an understanding achieved through theatrical experience. First and foremost, the plays are to be read aloud, acted out and enjoyed.

Seven Plays of Mystery & Suspense

Heat Lightning

Robert F. Carroll

HEAT LIGHTNING is a melodrama with all the ingredients of a good thriller: a frightened young woman running from a killer, a lonely spot, a dark and stormy night. The play opens on a shrill note of terror which doesn't let up until the curtain falls. As you read, let your imagination bring the play to life in the theater of your mind. That way you will see the dimly-lit bus station, hear the storm outside and glimpse, through a dark window, the brilliant flashes of lightning.

Vocabulary Preview

DRAB (DRAB) dull; cheerless
   It was a *drab* day, without a single ray of sunlight.
DISCARDED (dis-KARD-ed) cast aside; rejected
   On the street lay a *discarded* envelope, thrown carelessly aside.
FEEBLY (FEEB-lee) weakly
   Feebly the sick man motioned for the nurse to approach.
DISHEVELED (di-SHEV-uld) hanging in loose disorder
   After the storm, her clothes were drenched and her hair was *disheveled*.
VICIOUSLY (VISH-us-lee) in an evil or spiteful way
   Angered by the attack of the bear, the snake struck *viciously* back.

1

NONDESCRIPT (non-duh-SKRIPT) of no definite or particular kind
   His *nondescript* appearance made him hard to describe.
PIERCING (PEERS-ing) loud; shrill
   Her *piercing* voice seemed to cut through the noise in the room.

Characters

   Girl
   First Man
   Second Man

Setting

   The interior of a bus station

Heat Lightning

The drab interior of a bus station along a deserted highway somewhere in the midwest. There are two long benches stage Right, back to back; one faces the audience and one faces the rear wall. A door up Center leads out onto the road. It has a single glass pane in the top, and the bottom is wooden. Two doors, up Left and down Left. Up Left door reads "Men"; down Left door reads "Women." The room is lighted by an overhanging light with a dull green shade. A large bus schedule on the wall up Right Center. A window is up Right of Center and another at Right.

The sound of heavy RAIN can be heard outside. LIGHTNING flashes outside followed by large bursts of THUNDER. With each flash of lightning the light in the room dims almost to the point of going out, but somehow feebly struggles back to its full strength.

When the Curtain rises the stage is bare. Then a Man enters from the Men's room. He is a pleasant-looking man of about thirty-five. He takes off his hat and shakes the water from it; puts it on the bench downstage. He glances at the door up Center. Moves to it and peers out the glass; turns and moves to the Schedule on the wall and reads it. He then moves downstage and sits on the bench facing the audience. He picks up a discarded newspaper that lies on the seat beside him. He glances back at the door, then turns his attention once more to the paper and begins going through it casually.

The door up Center suddenly bursts open and a Girl of about twenty-three rushes into the room. She is sobbing and is out of breath. She throws her body against the door, slamming it. The Man turns about quickly. She throws the bolt into place and turns slowly, seeing the Man. The Girl's clothes are wet and muddy. Her hair is disheveled. She sobs and rushes to the Man quickly.

GIRL. (*Hysterically.*) Thank goodness! You're here! Oh, thank goodness!

(*She almost falls and the Man catches her.*)

MAN. My dear! What is it?

GIRL. Help me. Oh, please—please help me!

MAN. My word! You're in a terrible state. What has happened?

GIRL. Don't let him in. Please. He's after me. Please don't let him in.

MAN. Who? Who's after you?

GIRL. He'll be here any minute. Please—help me!

(*The Girl looks to the Center door. The LIGHTNING flashes and the LIGHT dims slowly. The Girl looks at the light and begins sobbing again.*)

MAN. Please, my dear, try to tell me what happened. You've locked the door. No one can come in. Now try to calm yourself.

(*The LIGHT has recovered again.*)

GIRL. You're waiting for the bus, aren't you? Oh, don't leave me! (*She rushes into his arms.*)

MAN. There, my dear! Of course I won't leave you!

GIRL. The bus. What time—Oh, tell me it will be here soon.

MAN. The last one's due any time now. The storm has probably slowed it down. Now, listen to me. I shall do whatever I can for you, but you must tell me what has happened.

GIRL. Yes—Yes—I must get hold of myself.

MAN. Here. Sit down. (*He brings her down to the bench facing the audience.*) There, now, that's better, isn't it? Now—

GIRL. I was at a party. I—I could have stayed all night with a friend, but I thought I had enough gas to get home—

MAN. Where do you live?

GIRL. About eight miles from here.

MAN. I see.

GIRL. About a mile from here, I suppose—I don't really know, I ran out of gas— I took my flashlight and locked the car and started walking down the road. There are so few cars this time of the morning, but I thought—anyway—I knew I could get the bus when it came along and then—go back for the car later. (*She breaks off and glances at the door again. She shudders at her own thoughts.*)

MAN. Come on, now. You were doing fine.

GIRL. I must have walked—I don't know—just a little way, when I noticed a car pulled off into a lane. I saw the rear light burning. I wanted to call to them. I thought I'd just call out to them and ask if they could help me—if they might let me have some gas.

MAN. Did you?

GIRL. No—I—I didn't get the chance to. I walked near enough to the car to be heard if I called, but—before I could call out, I saw someone. The

front door of the car was open and someone was standing by it. A man
—he hadn't heard me—he was—he was pulling something out of the
car. I couldn't tell what it was at first—and then the lightning—and I—I
saw her hand and then—her head—her hair was light and long and it
dragged in the mud.

MAN.   This is dreadful!

(*There is a flash of LIGHTNING and a crash of THUNDER.*)

GIRL.   He'll be here. He'll be here. I'm scared. Oh, I'm scared.

MAN.   Did he see you?

GIRL.   Maybe my flashlight—maybe I screamed—I don't know—I don't think
I screamed. I was too frightened. He looked up—I knew he saw me. I
dropped the flashlight and started running. I could hear him behind me. I
could hear the water splashing under his feet as he ran. I knew he was
behind me—I was afraid I was going to faint. I ran crazylike all over the
road—then I ran off the road and into the woods—I circled round and
round hoping I'd lose him, but I kept hearing something behind me—I
ran until I fell—I knew there was no use—I couldn't keep it up—but then
I realized I must have lost him—because I didn't hear him anymore.

MAN.   And you came straight here, then?

GIRL.   Yes—Yes—Oh, he's still out there—somewhere. He'll be here. I know
he will.

MAN.   The bus will be here soon and you'll be all right.

GIRL.   Yes. Oh, please let it come quickly.

MAN.   You'll have to get to the police immediately.

GIRL.   No—I couldn't. I don't want to—I'm afraid.

MAN.   But you must. It's your duty. This is a dreadful thing.

GIRL.   I know, but—what could I tell them?

MAN.   Tell them what you told me just now.

GIRL.   That wouldn't be enough—they'd want me to describe him. Maybe
identify him. I couldn't—I just couldn't.

MAN.   Are you sure you couldn't think of something that might give them a
lead? Anything?

GIRL.   I don't even know what he looked like. I couldn't see him very well
—I was so frightened.

MAN.   Nevertheless you've got to go to the police.

GIRL.   I don't know—I—

MAN.   They'll ask you a lot of questions, of course, but I'm sure you can
answer most of them. After you tell them the story the way you told it to

me, there'll be routine questions, but they'll be simple. They'll probably ask you something like—was he wearing a hat? How was he dressed?

GIRL.   I don't even know that!

MAN.   Or—was he tall? Was he short? How would you describe him generally?

GIRL.   I don't know—I swear—I just don't know.

MAN.   In the lightning—are you sure you didn't see his face at all?

GIRL.   I don't remember. Maybe he was wearing a hat or something. I don't remember seeing his face.

MAN.   But you saw the girl.

GIRL.   No—I didn't.

MAN.   But you said her hair was light—and you saw her hand.

GIRL.   Yes, I did. In the lightning, I think— Yes.

MAN.   But you don't remember seeing him?

GIRL.   No—I don't. (*She begins sobbing.*)

MAN.   I'm sorry—I shouldn't be going on like this—you are much too upset to even think any more about it. Don't worry about it anymore. Something will come to you later—that you've forgotten about right now. You'll see.

GIRL.   Perhaps.

MAN.   Your flashlight—for instance. You could identify that, couldn't you?

GIRL.   Yes—but—

MAN.   There, you see! Now—look— (*Points to Women's room.*) Go in there, and dry your eyes and fix yourself up. You'll feel much better.

GIRL.   You won't leave, will you?

MAN.   Of course not, my dear. I'll be right here!

(*She moves toward the door up Left. There is a brilliant flash of LIGHTNING. The LIGHT begins to dim. The Girl looks toward the Center door. There is a second flash of LIGHTNING illuminating the Center door. The Girl screams. In the flash of lightning, a man's face can be seen pressed against the glass outside the door. The door rattles viciously. The LIGHT in the room has almost dimmed out.*)

MAN.   (*Pushing her toward Women's room.*) Get in there. Stay until I tell you to come out.

(*The Man pushes her into the room quickly.*)

SECOND MAN.   (*Outside the door. Rattles the door viciously once more.*) Let me in. Open this door. Let me in!

MAN. What do you want?

SECOND MAN. (*Outside*.) I want to get out of this storm. What do you think I want? What's the idea of locking this door? You think you own this place? (*The Man goes to the door slowly, throws back the bolt and the Second Man enters quickly. He is a nondescript sort of person. Tall, nice-looking and about thirty years of age. He looks about the room as he enters.*) You've got no right to lock that door—keeping people outside in this kind of weather. (*The Second Man moves up to the Schedule on the wall.*) Has there been a bus?

MAN. No—not yet.

SECOND MAN. Late, huh? Good.

MAN. Why?

SECOND MAN. Why? I'd have missed it if it were on time—wouldn't I?

MAN. Yes—of course—how stupid of me.

SECOND MAN. There's someone else here, isn't there?

MAN. What do you mean?

SECOND MAN. I saw somebody else when I looked in.

MAN. There—

SECOND MAN. A girl, wasn't it?

(*The two Men look at each other a moment; then the First Man walks to the door where the Girl has gone and knocks on it. The door opens slowly and the Girl enters. When she sees the Second Man standing in the room, she starts to cry out, but the Man puts his finger to his lip conveying silence to her and then guides her downstage to the bench.*)

SECOND MAN. I thought you said—

MAN. I didn't say anything.

SECOND MAN. You tried to tell me there was no one else here. I thought there was—

MAN. Did you?

SECOND MAN. Yeah, I was sure there was. What was the idea of lying?

MAN. I wasn't conscious of lying about anything.

SECOND MAN. Yeah? I guess I'm imaginin' things. Oh, well—forget it. How far you going?

MAN. Just into town.

SECOND MAN. How about you, miss?

GIRL. Not far.

(*The Second Man starts moving down toward the Girl. She sees him coming, and moves over to the wall, appearing to read the Schedule.*)

SECOND MAN.   It's pretty late, isn't it? I was in luck, don't you think? I told that to our friend here, but he didn't get it. (*To First Man.*) I'll bet she's smarter than you are.

MAN.   Yes—I suppose she might—be.

SECOND MAN.   (*Noticing the Girl's nervousness.*) Say, you look pretty nervous about something. Storm upset your plans? You can expect storms to slow up buses. If people were smart they wouldn't be out on a night like this. Just try to get somewhere when it storms—can't be done—especially if you're in a hurry.

GIRL.   I'm—I'm in no particular hurry.

SECOND MAN.   Well, I sure am—but there's nothing I can do about it—I guess.

(*There is another flash of LIGHTNING and the LIGHT dims very low again. The Girl is pressed against the Right window in fear. The LIGHT recovers.*)

SECOND MAN.   Say—you're really upset, aren't you? Has somebody been bothering you? (*The Second Man moves toward her again.*)

GIRL.   It's—it's just the storm.

SECOND MAN.   Afraid of storms?

GIRL.   Yes—I—am.

(*The Girl seems as if she is about to faint. The First Man pushes ahead of the Second Man and takes her by the arm and leads her down to the bench.*)

MAN.   She'll be all right. Why don't you leave her alone?

SECOND MAN.   Yeah! Sure! (*He moves away, watching the Girl.*)

(*There is another brilliant flash of LIGHTNING and a crack of THUNDER. The LIGHT dims slowly and goes out. The Girl lets out a muffled cry.*)

MAN.   Here! Have a cigarette, my dear.

(*The Man strikes a match, lights her cigarette and his. The Second Man pushes his head between them.*)

SECOND MAN.   Don't mind three on a match, do you?

MAN.   No, of course not. (*Gives him a light.*)

(*The LIGHT comes up slowly.*)

SECOND MAN.   Thanks. (*He strolls up toward the Center door.*) What a night! Always wonder what brings people out on nights like this. Wouldn't catch me out if it weren't pretty important. (*To Man.*) How about you?

MAN. I have early business in town.

SECOND MAN. (*To Girl.*) And you?

GIRL. I was visiting—with friends. I should have stayed the night.

SECOND MAN. Oh! You're not together, then?

MAN. Er—no—

SECOND MAN. I see. (*He moves down toward the Girl.*) How far did you say you were going?

GIRL. Not far—about eight miles.

(*The Second Man sits beside her and she moves away suspiciously.*)

SECOND MAN. I never saw anybody so afraid of a storm.

GIRL. It's the lightning—I—

SECOND MAN. Lightning. I used to be afraid of it, when I was a kid, but I got over it. All by myself too. (*He takes the Girl's arm.*) Look! Come here. I'll show you. (*He leads her up to the window rear Right.*) Watch the sky the next time there's a big flash. One of the really beautiful sights in this world if you look at it right—like a great big Fourth of July. (*There is now a brilliant flash of LIGHTNING.*) Look! See! What did I tell you? It's just like it was cutting the whole world in two. (*The Girl breaks away and goes Right.*) You wouldn't even watch it. You'll never get over being afraid of things if you won't face them.

GIRL. I can't.

(*There is the hum of a MOTOR in the distance. They All listen. The Second Man goes to the window.*)

SECOND MAN. I guess that's it— Yep—Looks empty.

GIRL. Empty!

(*There is the sound of BRAKES being applied. Each waits for the other to make the first move.*)

SECOND MAN. Well—are we going?

MAN. No!

SECOND MAN. What?

MAN. I'm not going!

SECOND MAN. Why?

MAN. I don't see that I have to give you a reason for what I do.

SECOND MAN. No—I guess you don't at that— (*He looks at the Girl, then moves to her, reaching for her arm.*) Well, in that case, I guess we'll just keep each other company, won't we?

(*The Girl is stunned. She looks to the First Man, who stands behind the*

Second Man. The First Man shakes his head "no." There is the sound of a HORN outside.)

GIRL.   (*Backing away from the Second Man.*) No— No— I don't think I'll go either. I'll wait—

SECOND MAN.   I think you'd better come on. We'll have it all to ourselves.

GIRL.   No— No— I won't. Leave me alone. I'm going to stay here—with him.

SECOND MAN.   (*Looks from one to the other.*) I get it. Waiting for a bus! (*He laughs.*) No wonder you had the door locked! (*The Second Man exits laughing.*)

(*The Girl rushes after him, slamming the door and throwing the bolt once more. She listens to the sound of the BUS pulling away. Then she turns quickly to the Man.*)

GIRL.   Thank goodness!

MAN.   I tried to tell him you weren't here.

GIRL.   But you let him in—why?

MAN.   He was making such a disturbance out there. Besides there was really no way to tell for certain that—

GIRL.   No—He's gone— He's gone— I guess it wasn't— No— I somehow don't think it was—

MAN.   You don't think it was he?

GIRL.   No—I—don't—

MAN.   You remember something, then?

GIRL.   I seem— No— No—

MAN.   Yes— You do! You know that wasn't the man. Why? That's a step to remembering.

GIRL.   No—only that he—left. He left—

MAN.   Yes, you do! I knew it would come back slowly—that you'd remember something.

GIRL.   No!

MAN.   First, you would say— That *wasn't* the man because I remember—and then later— That *was* the man because I remember. Yes. You would remember!

GIRL.   No! (*There is another brilliant flash of LIGHTNING and the LIGHT begins to dim.*) Oh—no—the light—No!

MAN.   Don't worry, my dear. You'll have light.

(*He has taken a flashlight from his coat pocket. The Girl stares at it as the LIGHTNING crashes again and the already very dim LIGHT dies com-*

pletely. The piercing light of the flashlight is the only light in the room. The Girl runs up to the Center door and pulls at it; she doesn't have time to throw the bolt before the Man is almost on her. The light plays crazily over her. She runs Right and the light follows, jumping its crazy pattern about her. She runs downstage, but she can't escape it. She runs up Left and is pressed into the corner facing the Man as he approaches. She gropes wildly about the wall. The light dances about her face, blinding her, as he comes nearer and nearer. She shuts her eyes against its brightness. She screams terribly — as the Curtain falls.)

END

Looking into the Plot

1. Arrange these incidents in the order in which they are experienced by the Girl:
   (a) The Girl sees a man dragging a body from a car.
   (b) She sees a man's face at the window of the waiting room.
   (c) The bus leaves without the Girl.
   (d) The Girl enters the station waiting room weeping hysterically.
   (e) The Girl's car runs out of gas.
   (f) As the Girl enters, the First Man is sitting on a bench, reading a newspaper, his hat beside him.
   (g) The First Man questions the Girl about what she remembers.
2. The Girl is very frightened as she enters the station, not only because she has seen a murdered woman, but because she was herself seen. Who saw her? Why did she run?
3. Why is the Second Man's appearance so frightening? Where does his face first appear? Why doesn't he just come in through the door?
4. When the bus appears the Girl is terrified of entering it. Why? How does the First Man's decision increase her fearfulness?
5. At what point do you know she has made the wrong choice?

Thinking It Through

1. We don't see the First Man arrive at the station; we see him only as he comes out of the men's room. What is his first action? What does it tell us about how long he has been at the station? Why is this information important?

2. The First Man urges the Girl to go to the police and tell them what she knows and remembers. What is he really trying to find out?
3. The two men behave differently toward the Girl: the First Man seems gentle and concerned; the Second Man is brusque, almost rough in his speech and actions. How does the Girl respond to each? What is ironic about her reaction?
4. The First Man takes a calculated risk in announcing that he is not going on the bus. What two choices does the Girl have? Was there a chance she might decide not to remain? Explain.
5. The importance of light is symbolically represented in the play by the flashlight. How does the sight of it at the end of the play finally help the Girl "see the light"? How does this realization lead to darkness?
6. Heat lightning refers to the flashes of light without thunder or rain seen near the horizon, especially at the end of a hot day. The title of this play, then, does not refer to the storm raging outside the bus station. Rather it refers to a special kind of pressure experienced by two of the characters. Explain the relevance of the title to the actions and interactions of these characters.
7. For further reading you might enjoy the following tales of terror.
   a. The master of the horror tale is Edgar Allan Poe. One of his most famous stories is "The Cask of Amontillado," in which, ironically, a person trusts his enemy.
   b. In the short story "The Lady or the Tiger?" by Frank Stockton, the central character must make a choice that may mean certain death.
   c. "Sorry, Wrong Number" by Lucille Fletcher is a short play of mounting terror, similar to "Heat Lightning" in its creation of suspense and its unexpected ending.
   d. "Angel Street" by Patrick Hamilton is a full-length mystery play, later made into the movie *Gaslight*. Here, suspense is created by the machinations of an evil husband bent on the psychological destruction of his wife.

Building Vocabulary

The following sentences are based on those in the play. Decide which of the words following the sentences best fits each blank. Write your answers on a separate sheet of paper.

1. The play opens on the _____ interior of a dusty, deserted waiting room.

2. The Man picks up a _____ newspaper that has been left on the seat beside him.

3. The Girl's clothes are wet and muddy, her hair _____.

4. A man's face is seen at the window and then the door rattles _____.

5. A Second Man enters the bus station. He is a _____ person with no distinguishing features or mannerisms.

nondescript	viciously	feebly
piercing	drab	disheveled
	discarded	

Writing Projects

1. Write a **plot summary** of the play. Use the list of events you made up for Exercise #1 in "Looking into the Plot" (page 11). Be sure to use all of the events in your list. (*For help with this assignment see Writing Manual, p. 202.*)

2. Think up a new ending for "Heat Lightning." Then write your version, making up new lines of **dialogue** for the characters. Begin with this stage direction (page 9): *There is the hum of a MOTOR in the distance. They All listen. The Second Man goes to the window. (For help with this assignment see Writing Manual, p. 209.)*

Flight into
DANGER

Flight into Danger

Arthur Hailey

AIRCRAFT DISASTER stories always make powerful and suspenseful reading. If there is a master of this sort of chair-gripper, it is Arthur Hailey, author of the best-selling novel *Airport*. The following drama, written in the 1950s, was itself a best seller—expanded into a movie and rewritten as a novel.

While a plane in danger usually means turbulent weather, too little fuel or mechanical problems, the airliner in "Flight into Danger" is mechanically perfect; there is plenty of fuel and the weather is calm. Yet something—an unexpected calamity on board the plane—puts this craft and its 56 passengers in mortal danger.

The story is set in Canada. There are studio scenes of an airport passenger terminal, control room and tower as well as the passenger cabin and the captain's flight deck of a plane. Film "footage" of the exterior of a plane taking off and in flight adds to the realism.

Try to visualize as you read. Begin with a clear picture of the passenger lobby of the Winnipeg Air Terminal where George Spencer buys the last seat available on a chartered DC-4 headed for Vancouver.

Vocabulary Preview

EXUBERANT (eg-ZOO-buh-runt) full of high spirits; joyous
   The fans were *exuberant* when their home team won.

EXTRAVAGANCE (ek-STRAV-uh-guns) something costly and self-indulgent
> His buying expensive records was an *extravagance*.

PLACID (PLAS-ud) calm; tranquil; smooth
> The *placid* waters of the lake gave it its name.

SOLICITOUSLY (suh-LIS-uh-tus-lee) with concerned attention; in a caring manner
> The woman spoke *solicitously* to the ill child.

SIMULTANEOUSLY (sy-mul-TAY-nee-us-lee) at the same time
> The alarm clock and the doorbell rang *simultaneously*.

STRIDENTLY (STRYD-unt-lee) in a loud and shrill manner; harshly noisy
> The blue jay scolded *stridently* when anyone came near its nest.

DILUTE (dy-LOOT) to thin out or weaken
> He was told to *dilute* the concentrate by adding three cups of water.

TOXIC (TOK-sik) harmful; deadly; poisonous
> The leaves and flowers of some plants are *toxic* if eaten.

DIVERT (di-VURT) to turn aside
> The police *diverted* crowds from the accident scene.

SLUGGISH (SLUG-ish) slow; lacking in vigor and energy
> On cold mornings the engine was *sluggish* and often stalled.

Other Words You Will Need to Know

MANIFEST (MAN-uh-fest) a list of passengers and cargo for a particular flight
AFT rear section of an airplane
GALLEY (GAL-lee) kitchen of an airplane
EMETIC (ih-MET-uk) a medicine causing one to vomit
KNOT (NOT) a unit of speed for airplanes and boats
MAY DAY the international radio distress call

Characters

Aboard Flight 714:

THE PASSENGERS:

> George Spencer, *factory salesman, about thirty-five*
> Dr. Frank Baird, *medical doctor, fifty-five*
> Seven Male Passengers
> Two Women Passengers

THE CREW:
>   Captain
>   First Officer
>   Stewardess

At Vancouver Airport:
>   Captain Martin Treleaven
>   Airport Controller
>   Harry Burdick, *agent for charter airplane flight*
>   Switchboard Operator
>   Radio Operator
>   Tower Controller
>   Teletype Operator

At Winnipeg Airport:
>   First Passenger Agent
>   Second Passenger Agent

Flight into Danger   ACT ONE

FADE IN:

The passenger lobby of Winnipeg Air Terminal at night. At the departure counter of Cross-Canada Airlines a male passenger agent in uniform (First Agent) is checking a manifest. He reaches for P.A. mike.

FIRST AGENT.   Flight 98, direct fleetliner service to Vancouver, with connections for Victoria, Seattle, and Honolulu, leaving immediately through gate four. No smoking. All aboard, please.

(During the announcement George Spencer enters through the main lobby doorway. About thirty-five, he is a senior factory salesman for a motor-truck manufacturer. Spencer pauses to look for the Cross-Canada counter, then hastens toward it, arriving as the announcement concludes.)

SPENCER.   Is there space on flight 98 for Vancouver?

FIRST AGENT.   Sorry, sir, that flight is full. Did you check with reservations?

SPENCER.   Didn't have time. I came straight out on the chance you might have a "no show" seat.

FIRST AGENT.   With the big football game on tomorrow in Vancouver, I don't think you'll have much chance of getting out before tomorrow afternoon.

SPENCER.   That's no good. I've got to be in Vancouver tomorrow by midday.

FIRST AGENT.   *(Hesitates.)* Look, I'm not supposed to tell you this, but there's a charter flight in from Toronto. They're going out to the coast for the game. I did hear they were a few seats light.

SPENCER.   Who's in charge? Where do I find him?

FIRST AGENT.   Ask at the desk over there. They call themselves Maple Leaf Air Charter. But mind, I didn't send you.

SPENCER.   *(Smiles.)* Okay, thanks.

(Spencer crosses to another departure counter which has a cardboard sign hanging behind it — Maple Leaf Air Charter. Behind the desk is an agent in a lounge suit. He is checking a manifest.)

SPENCER.   Excuse me.

SECOND AGENT.   Yes?

SPENCER.   I was told you might have space on a flight to Vancouver.

SECOND AGENT.   Yes, there's one seat left. The flight's leaving right away though.

SPENCER. That's what I want.

SECOND AGENT. Very well, sir. Your name, please?

SPENCER. Spencer—George Spencer.

SECOND AGENT. That'll be fifty-five dollars for the one-way trip.

SPENCER. Will you take my air travel card?

SECOND AGENT. No, sir. Just old-fashioned cash.

SPENCER. All right. (*Produces wallet and counts out bills.*)

SECOND AGENT. (*Handing over ticket.*) Do you have any bags?

SPENCER. One. Right here.

SECOND AGENT. All the baggage is aboard. Would you mind keeping that with you?

SPENCER. Be glad to.

SECOND AGENT. Okay, Mr. Spencer. Your ticket is your boarding pass. Go through gate three and ask the commissionaire for Flight 714. Better hurry.

SPENCER. Thanks a lot. Good night.

SECOND AGENT. Good night.

(*Exit Spencer. Enter Stewardess.*)

SECOND AGENT. Hi, Janet. Did the meals get aboard?

STEWARDESS. Yes, they've just put them on. What was the trouble.

SECOND AGENT. Couldn't get service from the regular caterers here. We had to go to some outfit the other side of town. That's what held us up.

STEWARDESS. Are we all clear now?

SECOND AGENT. Yes, here's everything you'll need. (*Hands over papers.*) There's one more passenger. He's just gone aboard. So that's fifty-six souls in your lovely little hands.

STEWARDESS. I'll try not to drop any.

SECOND AGENT. (*Reaching for coat.*) Well, I'm off home.

STEWARDESS. (*As she leaves.*) 'Night.

SECOND AGENT. (*Pulling on coat.*) 'Night, Janet. (*Calls after her.*) Don't forget to cheer for the Blue Bombers tomorrow.

(*Stewardess waves and smiles.*)

DISSOLVE TO:

The passenger cabin of a DC-4 airliner. There is one empty aisle seat. Seated next to it is Dr. Frank Baird, 55. George Spencer enters, sees the unoccupied seat, and comes toward it.

SPENCER. Pardon me, is this anyone's seat?

BAIRD. No.

SPENCER. Thanks.

(*Spencer sheds his topcoat and puts it on the rack above the seats. Meanwhile the plane's motors can be heard starting.*)

CUT TO:

Film Insert: Four-engined airplane exterior. Night: The motors starting.

CUT TO:

The passenger cabin.

BAIRD. I presume you're going to the big game like the rest of us.

SPENCER. I'm ashamed to admit it, but I'd forgotten about the game.

BAIRD. I wouldn't say that too loudly if I were you. Some of the more exuberant fans might tear you limb from limb.

SPENCER. I'll keep my voice down. (*Pleasantly.*) Matter of fact, I'm making a sales trip to the coast.

BAIRD. What do you sell?

SPENCER. Trucks.

BAIRD. Trucks?

SPENCER. That's right. I'm what the local salesmen call the son-of-a-gun from head office with the special prices . . . Need any trucks? How about forty? Give you a real good discount today.

BAIRD. (*Laughs.*) I couldn't use that many, I'm afraid. Not in my line of work.

SPENCER. Which is?

BAIRD. Medicine.

SPENCER. You mean you're a doctor.

BAIRD. That's right. Can't buy one truck, leave alone forty. Football is the one extravagance I allow myself.

SPENCER. Delighted to hear it, Doctor. Now I can relax.

(*As he speaks, the run-up of the aircraft engines begins, increasing to a heavy roar.*)

BAIRD. (*Raising his voice.*) Do you think you *can* in this racket? I never can figure out why they make all this noise before take-off.

SPENCER. (*Shouting, as noise increases.*) It's the normal run-up of the engines. Airplane engines don't use battery ignition like you have in your car. They run on magneto ignition, and each of the magnetos is tested separately. If they're okay and the motors are giving all the power they should—away you go!

BAIRD. You sound as if you know something about it.

SPENCER. I'm pretty rusty now. I used to fly fighters in the air force. But that was ten years ago. Reckon I've forgotten most of it . . . Well, there we go.

(*The tempo of the motors increases. Baird and Spencer lean toward the window to watch the take-off, although it is dark outside.*)

CUT TO:

Film Insert: Airplane taking off. Night.

CUT TO:

The passenger cabin. The noise of the motors is reduced slightly and the two men relax in their seats. Spencer reaches for cigarettes.

SPENCER. Smoke?

BAIRD. Thank you.

(*They light up. Stewardess enters from aft of airplane and reaches for two pillows from the rack above.*)

STEWARDESS. We were held up at Winnipeg, sir, and we haven't served dinner yet. Would you care for some?

SPENCER. Yes, please.

(*Stewardess puts a pillow on his lap.*)

STEWARDESS. (*To Baird.*) And you, sir?

BAIRD. Thank you, yes. (*To Spencer.*) It's a bit late for dinner, but it'll pass the time away.

STEWARDESS. There's lamb chop or grilled halibut.

BAIRD. I'll take the lamb.

SPENCER. Yes, I'll have that, too.

STEWARDESS. Thank you, sir.

BAIRD. (*To Spencer.*) Tell me . . . By the way, my name is Baird.

SPENCER. Spencer. George Spencer.

(*They shake hands.*)

BAIRD. How'd'do. Tell me, when you make a sales trip like this do you . . .

(*Fade voices and pan with the Stewardess, returning aft. Entering the airplane's tiny galley she picks up a telephone and presses a call button.*)

VOICE OF FIRST OFFICER. Flight deck.

STEWARDESS. I'm finally serving the dinners. What'll "youall" have—lamb chops or grilled halibut?

VOICE OF FIRST OFFICER.   Just a minute. (*Pause.*) Skipper says he'll have the lamb . . . Oh, hold it! . . . No, he's changed his mind. Says he'll take the halibut. Make it two fish, Janet.

STEWARDESS.   Okay.

(*Stewardess hangs up the phone and begins to arrange meal trays.*)

CUT TO:

Spencer and Baird.

SPENCER.   No, I hadn't expected to go west again this quickly.

BAIRD.   You have my sympathy. I prescribe my travel in small doses.

(*Stewardess enters and puts meal tray on pillow.*)

Oh, thank you.

STEWARDESS.   Will you have coffee, tea, or milk, sir?

BAIRD.   Coffee, please.

STEWARDESS.   I'll bring it later.

BAIRD.   That'll be fine. (*To Spencer.*) Tell me, do you follow football at all?

SPENCER.   A little. Hockey's my game, though. Who are you for tomorrow?

BAIRD.   The Argos, naturally. (*As Stewardess brings second tray.*) Thank you, dear.

STEWARDESS.   Will you have coffee, tea, or—

SPENCER.   I'll have coffee too. No cream.

(*Stewardess nods and exits.*)

(*To Baird.*) Must be a calm night outside. No trouble in keeping the dinner steady.

BAIRD.   (*Looking out of window.*) It is calm. Not a cloud in sight. Must be a monotonous business flying these things, once they're off the ground.

SPENCER.   It varies, I guess.

AUDIO:

FADE UP THE ROAR OF MOTORS

DISSOLVE TO:

Film Insert: Airplane in level flight, night.

DISSOLVE TO:

The aircraft flight deck. The Captain is seated on left, First Officer on right. Neither is touching the controls.

FIRST OFFICER.   (*Into radio mike.*) Height 16,000 feet. Course 285 true. ETA Vancouver 0505 Pacific Standard. Over.

VOICE ON RADIO.   Flight 714. This is Winnipeg Control. Roger. Out.

(*The First Officer reaches for a log sheet and makes a notation, then relaxes in his seat.*)

FIRST OFFICER.   Got any plans for Vancouver?

CAPTAIN.   Yes, I'm going to sleep for two whole days.

(*The Stewardess enters with a meal tray.*)

STEWARDESS.   Who's first?

CAPTAIN.   You take yours, Harry.

(*Stewardess produces a pillow and the First Officer slides back his seat, well clear of the control column. He places the pillow on his knees and accepts the tray.*)

FIRST OFFICER.   Thanks, honey.

CAPTAIN.   Everything all right at the back, Janet? How are the football fans?

STEWARDESS.   They tired themselves out on the way from Toronto. Looks like a peaceful, placid night.

FIRST OFFICER.   (*With a mouth full of food, raising fork for emphasis.*) Aha! Those are the sort of nights to beware of. It's in the quiet times that trouble brews. I'll bet you right now that somebody's getting ready to be sick.

STEWARDESS.   That'll be when you're doing the flying. Or have you finally learned how to hold this thing steady? (*To Captain.*) How's the weather?

CAPTAIN.   General fog east of the mountains, extending pretty well as far as Manitoba. But it's clear to the west. Should be rockaby smooth the whole way.

STEWARDESS.   Good. Well, keep junior here off the controls while I serve coffee.

(*Exits.*)

FIRST OFFICER.   (*Calling after her.*) Mark my words, woman! Stay close to that mop and pail.

CAPTAIN.   How's the fish?

FIRST OFFICER.   (*Hungrily.*) Not bad. Not bad at all. If there were about three times as much it might be a square meal.

AUDIO:

FADE VOICES INTO ROAR OF MOTORS.

DISSOLVE TO:

The passenger cabin. Spencer and Baird are concluding their meal. Baird puts down a coffee cup and wipes his mouth with a napkin. Then he reaches up and presses a call button above his head. There is a soft "ping," and the Stewardess enters.

STEWARDESS. Yes, sir?

BAIRD. That was very enjoyable. Now if you'll take the tray I think I'll try to sleep.

STEWARDESS. Surely. *(To Spencer.)* Will you have more coffee, sir?

SPENCER. No thanks.

(Stewardess picks up the second tray and goes aft. Spencer yawns.)

Let me know if the noise keeps you awake. If it does, I'll have the engines stopped.

BAIRD. *(Chuckles.)* Well, at least there won't be any night calls—I hope.

(Baird reaches up and switches off the overhead reading lights so that both seats are in semi-darkness. The two men prepare to sleep.)

DISSOLVE TO:

Film Insert: Airplane in level flight, night.

DISSOLVE TO:

The passenger cabin. The Captain emerges from the flight deck and strolls aft, saying "Good evening" to one or two people who glance up as he goes by. He passes Spencer and Baird, who are sleeping. As the Captain progresses, the Stewardess can be seen at the rear of the cabin. She is bending solicitously over a woman passenger, her hand on the woman's forehead. The Captain approaches.

CAPTAIN. Something wrong, Miss Burns?

STEWARDESS. This lady is feeling a little unwell. I was going to get her some aspirin. *(To the Woman Passenger.)* I'll be back in a moment.

CAPTAIN. Sorry to hear that. What seems to be the trouble?

(The Woman Passenger has her head back and her mouth open. A strand of hair has fallen across her face, and she is obviously in pain.)

FIRST WOMAN PASSENGER. *(Speaking with effort.)* I'm sorry to be such a nuisance, but it hit me all of a sudden . . . just a few minutes ago . . . dizziness and nausea and a sharp pain . . . *(Indicating abdomen.)* down here

CAPTAIN. Well, I think the Stewardess will be able to help you.

(Stewardess returns.)

STEWARDESS. Now, here you are; try these.

(*She hands over two aspirins and a cup of water. The passenger takes them, then puts her head back on the seat rest.*)

FIRST WOMAN PASSENGER.   Thank you very much.

(*She smiles faintly at the Captain.*)

CAPTAIN.   (*Quietly, taking Stewardess aside.*) If she gets any worse you'd better let me know and I'll radio ahead. But we've still five hours' flying to the coast. Is there a doctor on board, do you know?

STEWARDESS.   There was no one listed as a doctor on the manifest. But I can go around and ask.

CAPTAIN.   (*Looks around.*) Well, most everybody's sleeping now. We'd better not disturb them unless we have to. See how she is in the next half hour or so. (*Captain bends down and puts a hand on the woman's shoulder.*) Try to rest, madam, if you can. Miss Burns will take good care of you.

(*The Captain nods to Stewardess and begins his return to the flight deck. The Stewardess arranges blanket around the woman passenger. Spencer and Baird are still sleeping as the Captain passes.*)

DISSOLVE TO:

Film Insert: Airplane in level flight, night.

DISSOLVE TO:

The passenger cabin. Spencer stirs and wakes. Then he glances forward to where the Stewardess is leaning over another section of seats, and her voice can be heard softly.

STEWARDESS.   I'm sorry to disturb you, but we're trying to find out if there's a doctor on board.

FIRST MALE PASSENGER.   Not me, I'm afraid. Is something wrong?

STEWARDESS.   One of the passengers is feeling unwell. It's nothing too serious. (*Moving on to the next pair of seats.*) I'm sorry to disturb you, but we're trying to find out if there's a doctor on board.

(*There is an indistinct answer from the two people just questioned, then Spencer sits forward and calls the Stewardess.*)

SPENCER.   Stewardess! (*Indicating Baird, who is still sleeping.*) This gentleman is a doctor.

STEWARDESS.   Thank you. I think we'd better wake him. I have two passengers who are quite sick.

SPENCER.   All right. (*Shaking Baird's arm.*) Doctor! Doctor! Wake up!

BAIRD. Um . . . Um . . . What is it?

STEWARDESS. Doctor, I'm sorry to disturb you. But we have two passengers who seem quite sick. I wonder if you'd take a look at them.

BAIRD. (*Sleepily.*) Yes . . . yes . . . of course.

(*Spencer moves out of seat to permit Baird to reach the aisle. Baird then follows the Stewardess aft to the first Woman Passenger. Although a blanket is around her, the woman is shivering and gasping, with her head back and eyes closed. The doctor places a hand on her forehead, and she opens her eyes.*)

STEWARDESS. This gentleman is a doctor. He's going to help us.

FIRST WOMAN PASSENGER. Oh, Doctor . . . !

BAIRD. Now just relax.

(*He makes a quick external examination, first checking pulse, then taking a small pen-type flashlight from his pocket and looking into her eyes. He then loosens the blanket and the woman's coat beneath the blanket. As he places a hand on her abdomen she gasps with pain.*)

BAIRD. Hurt you there? (*With an effort she nods.*) There?

FIRST WOMAN PASSENGER. Oh, yes! Yes!

(*Baird replaces the coat and blanket, then turns to the Stewardess.*)

BAIRD. (*With authority.*) Please tell the captain we must land at once. This woman has to be gotten to a hospital immediately.

STEWARDESS. Do you know what's wrong, Doctor?

BAIRD. I can't tell. I've no means of making a proper diagnosis. But it's serious enough to land at the nearest city with hospital facilities. You can tell your captain that.

STEWARDESS. Very well, Doctor. (*Moving across the aisle and forward.*) While I'm gone will you take a look at this gentleman here? He's also complained of sickness and stomach pains.

(*Baird goes to a male passenger indicated by the Stewardess. The man is sitting forward and resting his head on the back of the seat ahead of him. He is retching.*)

BAIRD. I'm a doctor. Will you put your head back, please?

(*The man groans, but follows the doctor's instruction. He is obviously weak. Baird makes another quick examination, then pauses thoughtfully.*)

BAIRD. What have you had to eat in the last twenty-four hours?

SECOND MALE PASSENGER. (*With effort.*) Just the usual meals . . . breakfast . . . bacon and eggs . . . salad for lunch . . . couple of sandwiches at the airport . . . then dinner here.

(*The Stewardess enters. Followed by the Captain.*)

BAIRD. (*To Stewardess.*) Keep him warm. Get blankets around him. (*To Captain.*) How quickly can we land, Captain?

CAPTAIN. That's the trouble. I've just been talking to Calgary. There was light fog over the prairies earlier, but now it's thickened and everything is closed in this side of the mountains. It's clear at the coast, and we'll have to go through.

BAIRD. Is that faster than turning back?

CAPTAIN. It would take us longer to go back now than to go on.

BAIRD. Then how soon do you expect to land?

CAPTAIN. At about 5 A.M. Pacific time. (*As Baird glances at his watch.*) You need to put your watch back two hours because of the changes of time. We'll be landing in three hours forty-five minutes from now.

BAIRD. Then I'll have to do what I can for these people. Can my bag be reached? I checked it at Toronto.

CAPTAIN. We can get it. Let me have your tags, Doctor.

(*Baird takes out a wallet and selects two baggage tags which he hands to Captain.*)

BAIRD. There are two bags. It's the small overnight case I want.

(*As he finishes speaking the airplane lurches violently. Baird and the Stewardess and the Captain are thrown sharply to one side. Simultaneously the telephone in the galley buzzes several times. As the three recover their balance the Stewardess answers the phone quickly.*)

STEWARDESS. Yes?

FIRST OFFICER'S VOICE. (*Under strain.*) Come forward quickly. I'm sick!

STEWARDESS. The First Officer is sick. He says come quickly.

CAPTAIN. (*To Baird.*) You'd better come too.

(*The Captain and Baird move quickly forward, passing through the flight deck door.*)

CUT TO:

The flight deck. The First Officer is at the controls on the right-hand side. He is retching and shuddering, flying the airplane by will power and nothing else. The Captain promptly slides into the left-hand seat and takes the controls.)

CAPTAIN. Get him out of there!

(*Together Baird and the Stewardess lift the First Officer from his seat, and, as they do, he collapses. They lower him to the floor, and the Stewardess reaches for a pillow and blankets. Baird makes the same quick examination he used in the two previous cases. Meanwhile the Captain has steadied the aircraft, and now he snaps over a button to engage the automatic pilot. He releases the controls and turns to the others, though without leaving his seat.*)

CAPTAIN. He must have been changing course when it happened. We're back on auto pilot now. Now, Doctor, what is it? What's happening?

BAIRD. There's a common denominator in these attacks. There has to be. And the most likely thing is food. (*To Stewardess.*) How long is it since we had dinner?

STEWARDESS. Two and a half to three hours.

BAIRD. Now then, what did you serve?

STEWARDESS. Well, the main course was a choice of fish or meat.

BAIRD. I remember that I ate meat. (*Indicating First Officer.*) What did he have?

STEWARDESS. (*Faintly, with dawning alarm.*) Fish.

BAIRD. Do you remember what the other two passengers had?

STEWARDESS. No.

BAIRD. Then go back quickly and find out, please.

(*As the Stewardess exits Baird kneels beside First Officer, who is moaning.*)

BAIRD. Try to relax. I'll give you something in a few minutes to help the pain. You'll feel better if you stay warm.

(*Baird arranges the blanket around the First Officer. Now the Stewardess reappears.*)

STEWARDESS. (*Alarmed.*) Doctor, both those passengers had fish. And there are three more cases now. And they ate fish too. Can you come?

BAIRD. Yes, but I need that bag of mine.

CAPTAIN. Janet, take these tags and get one of the passengers to help you. (*Hands over Baird's luggage tags.*) Doctor, I'm going to get on the radio and report what's happening to Vancouver. Is there anything you want to add?

BAIRD. Yes. Tell them we have three serious cases of suspected food poisoning, and there appear to be others. When we land we'll want ambulances and medical help waiting, and the hospitals should be warned. Tell them we're not sure, but we suspect the poisoning may have been caused by fish served on board. You'd better suggest they put a ban on serving all food which originated wherever ours came from until we've established the source for sure.

CAPTAIN.   Right.

(*He reaches for the radio mike, and Baird turns to go aft. But suddenly a thought strikes the captain.*)

Doctor, I've just remembered . . .

BAIRD.   Yes.

CAPTAIN.   (*Quietly.*) I ate fish.

BAIRD.   When?

CAPTAIN.   I'd say about half an hour after he did. (*Pointing to First Officer.*) Maybe a little longer. Is there anything I can do?

BAIRD.   It doesn't follow that everyone will be affected. There's often no logic to these things. You feel all right now?

CAPTAIN.   Yes.

BAIRD.   You'd better not take any chances. Your food can't be completely digested yet. As soon as I get my bag I'll give you something to help you get rid of it.

CAPTAIN.   Then hurry, Doctor. For Pete's sake, hurry! (*Into mike.*) Vancouver control. This is Maple Leaf Charter Flight 714. I have an emergency message. Do you read? Over.

VOICE ON RADIO.   (*Vancouver Operator.*) Go ahead, 714.

CAPTAIN.   We have serious food poisoning on board. Several passengers and the First Officer are seriously ill . . .

DISSOLVE TO:

The luggage compartment below the flight deck. A passenger is hurriedly passing up bags to the Stewardess. Baird is looking down from above.

BAIRD.   That's it! That's it down there! Let me have it!

FADE OUT

END OF ACT ONE

ACT TWO

FADE IN:

The control room, Vancouver Airport. At a radio panel an Operator, wearing headphones, is transcribing a message on a typewriter. Part way through the message he presses a button on the panel and a bell rings stridently, signaling an emergency. At once an Airport Controller appears behind the operator and reads the message as it continues to come in. Nearby is a telephone switchboard manned by an operator, and a battery of teletypes clattering noisily.

CONTROLLER. *(Over his shoulder, to Switchboard Operator.)* Get me area traffic control, then clear the teletype circuit to Winnipeg. Priority message. *(Stepping back to take phone.)* Vancouver Controller here. I've an emergency report from Maple Leaf Charter Flight 714, ex-Winnipeg for Vancouver. There's serious food poisoning among the passengers, and the First Officer is down too. They're asking for all levels below them to be cleared, and priority approach and landing. ETA is 0505 . . . Roger. We'll keep you posted. *(To a Teletype Operator, who has appeared.)* Got Winnipeg? *(As Teletype Operator nods.)* Send this message. Controller Winnipeg. Urgent. Maple Leaf Charter Flight 714 reports serious food poisoning among passengers believed due to fish dinner served on flight. Imperative check source and suspend all other food service originating same place. That's all. *(To Switchboard Operator.)* Get me the local agent for Maple Leaf Charter. Burdick's his name—call his home. And after that I want the city police—the senior officer on duty.

(Controller crosses to radio control panel and reads message which is just being completed.)

(To Radio Operator.) Acknowledge. Say that all altitudes below them are being cleared and they'll be advised of landing instructions here. Ask them to keep us posted on condition of the passengers.

SWITCHBOARD OPERATOR. Mr. Burdick is here at the airport. I have him on the line now.

CONTROLLER. Good. Controller here. Burdick, we've got an emergency on one of your flights—714, ex-Toronto and Winnipeg. *(Pause.)* No the aircraft is all right. There's food poisoning among the passengers, and the First Officer has it too. You'd better come over. *(Replaces phone. Then to Switchboard Operator.)* Have you got the police yet? *(As Operator nods.)* Right, put it on this line. Hello, this is the Controller, Vancouver

Airport. Who am I speaking to, please? (*Pause.*) Inspector, we have an emergency on an incoming flight. Several of the passengers are seriously ill, and we need ambulances and doctors out here at the airport. (*Pause.*) Six people for sure, maybe more. The flight will be landing at five minutes past five local time—that's in about three and a half hours. Now, will you get the ambulances, set up traffic control, and alert the hospitals? Right. We'll call you again as soon as there's anything definite.

(*During the above, Harry Burdick, local manager of Maple Leaf Air Charter, has entered.*)

BURDICK. Where's the message?

(*Radio Operator hands him a copy which Burdick reads.*)

BURDICK. (*To Radio Operator.*) How's the weather at Calgary? It might be quicker to go in there.

CONTROLLER. No dice! There's fog down to the deck everywhere east of the Rockies. They'll have to come through.

BURDICK. Let me see the last position report. (*As Controller passes a clip board.*) You say you've got medical help coming?

CONTROLLER. The city police are working on it now.

BURDICK. That message! They say the First Officer is down. What about the Captain? Ask if he's affected, and ask if there's a doctor on board. Tell them we're getting medical advice here in case they need it.

CONTROLLER. I'll take care of that.

BURDICK. (*To Switchboard Operator.*) Will you get me Doctor Knudsen, please? You'll find his home number on the emergency list.

CONTROLLER. (*Into radio mike.*) Flight 714, this is Vancouver.

DISSOLVE TO:

The airplane passenger cabin. Baird is leaning over another prostrate passenger. The main lighting is on in the cabin, and other passengers, so far not affected, are watching, with varying degrees of concern and anxiety. Some have remained in their seats, others have clustered in the aisle. The doctor has obtained his bag and it is open beside him. The Stewardess is attending to another passenger nearby.

BAIRD. (*To Stewardess.*) I think I'd better talk to everyone and tell them the story. (*Moving to center of cabin, he raises his voice.*) Ladies and gentlemen, may I have your attention, please? If you can't hear me, perhaps you would come a little closer. (*Pause, as passengers move in.*) My name is Baird, and I am a doctor. I think it's time that everyone knew what is happening. So far as I can tell, we have several cases of food poisoning, and we believe that the cause of it was the fish which was served for dinner.

SECOND WOMAN PASSENGER. (*With alarm, to man beside her.*) Hector! We both had fish!

BAIRD. Now, there is no immediate cause for alarm or panic, and even if you did eat fish for dinner, it doesn't follow that you are going to be affected too. There's seldom any logic to these things. However, we *are* going to take some precautions, and the Stewardess and I are coming around to everyone, and I want you to tell us if you ate fish. If you did we'll tell you what to do to help yourselves. Now, if you'll go back to your seats we'll begin right away. (*To Stewardess, as passengers move back to their seats.*) All we can do now is to give immediate first aid.

STEWARDESS. What should that be, Doctor?

BAIRD. Two things. First, everyone who ate fish must drink several glasses of water. That will help to dilute the poison. After that we'll give an emetic. I have some emetic pills in my bag, and if there aren't enough we'll have to rely on salt. Do you have salt in the galley?

STEWARDESS. A few small packets which go with the lunches, but we can break them open.

BAIRD. All right. We'll see how far the pills will go first. I'll start at the back here. Meanwhile you begin giving drinking water to the passengers already affected and get some to the First Officer too. I'll ask someone to help you.

FIRST MALE PASSENGER. Can I help, Doctor?

BAIRD. What did you eat for dinner—fish or meat?

FIRST MALE PASSENGER. Meat.

BAIRD. All right. Will you help the Stewardess bring glasses of water to the people who are sick? I want them to drink at least three glasses each— more if they can.

STEWARDESS. (*Going to galley.*) We'll use these cups. There's drinking water here and at the rear.

FIRST MALE PASSENGER. All right, let's get started.

BAIRD. (*To Stewardess.*) The Captain! Before you do anything else you'd better get him on to drinking water, and give him two emetic pills. Here. (*Takes bottle from his bag and shakes out the pills.*) Tell him they'll make him feel sick, and the sooner he is, the better.

STEWARDESS. Very well, Doctor.

SECOND WOMAN PASSENGER.   (*Frightened.*) Doctor! Doctor! I heard you say the pilots are ill. What will happen to us if they can't fly the plane? (*To husband.*) Hector, I'm frightened.

THIRD MALE PASSENGER.   Take it easy, my dear. Nothing has happened so far, and the doctor is doing all he can.

BAIRD.   I don't think you'll have any reason to worry, madam. It's quite true that both of the pilots had the fish which we believe may have caused the trouble. But only the first officer is affected. Now, did you and your husband eat fish or meat?

THIRD MALE PASSENGER.   Fish. We both ate fish.

BAIRD.   Then will you both drink at least three—better make it four—of those cups of water which the other gentleman is bringing around. After that, take one of these pills each. (*Smiling.*) I think you'll find there are little containers under your seat. Use those. (*Goes to the rear of plane.*)

FOURTH MALE PASSENGER.   (*In broad English Yorkshire accent.*) How's it comin', Doc? Everything under control?

BAIRD.   I think we're holding our own. What did you have for dinner?

FOURTH MALE PASSENGER.   Ah had the bloomin' fish. Didn't like it neither. Fine how d'you do this is. Coom all this way t'see our team win, and now it looks like ah'm headed for a mortuary slab.

BAIRD.   It really isn't as bad as that, you know. But just as a precaution, drink four cups of water—it's being brought around now—and after that take this pill. It'll make you feel sick.

FOURTH MALE PASSENGER.   (*Pulls carton under seat and holds it up.*) It's the last time I ride on a bloomin' airplane! What a service! They give you your dinner and then coom round and ask for it back.

BAIRD.   What did you have for dinner, please—meat or fish?

SECOND MALE PASSENGER.   Meat, Doctor.

FIFTH MALE PASSENGER.   Yes, I had meat too.

BAIRD.   All right, we won't worry about you.

SIXTH MALE PASSENGER.   I had meat, Doctor.

SEVENTH MALE PASSENGER.   I had fish.

BAIRD.   Very well, will you drink at least four cups of water, please? It'll be brought around to you. Then take this pill.

SIXTH MALE PASSENGER.   (*Slow speaking, a little dull witted.*) What's caused this food poisoning, Doctor?

BAIRD.   Well, it can either be caused through spoilage of the food, or some kind of bacteria—the medical word is staphylococcus poisoning.

SIXTH MALE PASSENGER. (*Nodding knowledgeably.*) Oh yes . . . staphylo . . . I *see.*

BAIRD. Either that, or some toxic substance may have gotten into the food during its preparation.

SEVENTH MALE PASSENGER. Which kind do you think this is, Doctor?

BAIRD. From the effect I suspect a toxic substance.

SEVENTH MALE PASSENGER. And you don't know what it is?

BAIRD. We won't know until we make laboratory tests. Actually, with modern food-handling methods—the chances of this happening are probably a million to one against.

STEWARDESS. (*Entering.*) I couldn't get the First Officer to take more than a little water, Doctor. He seems pretty bad.

BAIRD. I'll go to him now. Have you checked all the passengers in the front portion?

STEWARDESS. Yes, and there are two new cases—the same symptoms as the others.

BAIRD. I'll attend to them—after I've looked at the First Officer.

STEWARDESS. Do you think . . .

(*Before the sentence is completed the galley telephone buzzes insistently. Baird and the Stewardess exchange glances quickly, then, without waiting to answer the phone, race to the flight deck door.*)

CUT TO:

The flight deck. The Captain is in the left-hand seat. Sweat pouring down his face, he is racked by retching, and his right hand is on his stomach. Yet he is fighting against the pain and attempting to reach the radio transmitter mike. But he doesn't make it, and, as Baird and the Stewardess reach him, he falls back in his seat.

CAPTAIN. (*Weakly.*) I did what you said . . . guess it was too late. . . . You've got to give me something, Doctor . . . so I can hold out . . . till I get this airplane on the ground. . . . You understand? . . . It'll fly itself on this course . . . but I've got to take it in. . . . Get on the radio. . . . Tell control . . .

(*During the above Baird and the Stewardess have been helping the Captain from his seat. Now he collapses into unconsciousness, and Baird goes down beside him. The doctor has a stethoscope now and uses it.*)

BAIRD. Get blankets over him. Keep him warm. There's probably a reaction because he tried to fight it off so long.

STEWARDESS. (*Alarmed.*) Can you do what he said? Can you bring him around long enough to land?

BAIRD. (*Bluntly.*) You're part of this crew, so I'll tell you how things are. Unless I can get him to a hospital quickly I'm not even sure I can save his life. And that goes for the others too.

STEWARDESS. But—

BAIRD. I know what you're thinking, and I've thought of it too. How many passengers are there on board?

STEWARDESS. Fifty-six.

BAIRD. And how many fish dinners did you serve?

STEWARDESS. (*Composing herself.*) Probably about fifteen. More people ate meat than fish, and some didn't eat at all because it was so late.

BAIRD. And you?

STEWARDESS. I had meat.

BAIRD. (*Quietly.*) My dear, did you ever hear the term "long odds"?

STEWARDESS. Yes, but I'm not sure what it means.

BAIRD. I'll give you an example. Out of a total field of fifty-five, our chance of safety depends on there being one person back there who not only is qualified to land this airplane, but who didn't choose fish for dinner tonight.

(*After her initial alarm the Stewardess is calm now, and competent. She looks Baird in the eye and even manages a slight smile.*)

STEWARDESS. Then I suppose I should begin asking.

BAIRD. (*Thoughtfully.*) Yes, but there's no sense in starting a panic. (*Decisively.*) You'd better do it this way. Say that the First Officer is sick and the Captain wondered if there's someone with flying experience who could help him with the radio.

STEWARDESS. Very well, Doctor. (*She turns to go.*)

BAIRD. Wait! The man who was sitting beside me! He said something about flying in the war. And we both ate meat. Get him first! But still go around to the others. There may be someone else with more experience.

(*Stewardess exits and Baird busies himself with the First Officer and the Captain. After a moment, George Spencer enters.*)

SPENCER. The Stewardess said— (*Then, as he sees the two pilots*) . . . No! Not both pilots!

BAIRD. Can *you* fly this airplane—and land it?

SPENCER. No! No! Not a chance! Of course not!

BAIRD.   But you told me you flew in the war.

SPENCER.   So I did. But that was fighters—little combat airplanes, not a great ship like this. I flew airplanes which had one engine. This has four. Flying characteristics are different. Controls don't react the same way. It's another kind of flying altogether. And besides that, I haven't touched an airplane for over ten years.

BAIRD.   (*Grimly.*) Then let's hope there's someone else on board who can do the job . . . because neither of these men can.

(*Stewardess enters and pauses.*)

STEWARDESS.   (*Quietly.*) There's no one else.

BAIRD.   Mr. Spencer, I know nothing of flying. I have no means of evaluating what you tell me. All I know is this: that among the people on this airplane who are physically able to fly it, you are the only one with any kind of qualification to do so. What do you suggest?

SPENCER.   (*Desperately.*) Isn't there a chance—of either pilot recovering?

BAIRD.   I'll tell you what I just told the Stewardess here. Unless I can get them to a hospital quickly, I can't even be sure of saving their lives.

(*There is a pause.*)

SPENCER.   Well—I guess I just got drafted. If either of you are any good at praying, you can start any time.

(*He slips into the left-hand seat.*)

Let's take a look. Altitude 16,000. Course 290. The ship's on automatic pilot—we can be thankful for that. Air speed 210 knots. (*Touching the various controls.*) Throttles, pitch, mixture, landing gear, flaps, and the flap indicator. We'll need a check list for landing, but we'll get that on the radio. Well, maybe we'd better tell the world about our problems. (*To Stewardess.*) Do you know how to work this radio? They've added a lot of gizmos since my flying days.

STEWARDESS.   (*Pointing.*) It's this panel up here they use to talk to the ground, but I'm not sure which switches you have to set.

SPENCER.   Ah yes, here's the channel selector. Maybe we'd better leave it where it is. Oh, and here we are—"transmit."

(*He flicks a switch, and a small light glows on the radio control panel.*)

Now we're in business.

(*He picks up the mike and headset beside him, then turns to the other two.*)

Look, whatever happens I'm going to need another pair of hands here. Doc, I guess you'll be needed back with the others, so I think the best choice is Miss Canada here. How about it?

STEWARDESS.   But I know nothing about all this!

SPENCER.   Then that'll make us a real good pair. But I'll tell you what to do ahead of time. Better get in that other seat and strap yourself in. That all right with you, Doc?

BAIRD.   Yes, do that. I'll take care of things in the back. And I'd better go there now. Good luck!

SPENCER.   Good luck to *you*. We're all going to need it.

(*Baird exits.*)

SPENCER.   What's your name?

STEWARDESS.   Janet.

SPENCER.   Okay, Janet. Let's see if I can remember how to send out a distress message . . . Better put on that headset beside you. (*Into mike.*) May Day! May Day! May Day! (*To Stewardess.*) What's our flight number?

STEWARDESS.   714.

SPENCER.   (*Into mike.*) This is Flight 714, Maple Leaf Air Charter, in distress. Come in anyone. Over.

VOICE ON RADIO.   (*Immediately, crisply.*) This is Calgary, 714. Go ahead!

VOICE ON RADIO.   (*Vancouver Operator.*) Vancouver here 714. All other aircraft stay off the air. Over.

SPENCER.   Thank you Calgary and Vancouver. This message is for Vancouver. This aircraft is in distress. Both pilots and some passengers— (*To Stewardess.*) How many passengers?

STEWARDESS.   It was seven a few minutes ago. It may be more now.

SPENCER.   Correction. At least seven passengers are suffering from food poisoning. Both pilots are unconscious and in serious condition. We have a doctor on board who says that neither pilot can be revived. Did you get that Vancouver? (*Pause.*) Now we come to the interesting bit. My name is Spencer, George Spencer. I am a passenger on this airplane. Correction: I *was* a passenger. I have about a thousand hours total flying time, but all of it was on single-engine fighters. And also I haven't flown an airplane for ten years. Now, then, Vancouver, you'd better get someone on this radio who can give me some instructions about flying this machine. Our altitude is 16,000, course 290 magnetic, air speed 210 knots. We are on automatic pilot. Your move, Vancouver.

Over. (*To Stewardess.*) You want to take a bet that that stirred up a little flurry down below?

(*The Stewardess shakes her head, but does not reply.*)

DISSOLVE TO:

The control room, Vancouver.

(*The Controller is putting down a phone as the Radio Operator brings a message to him. He reads the message.*)

CONTROLLER. Oh no! (*To Radio Operator.*) Ask if— No, let me talk to them.

(*Controller goes to panel and takes the transmitter mike. The Radio Operator turns a switch and nods.*)

CONTROLLER. (*Tensely.*) Flight 714. This is Vancouver control. Please check with your doctor on board for any possibility of either pilot recovering. Ask him to do everything possible to revive one of the pilots, even if it means neglecting other people. Over.

SPENCER'S VOICE ON RADIO. Vancouver, this is 714, Spencer speaking. I understand your message. But the doctor says there is no possibility whatever of either pilot recovering to make the landing. He says they are critically ill and may die unless they get hospital treatment soon. Over.

CONTROLLER. All right, 714. Stand by, please.

(*He pauses momentarily to consider the next course of action. Then briskly to Switchboard Operator.*)

Get me area traffic control—fast. (*Into phone.*) Vancouver controller. The emergency we had! . . . Right now it looks like it's shaping up for a disaster.

FADE OUT

END OF ACT TWO

ACT THREE

FADE IN:

The control room, Vancouver. The atmosphere is one of restrained pandemonium. The Radio Operator is typing a message. The teletypes are busy. The Controller is on one telephone, and Harry Burdick on another. During what follows cut back and forth from one to the other.

CONTROLLER. (*Into phone.*) As of right now, hold everything taking off for the East. You've got forty-five minutes to clear any traffic for South, West, or North. After that, hold everything that's scheduled outward. On incoming traffic, accept anything you can get on the deck within the next forty-five minutes. Anything you can't get down by then for sure, divert away from this area. Hold it.

(*A messenger hands him a message which he scans. Then to messenger.*)

Tell the security officer. (*Into phone.*) If you've any flights coming in from the Pacific, divert them to Seattle. And any traffic inland is to stay well away from the east-west lane between Calgary and Vancouver. Got that? Right.

BURDICK. (*Into phone.*) Is that Cross-Canada Airlines? . . . Who's on duty in operations? . . . Let me talk to him. (*Pause.*) Mr. Gardner, it's Harry Burdick of Maple Leaf Charter. We have an incoming flight that's in bad trouble, and we need an experienced pilot to talk on the radio. Someone who's flown DC-4's. Can you help us? (*Pause.*) Captain Treleaven? Yes, I know him well. (*Pause.*) You mean he's with you now? (*Pause.*) Can he come over to control right away? (*Pause.*) Thank you. Thank you very much. (*To Switchboard Operator.*) Get me Montreal. I want to talk with Mr. Barney Whitmore. You may have to try Maple Leaf Air Charter office first, and someone there'll have his home number. Tell them the call is urgent.

SWITCHBOARD OPERATOR. Right. (*To Controller.*) I've got the fire chief.

CONTROLLER. (*Into phone.*) Chief, we have an emergency. It's Flight 714, due here at 0505. It may be a crash landing. Have everything you've got stand by. If you have men off duty call them in. Take your instructions from the tower. They'll tell you which runway we're using. And notify the city fire department. They may want to move equipment into this area. Right. (*To Switchboard Operator.*) Now get me the city police again —Inspector Moyse.

SWITCHBOARD OPERATOR. I have Seattle and Calgary waiting. They both received the message from Flight 714 and want to know if we got it clearly.

CONTROLLER. Tell them thank you, yes, and we're working the aircraft direct. But ask them to keep a listening watch in case we run into any reception trouble.

(*Another message is handed him. After reading, he passes it to Burdick.*)

There's bad weather moving in. That's all we need. (*To Switchboard Operator.*) Have you got the police? Right! (*Into phone.*) It's the Airport Controller again, Inspector. We're in bad trouble, and we may have a crash landing. We'll need every spare ambulance in the city out here— and doctors and nurses too. Will you arrange it? (*Pause.*) Yes, we do— fifty-six passengers and a crew of three. (*Pause.*) Yes, the same time— 0505. That's less than three hours.

BURDICK.   (*To switchboard.*) Is Montreal on the line yet? . . . Yes, give it to me . . . Hello. Hello. Is that you, Barney? . . . It's Harry Burdick in Vancouver. I'll give you this fast, Barney. Our flight from Toronto is in bad trouble. They have food poisoning on board, and both pilots and a lot of the passengers have passed out. There's a doctor on board, and he says there's no chance of recovery before they get to the hospital. (*Pause.*) It's a passenger doing the flying. He's just been on the radio. (*Pause.*) No, he isn't qualified. He flew single-engine fighters in the war, nothing since. (*Pause.*) I've asked him that. This doctor on board says there isn't a chance. (*Pause.*) What else can we do? We've got to talk him down. Cross-Canada is lending us a pilot. It's Captain Treleaven, one of their senior men. He's here now, just arrived. We'll get on the radio with a check list and try to bring him in. (*Pause.*) We'll do the best we can. (*Pause. Then impatiently.*) Of course it's a terrible risk, but can you think of something better? (*Pause.*) No, the papers aren't on to it yet, but don't worry, they will be soon. We can't help that now. (*Pause. Anxious to get off phone.*) That's all we know, Barney. It only just happened. I called you right away. ETA is 0505 Pacific time; that's just under two hours. I've got a lot to do, Barney. I'll have to get on with it. (*Pause. Nodding impatiently.*) I'll call you. I'll call you as soon as I know anything more . . . G'by.

(*During the foregoing Captain Martin Treleaven, forty-five, has entered. He is wearing airline uniform. As Burdick sees Treleaven, he beckons him, indicating that he should listen. To Treleaven.*)

Did you get that?

TRELEAVEN.   (*Calmly .*) Is that the whole story?

BURDICK.   That's everything we know. Now what I want you to do is get on the horn and talk this pilot down. You'll have to help him get the feel of the airplane on the way. You'll have to talk him around the circuit. You'll have to give him the cockpit check for landing, and—so help me!—you'll have to talk him onto the ground.

(*Captain Treleaven is a calm man, not easily perturbed. While Burdick has been talking, the Captain has been filling his pipe. Now, with methodical movements, he puts away his tobacco pouch and begins to light the pipe.*)

TRELEAVEN.　(*Quietly.*) You realize, of course, that the chances of a man who has only flown fighter airplanes, landing a four-engine passenger ship safely are about nine to one against.

BURDICK.　(*Rattled.*) Of course I know it! You heard what I told Whitmore. But do *you* have any other ideas?

TRELEAVEN.　No. I just wanted to be sure you knew what we were getting into, Harry . . . All right. Let's get started. Where do I go?

CONTROLLER.　Over here.

(*They cross to the radio panel, and the operator hands him the last message from the aircraft. When he has read it he takes the transmitter mike.*)

TRELEAVEN.　How does this thing work?

RADIO OPERATOR.　(*Turning a switch.*) You're on the air now.

TRELEAVEN.　(*Calmly.*) Hello, Flight 714. This is Vancouver, and my name is Martin Treleaven. I am a Cross-Canada Airlines captain, and my job right now is to help fly this airplane in. First of all, are you hearing me okay? Over.

VOICE OF SPENCER.　Yes, Captain, loud and clear. Go ahead, please.

TRELEAVEN.　Where's that message? (*As operator passes it. Into mike.*) I see that I'm talking to George Spencer. Well, George, I don't think you're going to have much trouble. These DC-4's handle easily, and we'll give you the drill for landing. But first of all, please tell me what your flying experience is. The message says you have flown single-engine fighters. What kind of airplanes were these, and did you fly multi-engine airplanes at all? Let's hear from you, George. Over.

CUT TO:
The flight deck.

SPENCER.　(*Into mike.*) Hello, Vancouver, this is 714. Glad to have you along, Captain. But let's not kid each other, please. We both know we need a lot of luck. About my flying. It was mostly on Spitfires and Mustangs. And I have around a thousand hours' total. And all of that was ten years ago. Over.

CUT TO:

The control room.

TRELEAVEN. (*Into mike.*) Don't worry about that, George. It's like riding a bicycle. You never forget it. Stand by.

CONTROLLER. (*To Treleaven.*) The air force has picked up the airplane on radar, and they'll be giving us courses to bring him in. Here's the first one. See if you can get him on that heading.

TRELEAVEN. (*Nods. Then into mike.*) 714, are you still on automatic pilot? If so, look for the auto pilot release switch. It's a push button on the control yoke and is plainly marked. Over.

CUT TO:

The flight deck.

SPENCER. (*Into mike.*) Yes, Vancouver. I see the auto-pilot switch. Over.

CUT TO:

The control room.

TRELEAVEN. (*Into mike.*) Now, George, in a minute you can unlock the automatic pilot and get the feel of the controls, and we're going to change your course a little. But first listen carefully. When you use the controls they will seem very heavy and sluggish compared with a fighter airplane. But don't worry, that's quite normal. You must take care, though, to watch your air speed carefully, and do not let it fall below 120 knots while your wheels and flaps are up. Otherwise you will stall. Now, do you have someone up there who can work the radio to leave you free for flying? Over.

CUT TO:

The flight deck.

SPENCER. (*Into mike.*) Yes, Vancouver. I have the Stewardess here with me, and she will take over the radio now. I am now going to unlock the automatic pilot. Over. (*To Stewardess as he depresses the auto-pilot release.*) Well, here we go.

(*Feeling the controls, Spencer eases into a left turn.*)

(*Then straightening out, he eases the control columns slightly forward and back.*)

CUT TO:

The control room.

TRELEAVEN'S VOICE.   Hello, 714. How are you making out, George? Have you got the feel of her yet?

CUT TO:

The flight deck.

SPENCER.   Tell him I'm on manual now and trying out some gentle turns.

STEWARDESS.   (*Into mike.*) Hello, Vancouver. We are on manual now and trying out some gentle turns.

CUT TO:

The control room.

TRELEAVEN.   (*Into mike.*) Hello, George Spencer. Try the effect of fore-and-aft control on your air speed. To begin with, close your throttles slightly and bring your air speed back to 160. Adjust the trim as you go along. But watch that air speed closely. Remember to keep it well above 120. Over.

CUT TO:

The flight deck.

SPENCER.   (*Tensely. Still feeling out the controls.*) Tell him okay.

STEWARDESS.   (*Into mike.*) Okay, Vancouver. We are doing as you say.

TRELEAVEN'S VOICE.   (*After a pause.*) Hello, 714. How does she handle, George?

SPENCER.   (*Disgustedly.*) Tell him sluggish like a wet sponge.

STEWARDESS.   Sluggish like a wet sponge, Vancouver.

CUT TO:

The control room.

(*There is a momentary relaxing of tension as Captain Treleaven and the group around him exchange grins.*)

TRELEAVEN.   (*Into mike.*) Hello, George Spencer. That would be a natural feeling, because you were used to handling smaller airplanes. The thing you have got to remember is that there is a bigger lag in the effect of control movements on air speed, compared with what you were used to before. Do you understand that? Over.

CUT TO:

The flight deck.

SPENCER.   Tell him I understand.

STEWARDESS.   (*Into mike.*) Hello, Vancouver. Yes, he understands. Over.

CUT TO:

The control room.

TRELEAVEN.   (*Into mike.*) Hello, George Spencer. Because of that lag in air speed you must avoid any violent movements of the controls, such as you used to make in your fighter airplanes. If you *do* move the controls violently, you will over-correct and be in trouble. Is that understood? Over.

CUT TO:

The flight deck.

SPENCER.   (*Nodding, beginning to perspire.*) Tell him—yes, I understand.

STEWARDESS.   (*Into mike.*) Yes, Vancouver. Your message is understood. Over.

CUT TO:

The control room.

TRELEAVEN.   (*Into mike.*) Hello, George Spencer. Now I want you to feel how the ship handles at lower speeds when the flaps and wheels are down. But don't do anything until I give you the instructions. Is that clear? Over.

CUT TO:

The flight deck.

SPENCER.   Tell him okay; let's have the instructions.

STEWARDESS.   (*Into mike.*) Hello, Vancouver. Yes, we understand. Go ahead with the instructions. Over.

TRELEAVEN'S VOICE.   First of all, throttle back slightly, get your air speed steady at 160 knots, and adjust your trim to maintain level flight. Then tell me when you're ready. Over.

SPENCER.   Watch that air speed, Janet. You'll have to call it off to me when we land, so you may as well start practicing.

STEWARDESS.   It's 200 now . . . 190 . . . 185 . . . 180 . . . 175 . . . 175 . . . 165 . . . 155 . . . 150 . . . (*Alarmed*) That's too low! He said 160!

SPENCER.   (*Tensely.*) I know. I know. Watch it! It's that lag on the air speed. I can't get used to.

STEWARDESS.   150 . . . 150 . . . 155 . . . 160 . . . 160 . . . It's steady on 160.

SPENCER.   Tell them.

STEWARDESS.   (*Into mike.*) Hello, Vancouver. This is 714. Our speed is steady at 160. Over.

CUT TO:

The control room.

TRELEAVEN. (*Into mike.*) Okay, 714. Now, George, I want you to put down twenty degrees of flap. But be careful not to make it any more. The flap lever is at the base of the control pedestal and is plainly marked. Twenty degrees will mean moving the lever down to the second notch. Over.

CUT TO:

The flight deck.

SPENCER. Janet, you'll have to put the flaps down. (*Pointing.*) There's the lever.

TRELEAVEN'S VOICE. Can you see the flap indicator, George? It's near the center of the main panel.

SPENCER. Here's the indicator he's talking about. When I tell you, push the lever down to the second notch and watch the dial. Okay?

STEWARDESS. Okay (*Then with alarm.*) Oh, look at the air speed! It's down to 125!

(*Spencer grimaces and pushes the control column forward.*)

SPENCER. (*Urgently.*) Call off the speed! Call off the speed!

STEWARDESS. 140 . . . 150 . . . 160 . . . 170 . . . 175 . . . Can't you get it back to 160?

SPENCER. (*Straining.*) I'm trying! I'm trying! (*Pause.*) There it is.

CUT TO:

The passenger cabin.

SECOND WOMAN PASSENGER. (*Frightened.*) Hector! We're going to crash! I know it! Oh, do something! Do something!

BAIRD. (*He appears at her elbow.*) Have her take this. It'll help calm her down. (*Gives pill and cup to Third Male Passenger.*) Try not to worry. That young man at the front is a very experienced pilot. He's just what they call "getting the feel" of the airplane.

(*He moves aft in the cabin.*)

FIRST MALE PASSENGER. Doctor!

BAIRD. Yes.

FIRST MALE PASSENGER. Tell us the truth, Doctor. Have we got a chance? Does this fellow know how to fly this thing?

BAIRD. We've got all kinds of chances. He's a very experienced pilot, but it's just that he's not used to flying this particular type and he's getting the feel of it.

FOURTH MALE PASSENGER. You didn't need none of them pills to make me sick. Never mind me dinner. Now ah'm workin' on yesterday's breakfast.

CUT TO:

The flight deck.

STEWARDESS. (*Into mike.*) Hello, Vancouver. Air speed is 160, and we are ready to put down the flaps. Over.

CUT TO:

The control room.

TRELEAVEN. (*Into mike.*) Okay, 714. Go ahead with your flaps. But be careful—only twenty degrees. Then, when you have twenty degrees down, bring back the air speed to 140, adjust your trim, and call me again. Over.

CUT TO:

The flight deck.

SPENCER. Okay, Janet—flaps down! Twenty degrees.

(*The Stewardess pushes down the flap lever to its second notch.*)

Tell them we've got the flaps down, and the air speed's coming to 140.

STEWARDESS. (*Into mike.*) Hello, Vancouver. This is 714. The flaps are down, and our air speed is 140.

CUT TO:

The control room.

TRELEAVEN. All right, 714. Now the next thing is to put the wheels down. Are you still maintaining level flight?

CUT TO:

The flight deck.

SPENCER. Tell him—more or less.

STEWARDESS. (*Into mike.*) Hello, Vancouver. More or less.

CUT TO:

The control room.

RADIO OPERATOR. This guy's got a sense of humor.

BURDICK. That's a *real* help.

TRELEAVEN. (*Into mike.*) Okay, 714. Try to keep your altitude steady and your speed at 140. Then when you *are* ready, put down the landing gear and let your speed come back to 120. You will have to advance your throttle setting to maintain that air speed, and also adjust your trim. Is that understood? Over.

CUT TO:

The flight deck.

SPENCER. Ask him—what about the propeller controls and mixture?

STEWARDESS. (*Into mike.*) Hello, Vancouver. What about the propeller controls and mixture? Over.

CUT TO:

The control room.

CONTROLLER. He's thinking, anyway.

TRELEAVEN. (*Into mike.*) Leave them alone for the time being. Just concentrate on holding that air speed steady with the wheels and flaps down. Over.

CUT TO:

The flight deck.

SPENCER. Wheels down, Janet, and call off the air speed.

STEWARDESS. (*Selects landing gear "down."*) 140 . . . 145 . . . 140 . . . 135 . . . 130 . . . 125 . . . 120 . . . 115 . . . The speed's too low!

SPENCER. Keep calling it!

STEWARDESS. 115 . . . 120 . . . 120 . . . Steady on 120.

CUT TO:

The control room.

TRELEAVEN. (*Into mike.*) Hello, George Spencer. Your wheels should be down by now, and look for three green lights to show that they're locked. Over.

CUT TO:

The flight deck.

SPENCER. Are they on?

STEWARDESS. Yes—all three lights are green.

SPENCER. Tell them.

STEWARDESS. (*Into mike.*) Hello, Vancouver. Yes, there are three green lights.

CUT TO:

The control room.

TRELEAVEN. Okay, 714, now let's put down full flap so that you can feel how the airplane will handle when you're landing. As soon as full flap is down, bring your air speed back to 110 knots and trim to hold it steady. Adjust your throttle setting to hold your altitude. Is that understood? Over.

CUT TO:

The flight deck.

SPENCER.   Tell him "yes."

STEWARDESS.   (*Into mike.*) Yes, Vancouver. That is understood.

SPENCER.   Full flap, Janet! Push the lever all the way down, and call off the air speed.

STEWARDESS.   120 . . . 115 . . . 115 . . . 110 . . . 110 . . .

SPENCER.   Okay, tell 'em we've got full flap and air speed 110, and she still handles like a sponge, only more so.

STEWARDESS.   (*Into mike.*) Hello, Vancouver. We have full flap, and air speed is 110. And the pilot says she still handles like a sponge, only more so.

CUT TO:

The control room.

(Again there is a momentary sense of relief.)

TRELEAVEN.   (*Into mike.*) That's nice going, George. Now I'm going to give you instructions for holding your height and air speed while you raise the flaps and landing gear. Then we'll run through the whole procedure again.

CUT TO:

The flight deck.

SPENCER.   Again! I don't know if my nerves'll stand it. (*Pause.*) All right. Tell him okay.

DISSOLVE TO:

Control room clock showing 2:55.

DISSOLVE TO:

Control room clock showing 5:20.

DISSOLVE TO:

The control room. Captain Treleaven is still seated in front of the transmitter, but has obviously been under strain. He now has his coat off and his tie loosened, and there is an empty carton of coffee beside him. Burdick and the Controller are in the background, watching tensely. A phone rings and the Controller answers it. He makes a note and passes it to Treleaven.

TRELEAVEN.   (*Into mike*). Hello, Flight 714. Our flying practice has slowed you down, and you are later than we expected. You are now twelve minutes flying time from Vancouver Airport, but it's getting light, so your landing will be in daylight. You should be able to see us at any minute. Do you see the airport beacon? Over.

STEWARDESS'S VOICE.   Yes, we see the airport beacon. Over.

TRELEAVEN.   Okay, George, now you've practiced everything we need for a landing. You've flown the ship with wheels and flaps down, and you know how she handles. Your fuel feeds are checked, and you're all set to come in. You won't hear from me again for a few minutes because I'm moving to the control tower so I'll be able to see you on the circuit and approach. Is that clear? Over.

STEWARDESS'S VOICE.   Yes, Vancouver, that is understood. Over.

TRELEAVEN.   All right, George. Continue to approach at two thousand feet on your present heading and wait for instructions. We'll let you know the runway to use at the last minute because the wind is shifting. Don't forget we want you to do at least one dummy run, and then go around again so you'll have practice in making the landing approach. Over.

(*He mops his forehead with a crumpled handkerchief.*)

CUT TO:
The flight deck.

(*Spencer, too, has his coat off and tie loosened. His hair is ruffled, and the strain is plainly beginning to tell on him. The Stewardess is still in the co-pilot's seat, and Baird is standing behind them both. The Stewardess is about to acknowledge the last radio message, but Spencer stops her.*)

SPENCER.   I'll take it, Janet. (*Into mike.*) No dice, Vancouver. We're coming straight in and the first time is "it." Dr. Baird is here beside me. He reports two of the passengers and the first officer are in critical condition, and we must land in the next few minutes. The doctor asks that you have stomach pumps and oxygen equipment ready. Over.

CUT TO:
The control room.

BURDICK.   He mustn't! We need time!

TRELEAVEN.   It's his decision. By all the rules he's in command of the airplane. (*Into mike.*) 714, your message is understood. Good luck to us all. Listening out. (*To Burdick and Controller.*) Let's go!

DISSOLVE TO:
The flight deck.

SPENCER.   This is it, Doctor. You'd better go back now and make sure everybody's strapped in tight. Are both the pilots in seats?

BAIRD.   Yes.

SPENCER.   How about the passengers who aren't sick? Are they worried?

BAIRD.   A little, but there's no panic. I exaggerated your qualifications. I'd better go. Good luck.

SPENCER.   (*With ironic grin.*) Thanks.

DISSOLVE TO:

The control tower, Vancouver Airport. It is a glass-enclosed area, with radio panels and other equipment, and access is by a stairway from below. It is now daylight, and the Tower Controller is looking skyward, using binoculars. There is the sound of hurried feet on the stairway and Treleaven, the Controller, and Burdick emerge in that order.

TOWER CONTROLLER.   There he is!

(*Treleaven picks up a second pair of binoculars, looks through them quickly, then puts them down.*)

TRELEAVEN.   All right—let's make our decision on the runway. What's it to be?

TOWER CONTROLLER.   Zero eight. It's pretty well into wind now, though there'll be a slight crosswind from the left. It's also the longest.

TRELEAVEN.   (*Into mike.*) Hello, Flight 714. This is Martin Treleaven in Vancouver tower. Do you read me? Over.

CUT TO:

The flight deck.

STEWARDESS.   (*Into mike.*) Yes, Vancouver Tower. Loud and clear. Over.

CUT TO:

The tower.

TRELEAVEN.   (*Crisply, authoritatively, yet calmly.*) From here on, do not acknowledge any further transmissions unless you wish to ask a question. You are now ready to join the airport circuit. The runway for landing is zero eight. That means you are now crosswind and will shortly make a left turn on to the downwind leg. Begin now to lose height to one thousand feet. Throttle back slightly and make your descent at 400 feet a minute. Let your air speed come back to 160 knots and hold it steady there. . . . Air speed 160.

CONTROLLER.   (*Reaching for phone.*) Runway is zero eight. All vehicles stand by near the extreme south end. Do not, repeat not, go down the runway until the aircraft has passed by you because it may swing off. Is that clear? (*Pause.*) Right.

CUT TO:

Film Insert: Fire trucks and ambulances are manned and move away with sirens wailing.

CUT TO:

The flight deck. Spencer is pushing the throttles forward, and the tempo of the motors increases.

SPENCER. Tell them we're at one thousand feet and leveling off.

STEWARDESS. (*Into mike.*) Vancouver Tower. We are now at one thousand feet and leveling off. Over.

TRELEAVEN'S VOICE. Now let's have twenty degrees of flap. Do not acknowledge this message.

SPENCER. Twenty degrees of flap, Janet.

(*The Stewardess reaches for flap lever and pushes it down while she watches the flap indicator.*)

TRELEAVEN'S VOICE. When you have your flaps down, bring your air speed back slowly to 140 knots, adjust your trim, and begin to make a left turn onto the downwind leg. When you have turned, fly parallel with the runway you see on your left. I repeat—air speed 140 and begin a left turn.

CUT TO:

Close-up of an instrument panel showing artificial horizon and air-speed indicator. The air speed first comes back to 140, goes slightly below it, then returns to 140. The artificial horizon tilts so that the airplane symbol is banked to the left.

CUT TO:

The flight deck.

(*Spencer has control yoke turned to the left and is adjusting the throttles.*)

CUT TO:

The tower.

TRELEAVEN. Watch your height! Don't make that turn so steep! Watch your height! More throttle! Keep the air speed on 140 and the nose up! Get back that height! You need a thousand feet!

CUT TO:

The flight deck.

(*Spencer eases the throttles open, and the tempo of the motors increases. He eases the control column forward, then pulls back again.*)

CUT TO:

Close-up of climb and descent indicator. The instrument first shows a descent of 500 feet per minute, then a climb of 600 feet, and then gradually begins to level off.

CUT TO:

The control tower. ·

(*Captain Treleaven is looking out through binoculars, the others anxiously behind him.*)

TRELEAVEN. (*Angrily.*) He can't fly the bloody thing! Of course he can't fly it! You're watching fifty people going to their deaths!

BURDICK. (*Shouting.*) Keep talking to him! Keep talking! Tell him what to do!

TRELEAVEN. (*Urgently, into mike.*) Spencer, you can't come straight in! You've got to do some circuits, and practice that approach. You've enough fuel left for three hours' flying. Stay up, man! Stay up!

CUT TO:

The flight deck.

SPENCER. Give it to me! (*Taking the mike. Then tensely.*) Listen, down there! I'm coming in! Do you hear me? . . . I'm coming in. There are people up here who'll die in less than an hour, never mind three. I may bend your precious airplane a bit, but I'll get it down. Now get on with the landing check. I'm putting the gear down now. (*To Stewardess.*) Wheels down, Janet!

(*The Stewardess selects landing gear "down," and Spencer reaches for the throttles.*)

CUT TO:

Film Insert: Airplane in flight, day. Its landing wheels come down.

CUT TO:

The flight deck.

STEWARDESS. (*Looks out of window, then back to Spencer.*) Wheels down and three green lights.

CUT TO:

The tower.

BURDICK. He may not be able to fly, but he's sure got guts.

TRELEAVEN. (*Into mike.*) Increase your throttle slightly to hold your air speed now that the wheels are down. Adjust your trim and keep that height at a thousand feet. Now check your propeller setting and your mixture—propellers to fully fine; mixture to full rich. I'll repeat that. Propellers to fully fine; mixture to full rich.

CUT TO:

The flight deck.

SPENCER. (*To himself, as he moves controls.*) Propellers fully fine. Mixture full rich. (*To Stewardess.*) Janet, let me hear the air speed.

STEWARDESS. 140 . . . 135 . . . 130 . . . 135 . . . 140 . . .

CUT TO:

The tower.

TRELEAVEN. (*Into mike.*) You are well downwind now. You can begin to make a left turn on the crosswind leg. As you turn, begin losing height to 800 feet and let your air speed come back to 120. I'll repeat that. Start a left turn. Lose height to 800. Air speed 120.

(*He picks up binoculars, then puts them down hurriedly and takes mike again.*)

You are losing height too fast! You are losing height too fast! Open up! Open! Hold your height now! Keep your air speed at 120.

CUT TO:

The flight deck.

STEWARDESS. 110 . . . 110 . . . 105 . . . 110 . . . 110 . . . 120 . . . 120 . . . Steady at 120.

SPENCER. What a blasted insensitive wagon this is! It doesn't respond! It doesn't respond at all!

STEWARDESS. 125 . . . 120 . . . 120 . . . Steady on 120.

CUT TO:

The tower.

TRELEAVEN. Start your turn into wind now to line up with the runway. Make it a gentle turn—you've plenty of time. As you turn, begin losing height, about 400 feet a minute. But be ready to correct if you lose height too fast. Adjust your trim as you go . . . That's right! . . . Keep turning! As soon as you've completed the turn, put down full flap and bring your air speed to 115. I'll repeat that. Let down 400 feet a minute. Full flap. Then air speed 115. (*To the others.*) Is everything ready on the field?

CONTROLLER. As ready as we'll ever be.

TRELEAVEN. Then this is it. In sixty seconds we'll know.

CUT TO:

The flight deck.

SPENCER. (*Muttering.*) Not quite yet . . . a little more . . . that should do it! (*As he straightens out of the turn.*) Janet, give me full flap!

(*The Stewardess reaches for the flap control, pushes it down and leaves it down.*)

Height and air speed!

STEWARDESS.　Seven hundred feet, speed 130 . . . 600 feet, speed 120 . . . 500 feet, speed 105 . . . We're going down too quickly!

SPENCER.　I know! I know!

(*He pushes throttles forward, and the tempo of the motors increases.*)

Keep watching it!

STEWARDESS.　450 feet, speed 100 . . . 400 feet, speed 100 . . .

CUT TO:

Film Insert: Airplane (DC-4) with wheels and flaps down, on a landing approach.

CUT TO:

The tower.

TRELEAVEN.　(*Urgently into mike.*) Open up! Open up! You're losing height too fast! (*Pause.*) Watch the air speed! Your nose is too high! Open up quickly or she'll stall. Open up, man! Open up!

BURDICK.　He heard you. He's recovering.

TRELEAVEN.　(*Into mike.*) Maintain that height until you get closer in to the runway. But be ready to ease off gently . . . You can start now . . . Let down again . . . That looks about right . . . But watch the air speed. Your nose is creeping up . . . (*More steadily.*) Now listen carefully, George. There's a slight crosswind on the runway, and your drift is to the right. Straighten up just before you touch down, and be ready with your right rudder as soon as you *are* down. And remember to cut the switches if you land too fast. (*Pause.*) All right, your approach is good . . . Get ready to round out—now! (*Pause. Then urgently.*) You're coming in too fast! Lift the nose up!

CUT TO:

The flight deck.

TRELEAVEN'S VOICE.　Lift the nose up! Back on the throttles! Throttles right back! Hold her off! Not too much! Not too much! Be ready for that crosswind! Ease her down, *now*! Ease her down!

CUT TO:

Film Insert: A landing wheel skimming over a runway and about to touch down. As it makes contact, rock picture to show instability.

CUT TO:

The flight deck.

(*There is a heavy thud, and Spencer and the Stewardess are jolted in their seats. There is another, another, and another. Everything shakes.*)

SPENCER.   (*Shouting.*) Cut the switches! Cut the switches!

(*The Stewardess reaches upward and pulls down the cage of the master switches. Instantly the heavy roar of motors stops, but there is still a whistling because the airplane is traveling fast. Spencer stretches out his legs as he puts his full strength into applying the airplane toe brakes, at the same time pulling back on the control column. There is a screaming of rubber on pavement, and Spencer and the Stewardess are thrown violently to the left. Then, except for the hum of the radio and gyros, there is silence as the airplane stops.*)

SPENCER.   (*Disgustedly.*) I groundlooped! I did a lousy stinking groundloop! We're turned right around the way we came!

STEWARDESS.   But we're all right! We're all right! You did it! You did it!

(*She leans over and kisses him. Spencer pulls off his radio headset. Outside there is a rising note of approaching sirens. Then, from the headset we hear Captain Treleaven's voice.*)

TRELEAVEN'S VOICE.   (*Exuberantly.*) Hello, George Spencer. That was probably the lousiest landing in the history of this airport. So don't ever ask us for a job as a pilot. But there are some people here who'd like to shake you by the hand, and later on we'll buy you a drink. Stay right where you are, George! We're coming over.

FADE OUT

THE END

Looking into the Plot

Overview

1. Three men struggle to save a plane and its passengers from disaster. Who are they? Which one comes forward in Act I? Act II? Act III?
2. Why is it impossible for the captain or his first officer to save the plane?
3. Arthur Hailey reminds us of the role that *chance* can play in human affairs. How is chance responsible for creating the dangerous situation on the plane? To what extent does chance play a part in the solution?

Act I

1. Early in the play, through natural-sounding conversations, the author presents the basic elements of his drama.
    (a) The flight agent and the stewardess talk about the cause of the plane's delay at Winnipeg. Why is this important?
    (b) Baird and Spencer talk together as any two strangers on a plane might. What important information do they reveal?
2. The reader learns what the captain and the first officer eat and who dines first. Why is this important?
3. What joking words of the first officer foreshadow the trouble to come?
4. The captain says that the weather is fine except for "fog east of the mountains." How is this fog important later in the play?
5. Through repeated references, the reader is kept aware of the passage of time and the plane's distance from its destination.
    (a) How much flying time is left when the first passenger falls ill?
    (b) How long is it before another passenger becomes ill and the doctor is awakened?
6. By the end of Act I, the writer has established a problem for his characters. How serious is their situation at this point? Which character seems to be taking charge? What does he do?

Act II

1. The scene shifts to Vancouver Airport. How much time has elapsed? How do you know?
2. What is George Spencer's first reaction to the idea of flying the plane? At what point does he change his mind? How does his behavior change once he seats himself at the controls?
3. Act II ends with Vancouver's reactions to the latest turn of events. What

are these reactions? What effect do they have on any confidence the audience might feel? Do you think this is a good way to end the act? Explain.

Act III

1. Act III begins with a preparation for disaster. What important steps does the controller take? What does Burdick do?
2. The audience meets Treleaven for the first time. What is most noticeable about his behavior?
3. Through Treleaven's directions and explanations, the author makes some of the complexities of flying seem clear to the reader. Why is it important for Spencer to keep his speed up to 120 knots? What else must he be careful about? Why do the controls feel "sluggish" to him?
4. How is the passage of time indicated in Act III?
5. Things seem to be going well as Spencer follows Treleaven's instructions. The audience, however, is not to be denied a last-minute, agonizing suspense. Why does Spencer refuse to try a practice run? How does the rapid alternation of scenes from Treleaven at the tower to Spencer in the cockpit keep the reader in suspense?
6. In the last few lines the writer releases the tension that has been building up throughout Act III. How does he do this? Is it likely people would react the way Spencer and Treleaven do?

Thinking It Through

1. Different people have different reactions to danger. What are some of the reactions of the people on Flight 714? Which of these reactions is the type that creates panic? Which serves to dispel it?
2. There are times when people must hide their own fear in order to encourage others. When is this true of the Stewardess? The doctor? Spencer? Treleaven? How does humor serve temporarily to ease the tension? Give examples.
3. The end of the play gives the reader a sense of tremendous human achievement against impossible odds. What qualities in the three men responsible for this achievement help to explain their success? Which of the three men faces the most difficult task? Explain your choice. Which of the three is the protagonist of the play? How can you tell?

Building Vocabulary

The following sentences are based on the play. Decide which of the words following the sentences best fits each blank. Write your answers on a separate sheet of paper.

1. The stewardess bent _____ over the sick passenger.

2. Some _____ substance got into the food during its preparation.

3. The controls of the DC-4 seemed heavy and _____ compared to a small fighter plane.

4. The emergency bell rang _____, shocking the officers into action.

5. The captain and the first officer reached for the controls _____.

6. The _____ fans will shout down any criticism of their team.

7. They expected no trouble on such a calm, _____ night.

simultaneously	solicitously	sluggish
toxic	extravagance	stridently
exuberant	placid	dilute

Writing Projects

1. Newspapers frequently report fascinating stories of rescue and survival in the face of overwhelming odds. Police and firefighters, for example, are called upon to supply first aid and sometimes deliver babies. Medics on ships and at army outposts perform emergency surgery. Miners, archeologists, explorers are trapped, in caves or on ice packs, and are rescued. Whole communities turn out to search for a lost child.

Look through a newspaper or magazine for a story that you find especially interesting and action-packed. Then **dramatize** a scene from it (make it into a short play, creating lines of dialogue for the characters). Start by making an outline. Determine which individuals mentioned in the news story will appear as characters. Figure out which one will be the protagonist. (*For help with this assignment see Writing Manual, p. 209.*)

2. An interesting exercise for the imagination is to write about an event the way another person might experience it. Instead of seeing it through your own eyes, you see it through the eyes of someone else. To do this, you must consider (1) how much the person actually sees and understands, and (2) what the person's thoughts and feelings are as he or she reacts to the event.

Write an account of Flight 714 from the **point of view** of one of the passengers. Remember that, as a passenger, your understanding of events and your view of things are limited. While you can see, for instance, the captain visiting the cabin and the stewardess and doctor attending to sick people, you do not know what is happening in the cockpit or the airport control room. (*For help with this assignment see Writing Manual, p. 202.*)

I Shot an Arrow

Rod Serling

FOR YEARS writers have thrilled their readers with adventure stories of men lost in the desert, in a steaming jungle, in arctic wilderness or on a lonely sea. Now the twentieth century space age offers a new and terrifying possibility—men lost in space.

"I Shot an Arrow" presents just such an idea. As in those earlier adventure stories, however, it is not the remote place itself that seems most important; rather, it is the behavior of the men who are lost there. How do people react when pushed to their limits? What qualities are most important in getting them through?

Rod Serling gives his answers to these questions in the play that follows. Join Colonel Donlin and his men in Spaceship *Arrow One* as they plunge into the unknown. Their story is an unforgettable one.

Vocabulary Preview

INFINITY (in-FIN-uh-tee) a concept of time or space without limits or end
   The sea was so vast that it seemed like an *infinity* of water.
MUSINGLY (MYOO-zing-lee) dreamily, as in deep thought
   The astronomer looked *musingly* out into space.
AWESOME (AW-sum) inspiring awe and wonder
   The three-hundred foot rocket on its launching pad was an *awesome* sight.
MALFUNCTION (mal-FUNC-shun) flaw in the performance of a mechanical device

61

A *malfunction* in the ship's engine sent it into port for repairs.

CESSATION (seh-SAY-shun) a pause; a stopping

The sudden *cessation* of wind brought a strange calm to the rain-soaked forest.

WARY (WAIR-ee) cautious; on one's guard

The astronaut was *wary* as he unlocked the space ship and set foot on a new terrain.

PROSTRATE (PROS-trayt) lying flat; lying with one's face to the ground

The marathon runner lay *prostrate* across the finish line, unable to move another inch.

PROTOTYPE (PROH-tuh-typ) the original or model after which something is formed.

The small plane he designed became a *prototype* for all future fighter planes.

DEMENTED (duh-MEN-tud) crazed; insane

The long, solitary space voyage caused even the strongest of men to feel *demented* at the end.

DELIBERATELY (duh-LIB-uh-rut-lee) slowly and carefully

Very *deliberately*, the astronaut approached the mysterious object.

Other Words You Will Need to Know

NEBULAE (NEB-yoo-lye) large bodies of gas or dust in outer space

VECTOR-PATH (VEK-tur PATH) the path an airplane or rocket takes to reach its destination

ASTEROID (AS-tuh-royd) a star-like celestial body

PROTOCOL (PROH-tuh-kol) formal military etiquette

Characters

In the Monitor Control Room

Langford, *chief of the control room*

Brandt, *technician in the television control room*

Members of the staff

Narrator

The Aircraft Crew

Colonel R. G. Donlin, *commander of* Arrow One *airship*

Flight Officer Corey, *member of flight crew*

Flight Officer Pierson, *member of flight crew*

Navigator Hudak, *crew member, hurt in the crash landing*

I Shot an Arrow

FADE IN:

Shot of the sky: the various nebulae and the planet bodies stand out in sharp, sparkling relief. The camera pans down and we see a huge rocket poised for launching, on it the lettering, "Arrow One."

NARRATOR'S VOICE. (*Offscreen.*) There is a fifth dimension beyond that which is known to man. It is a dimension as vast as space and as timeless as infinity. It is the middle ground between light and shadow, between science and superstition. And it lies between the pit of his fears and the summit of his knowledge. This is the dimension of imagination. It is an area we call The Twilight Zone.

DISSOLVE TO:

Interior of the Launching Control Room. It is night. The launching team is now busily engaged in the final seconds of the count down. The room consists mainly of television monitors, automatic controls, receivers and a large plotting chart.

BRANDT'S VOICE. (*Offscreen.*) Minus fifteen. Minus fourteen. Minus thirteen...

NARRATOR'S VOICE. Her name is *Arrow One*. She represents four and a half years of planning, preparation and training; and a thousand years of science and mathematics and the projected dreams and hopes of not only a nation but a world. She is the first manned aircraft into space. And this is the count down, the last five seconds before man shot an arrow into the air.

BRANDT'S VOICE. Minus three. Minus two. Minus one. Minus zero.

The camera pulls back to where a man wearing a head set and speaker is writing in the word "unreported" across the incomplete vector-path of an object labeled "Arrow One." Brandt is sitting at his paper-littered desk, confronted by Langford, obviously the man in authority.

LANGFORD. (*Excited.*) Well what do you mean we've lost it? I mean, with all the monitors we have going . . .

BRANDT. (*Cutting in.*) We could have fifteen thousand monitors, but the situation would be the same. We've lost contact. She's off her vector-path, off the radar screen. Just gone, completely gone.

LANGFORD. When did you first lose contact?

BRANDT. Less than a half hour ago. There was a short period of heavy interference. It was probably solar. We haven't been able to identify it yet. In any case, when it was over, the contact was broken.

LANGFORD.   Couldn't a change in their course account for that?

BRANDT.   (*Shakes his head.*) The course was preset. The pilot wouldn't change it without notifying us. Bob Donlin's commanding. This is a solid officer. And even if he did change course, the relay alarm system in the ship would have been activated. The change would have shown up here on the board.

LANGFORD.   (*Turns away, rubbing his jaw reflectively. He walks over to a radar screen, reaches out and flicks at it nervously with a finger.*) So an aircraft with an eight-man crew just disappears like a puff of smoke. One moment she's there; the next moment she's gone.

(*Musingly and softly.*)   I shot an arrow into the air
                                 It landed I know not where

An old rhyme for the age of space. Gentlemen, wherever you are . . . God help you!

FADE TO BLACK

FADE TO:

The barren, rocky face of a blistering desert. The mountains in the background are pure bedrock, jagged shapes from another world. The upper portion of a space aircraft comes into view, gradually taking shape through a cloud of smoke. A side panel of the ship shows the lettering, "Arrow One." The ship is nose down in the sand. In the foreground we see men carrying bodies of fellow crew members. Donlin, Pierson and Corey are pulling various crew members as far away from the ship as they can and laying them in the sand. Corey is the farthest away from the group, pulling another crew member across the sand by the arm pits, stumbling, falling with semi-exhaustion, then rising to pull him again.

PIERSON.   (*Shouting.*) Come on, Corey. Get him away from there, quick!

DONLIN.   (*Urgently.*) That all of them, Pierson?

PIERSON.   (*Looking up with a grimy, sweaty face.*) That's all of them, Colonel.

DONLIN.   All right. It's the forward hold. We'll try to get the supplies out.

The two men start back toward the ship and stop abruptly as an explosion rocks them back on their heels. (Cut to the space ship as it blows up.) The two men stare toward the burning and disappearing ship. Corey comes up to them expectantly, frightened. Donlin turns away.

Pierson walks over to the crew members who are lying in a row in the sand. He goes from one to the other finding only one man, Hudak, alive. He moves him away from the others, kneels over him and administers to him. Donlin turns toward him questioningly. Pierson rises.

PIERSON. They're all dead, sir, except Hudak.

(*Donlin walks over toward them. He looks from one body to the other, then kneels down beside Hudak, wipes the sweat from the man's face, takes his jacket and bunches it up as a pillow, gently puts it under the man's head. Corey's shadow crosses him and Donlin looks up to see Corey standing there, thin-lipped, accusative.*)

COREY. (*Tightly.*) We should have gotten the supplies, Colonel. We knew the ship might go up. So instead of food and water, we've got four dead men and another one dying.

PIERSON. We didn't know they were dead, Corey.

COREY. (*Turns to him savagely.*) Knock it off, Pierson. Maybe when your tongue starts swelling up you'll realize we pulled a rock here. We're playing undertaker instead of going in there and getting supplies.

DONLIN. (*Rises, to Pierson, softly.*) Let's cover them up, Pierson. We'll take fifteen or twenty minutes and then we'll bury them.

As Pierson covers each of the men in turn, Donlin sits down in the sand and pulls out a ledger book. Very slowly and deliberately he writes in it. Over the action we hear his voice.

DONLIN'S VOICE. First entry. Log. *Arrow One.* Colonel R. G. Donlin commanding. We have crash-landed on what appears to be an uncharted asteroid. Cause of malfunction and ultimate crash—unknown. There was an explosion. The electrical system went out. And that's all any of us can remember, "any of us" being Flight Officers Corey and Pierson and Navigator Hudak, who has been seriously hurt, and myself. The rest of the crew is dead. There is very little left of the aircraft. The radio is gone, the bulk of the supplies have been destroyed in the crash and, as of this moment, there is little certainty that we have been tracked and our whereabouts known.

COREY. (*He rips the book out of Donlin's hand. His eyes are wide, blazing; his face white.*) Begging the Colonel's pardon. This is no time to write your memoirs!

DONLIN. Corey, we're in bad shape and that's no mistake, but we're still a crew. As long as we're a crew there'll be discipline and there'll be protocol. And until I'm lying in a hole like the rest of those devils, we'll operate from the book! Now go over there and sit down.

COREY. (*Picks up the ledger and shakes it.*) Captain Donlin, it's hot, see? It's very hot and it makes it hard to think. So if you're going to expend all that energy, use it to figure a way out of here. A way to get back. A way to let them know where we are.

PIERSON. (*Shouting.*) Corey! (*He walks over to him and pulls him away.*) You heard the Captain. Get over there and sit down.

Corey turns away, walks over a few yards, sinks to his knees close to the prostrate form of Hudak. He studies the stricken man's face, then sinks down into a heap and just stares lifelessly across the desert.

PIERSON. Something's wrong with Corey, sir. The bump on his head, or whatever it was. He's not acting right.

Donlin nods, picks up the ledger, opens it, stares at it, then closes it and tosses it aside. He walks over to look down at Hudak. He takes out a canteen, kneels beside the man, tilts his head up and puts a little water into his mouth. We see Corey in the background watching.

COREY. How much water is there?

DONLIN. A five gallon can and what we have on us.

COREY. (*Pointing toward Hudak's figure.*) Then why waste it? He won't live through the day.

DONLIN. You the consulting surgeon, Corey?

COREY. (*Slowly rises.*) I'm one man out of three who's going to need water. And five gallons isn't gonna last very long.

DONLIN. If the situation were reversed, Corey, if that was you lying there, I'll give you good odds you wouldn't want to get written off, five gallons of water or no.

COREY. (*On his feet, close to Donlin.*) He's going to die, Captain.

DONLIN. (*Lashes out and grabs him.*) If he dies, he dies, Corey! But nobody gets behind to push. If he's thirsty, he gets water. If he's hot, we move him in the shade. And then if he goes, we'll give him a prayer or two. (*Without turning his eyes from Corey's face.*) Pierson!

PIERSON. Sir?

DONLIN. There's half a shovel near the packs. Let's start digging the graves. I'll relieve you in five minutes. Then Corey will relieve me.

He lets go of Corey's tunic. Corey turns to look toward Hudak on the ground.

PIERSON. (*Picks up the half a shovel.*) What's the matter, Corey. You want him on detail too?

Corey doesn't answer him. He walks over toward the gear that's been stowed in a circle in the sand. He stares down at the five gallon water can and wets his lips. He looks up to see Pierson staring at him and he turns away.

PIERSON. Colonel? That's odd. The size of the sun, I mean.

DONLIN. (*Nods.*) I noticed.

COREY. The size of the sun?

DONLIN. It's hardly any different than we knew it on Earth.

PIERSON. Which means whatever asteroid we've landed on is close to the Earth.

COREY. How close?

DONLIN. (*Shrugs.*) Pick a number.

PIERSON. (*Softly.*) Like that, huh?

DONLIN. (*Nods.*) Fifty thousand miles. A hundred thousand miles. Who knows?

(*He looks up toward the sun and closes his eyes and wipes his face.*)

Wherever we are, it's a cinch it isn't Heaven. We can count on that. (*He turns to look from Pierson to Corey.*) We can count on this, too. We've got maybe six, seven gallons of water and food concentrates for maybe four days. And that's it. So we might as well make our plans with this in mind.

COREY. What kind of plans?

DONLIN. We'll use this as a base and spread out in two man patrols. One man to stay behind and watch Hudak. (*He jerks his head toward the direction of the mountains.*) Maybe see what lies on the other side. We've got one thing in our favor. The air is perfect and there's no radiation count to speak of. (*He bends down and picks up a fragment of metal from the ship.*) It took four and a half years to build that ship. There wasn't any prototype. Just the one ship. The only one of its kind. And it took four and a half years to build her. So if they know where we are and want to come and get us, they've got to build another ship. (*He takes a deep breath. His eyes go down toward the sandy floor of the desert. He scrabbles it with his boot then looks up at the two men.*) So get comfortable, gentlemen. We've got a devil of a long wait.

DISSOLVE TO:

Four graves obviously freshly covered. The camera pans up until we're looking down on Pierson who stands close to Hudak, shading his eyes against the sun. Donlin and Corey walk slowly back toward the area.

DONLIN. (*Nods toward Hudak.*) How is he?

PIERSON. The same. Breathing seems shallower though. Did you see anything, Captain?

Donlin shakes his head. Corey, in the process of finishing a drink out of his canteen, takes it out of his mouth, wipes his face with his sleeve, screws on the top of the canteen.

COREY. Yeah, we saw something. Sand. Sand, rocks and those scrubby mountains over there. This isn't an asteroid; it's an eight ball. (*He shakes his head slowly, sinks to a sitting position on the sand.*) And hot, Pierson. Hot like nothing you've ever felt before.

PIERSON. (*Looks over to Donlin.*) It'll be cooler at night, sir. I'll head south toward the mountains. I'll look in that direction. (*A pause.*) If there is a night here!

Donlin nods, takes out a canteen, starts to unscrew it. Corey grabs his wrist.

COREY. Not this time, Colonel. Not this time. I want an even shake. I want a chance.

DONLIN. You're alive, Corey. That's a better shake than those four got.

COREY. I want to *stay* alive. So don't give him *my* water.

Donlin reaches over and firmly takes Corey's hand from his wrist and pushes it aside. Then he carries the canteen over toward Hudak's mouth. Corey bats the canteen out of his hand. Donlin, enraged, is on his feet and throws himself at Corey. The two men start to grapple in the sand. Donlin gets on top of Corey, his hands on his throat. The canteen is lying on its side, the water trickling out. Donlin, seeing this, gets up, grabs the canteen and puts the top back on and then just stands there, his eyes closed. Corey lies on his back, gingerly touching his throat.

PIERSON. (*In a strained voice.*) Colonel Donlin? (*As Donlin turns, Pierson is hunched over the body of Hudak.*) You'll be pleased to hear, Corey, he won't drink any more of your water! (*He reaches over to a crumpled top of a uniform that lies on the sand, picks it up and covers Hudak's face. Donlin walks over, stares down at the body, shakes his head slowly from side to side.*)

DONLIN.   You died a long way from home, boy. A long way from home. (*He turns to look at the other two.*) We'll wait till dark. Then we'll start taking some treks over the mountain and down to the flats in all four directions. This is home now, gentlemen. Such as it is.

PIERSON.   (*Sees Corey cutting the water canteen from Hudak's belt.*) Corey!

Corey reacts as if burnt and scrambles backwards. Pierson takes three steps over to him, his voice shaking with anger.

PIERSON.   For the record, Corey, there's just three of us now. And the big problem is going to be to stay alive. I mean the three of us! Something may be wrong with you, Corey. Something happened to you when you hit your head. I don't think you're responsible any more. But if I catch you filching just once, just once, Corey . . .

DONLIN.   (*Quietly, but with authority.*) Pierson, let's forget it.

PIERSON.   This dirty little grave robbing . . .

DONLIN.   (*Shouts.*) Pierson!

PIERSON.   (*Very quietly turning away.*) Yes, sir!

He goes over and sits down. Donlin does the same thing, stretching himself out in the sand, half covering his face with a jacket collar. Corey just remains there squatting, staring across at Pierson. Their eyes lock and there is a mutual challenge in the look.

FADE OUT

END ACT ONE

ACT TWO

FADE IN:

The desert at night. There is a campfire. The silence is almost incredible, a total cessation of noise. Donlin sits staring at the fire, rises, stirs it with a stick, then looks around the darkness trying to probe with his eyes. He looks up at the sky for a moment, then looks at his watch. He starts as he hears the sound of what appears to be the crunching of footsteps on sand.

DONLIN.   (*Calling out.*) Pierson? (*His eyes are narrow with suspicion and concern as he goes back to the fire and picks up his rifle.*)

Suddenly a figure, at first just a shrouded silhouette, appears in the gloom and then takes on a gradual dimension until we see Corey appear in the light. He looks totally bushed, bearded, sweaty. He walks on into the light of the campfire, half stumbles to his knees, then turns himself over so that he's lying on his back.

DONLIN. *(Staring down at him.)* Well?

COREY. *(Shakes his head.)* Nothing. Not a thing. I must have gone twelve, fifteen miles anyway. Sand flats, that's all there was. Just sand flats. I thought I could get some kind of a fix using the stars. But it's overcast.

DONLIN. *(Nods.)* I know. I thought of the same thing. *(A pause.)* What about Pierson?

Corey doesn't answer. He busily unscrews the top of his canteen, takes a long, long gulp, then very slowly and methodically screws the top back on, looks at Donlin again.

COREY. What about him?

DONLIN. You didn't see him? You didn't hear him at all?

COREY. He went south toward the mountains. I went west toward . . *(he grins ruefully)* I went west toward nothing. What time is it?

Donlin walks back toward the light and stares out into the dark desert beyond. Once again he checks his watch. He speaks with his back toward Corey.

DONLIN. He's been gone six hours. He should have been back by now.

He turns to stare at Corey who is once again drinking from the canteen. He screws back the top and throws the canteen on the ground. It lands with a heavy thud. Donlin stares at him; something freezes on his face. He runs to Corey, stops, stands above him his voice quiet but shaking.

DONLIN. Corey?

COREY. *(Looking up.)* Yeah?

DONLIN. You didn't hear Pierson or see him or anything?

COREY. *(Unflinching.)* I already told you, Captain. We went in different directions.

DONLIN. *(Leaning close to Corey.)* Corey, was it hot out there?

COREY. *(Nods.)* You know it.

DONLIN. Made you thirsty, didn't it.

COREY. *(Wary, now.)* I'm getting accustomed to it, Captain.

DONLIN. *(Slowly reaches over and picks up the canteen.)* Obviously. Very accustomed to it. So accustomed to it, Corey, that you didn't drink any water. You were out three hours and you didn't touch a drop.

COREY. Put me in for a medal.

Donlin lashes out with both hands and grabs him, pulling him so that their faces are only an inch apart.

DONLIN. Buddy, what I'm gonna give you can't be pinned on a uniform. I want to know why you started out three hours ago with half a canteen. (*He releases him, picks up the canteen and shakes it.*) And then come back with it three quarters full. Come on, Corey. I want to know where you left Pierson and what you did to him. (*Shouting in his face.*) Come on, Corey. *Come on!*

COREY. (*As his head goes down, Donlin pulls him upright by the hair.*) I found him. Face down. He must have . . . he must have fallen and hit his head on a rock. He was dead.

DONLIN. Where did this happen?

COREY. At the foot of the mountain. The sand was too deep heading west. I had to change directions.

DONLIN. You better change your story.

COREY. Captain, I swear, I didn't touch him. I found him. He was dead. I saw his canteen and I poured his water into mine. I knew you wouldn't believe me. That's why I told you I hadn't seen him.

Donlin releases him, their eyes locking. Then Donlin slowly gets to his feet, goes over to the fire and picks up his rifle. He points it toward Corey.

DONLIN. Up on your feet. We're going to bring him back.

COREY. You're out of your mind. It's seven or eight miles out there. I can't make it again. I'm dead, Captain.

DONLIN. Correction! You're almost dead. But you're not quite yet. Let's go, Corey. I want a conducted tour to Pierson's body. I want to see for myself. Let's move out!

DISSOLVE TO:

Shots of the two men clambering over sand dunes and down again. Corey is in the foreground. Behind him we see Donlin with the gun. Corey stops dead, staring down, his eyes wide with surprise and shock. Donlin comes up alongside. Corey turns to him.

COREY. This is where he was. I swear, this is where he was.

DONLIN. (*Tersely.*) But he's not here now.

The camera pans over the ground. We can see a furrow as if a man had dragged himself across the sand.

COREY.   Captain, look. He must have crawled away.

DONLIN.   You said he was dead!

COREY.   I was wrong. I must have been wrong.

DONLIN.   (*Holds the gun up.*) Where are the rocks, Corey? The rocks he hit his head on.

COREY.   (*Takes a step backwards.*) I don't know. But I swear . . . it was an accident or something. I didn't do anything to him. I swear to you, Captain. You've got to believe me. I didn't touch him.

DONLIN.   (*Stares around him and shouts.*) Pierson? (*A pause.*) Pierson, it's Captain Donlin. Pierson, answer me.

Donlin stumbles as he half runs in the direction of the furrow. Corey stands alone; his face suddenly looks set and determined. He hears Donlin's voice fading off as he calls, "Pierson, Pierson, Pierson." Then Corey slowly reaches into his pocket. He takes out a small wrench, grips it in his fist and starts out in the direction of Donlin's voice.

DISSOLVE TO:

The base of one of the small, rocky hills that loom up. We see the prostrate body of Pierson on the sand. He is propped up against the side of a rock, his eyes open, his breathing shallow. He's close to death. He looks up and weakly reacts to the men approaching him. Donlin runs to Pierson, throws himself down close to him, takes out his canteen, tilts the wounded man's head back and pours water through parched, cracked lips. Pierson's lips move soundlessly. He is desperately trying to say something.

DONLIN.   Pierson, you're all right, boy. We'll take you back now. You're going to be all right. What, Pierson? What are you trying to say.

Pierson, with desperation, weakly pounds Donlin's sleeve, and his head half turns to look toward the mountain behind them.

DONLIN.   What, Pierson, what? (*He looks in the direction of the mountain.*) Did you go up there, Pierson? You went up there, is that the idea?

Pierson nods.

DONLIN.   And what, Pierson? What did you see?

Pierson's lips move and his eyes dart around agonizingly. He calls on the strength that he no longer possesses; then his eyes close. He's obviously unable to vocalize. Then his face takes on a set, determined look. Slowly, with a shaking hand, he draws a line in the sand, then crisscrosses it with two other horizontal lines. He turns to stare into Donlin's face, a pleading look, as though silently begging the Colonel to understand what he means. Suddenly his fingers convulse, pull back into a fist, then the hand falls to one side, limp.

Donlin's face shows his agonized reaction to the death. Then he looks questioningly over to the symbol in the sand. As he looks up, he sees Corey standing there.

DONLIN.   He drew this. Some kind of a sign or a symbol of something. (*He looks up toward Corey.*) He was trying to tell us something. What do you suppose he . . .

Donlin's eyes travel up toward the mountain. He puts the carbine aside and starts to climb. As he starts to scramble up, Corey picks up the gun and holds it at his hip, pointing up toward Donlin.

COREY.   Colonel!

Donlin turns to stare down at him.

COREY.   Colonel, two men can live maybe five days. One man can live ten. You'll forgive me, Colonel . . .

DONLIN.   You killed Pierson, didn't you, Corey? You killed him.

Corey nods.

DONLIN.   (*Shakes his head slowly from side to side, in a whisper.*) Corey, you're demented. You're out of your mind. You've already killed once, you've already . . .

He's interrupted by the explosion of the carbine. He totters for a moment and then pitches forward on his face. He lands, lifeless. Corey stands there with a smoking gun.

COREY.   (*Very softly.*) Sorry, Colonel. Real sorry (*shakes his head*). No choice. No alternatives. Just had to be.

Then he slowly puts the carbine down and looks up toward the mountain, wipes his face, blinks his eyes, sits down with his back against the rock wall and slowly falls asleep.

DISSOLVE TO:

The foot of the mountain. It is day. The camera pans across the bodies of Pierson and Donlin to the huddled, sleeping figure of Corey who suddenly awakens with a start. He looks around him, startled, then gets to his feet, looks briefly at Donlin's body and walks a few feet to where Pierson lies. *He kneels down and studies the imprint that Pierson has made in the sand, the three lines. He reacts thoughtfully and reflectively. He rises again slowly and looks up toward the mountain and begins a slow climb toward the peak.*

DISSOLVE TO:

Corey is climbing hand over hand, scrambling at the rock and the outgrowths. He hoists himself onto a small flat rock and lies there for a long moment panting heavily. His eyes narrow suddenly. He listens to something and then gradually we hear it. It's the sound of engines. Corey jerks himself upright staring around wildly and then suddenly stops dead, staring down and ahead to the other side of the mountain, his mouth wide open, his eyes bugged.

COREY. Pierson. Pierson, now I know what you meant. Now I know what you were trying to describe. (*A pause.*) Telephone poles. Pierson, you were trying to draw a telephone pole!

The camera begins a giant sweep down the other side of the mountain until we see a four-lane, concrete highway. A sign in the foreground reads: "Reno, Nevada, 97 miles." Beyond that a sign which reads: "Nelson's Motel just up ahead. Gas - oil - eats." Then down the highway rolls a big truck and after a few moments in the opposite direction a big, flashy convertible. The camera sweeps back and we are looking up at Corey who starts to cry and laugh at the same time.

COREY. (*Shouts.*) Hey! Oh, no! Captain Donlin. Pierson. Hudak.

He whirls around and all the names die in his throat as he looks at the distant crumpled figures of the two dead men. He closes his eyes and the tears roll down his cheeks.

COREY. I know what happened. We never left the Earth. That's why nobody tracked us. We never left the Earth. We just . . . we just crashed back into it. (*He is lying on his face, sobbing.*) Donlin . . . Pierson . . . Hudak . . . I'm sorry. Please forgive me. I'm sorry.

The camera starts a slow dolly away until once again we are looking from the highway up toward the mountain at the small figure of the sobbing man who continues to cry out names and pleas for forgiveness. Over this we hear the Narrator's voice.

NARRATOR'S VOICE. Practical joke perpetrated by mother nature and a combination of improbable events. Practical joke wearing the trappings of nightmare, terror, desperation. Small human drama played out in a desert a hundred miles from Reno, Nevada, U.S.A., Continent of North America, the Earth and, of course, The Twilight Zone.

FADE OUT

THE END

Looking into the Plot

1. Arrange these incidents in the order in which they occur in the story:
   (a) Pierson draws a picture in the sand.
   (b) Hudak dies.
   (c) Donlin forces Corey at gun point to lead him to Pierson.
   (d) Corey wounds Pierson and leaves him to die.
   (e) The space ship explodes.
   (f) Corey weeps and asks forgiveness.
   (g) Donlin is shot and killed.
2. How many of the eight crew members survive the crash?
3. Why are Donlin and his men limited to such a small supply of water and food concentrates?
4. Both Donlin and Pierson see Corey's destructive behavior as something unnatural to him. How do they explain it?
5. Donlin and Pierson are convinced that they have landed on a distant asteroid. What similarities do they find between this "asteroid" and the earth?
6. What procedure does Donlin establish for exploring the "asteroid"? If adhered to strictly, would this procedure have saved the men? Why does it fail?
7. Who is the first one to learn that the "asteroid" is actually Earth? What evidence does he find? How does he attempt to communicate his discovery? Is he successful?

Thinking It Through

1. Colonel Donlin maintains his command over his crew in their new and dangerous situation. What is the first job he assigns to his men? What does this show about him?

2. It's not surprising that Donlin has earned a reputation among his superiors as a "solid officer." When his spaceship crashes, he shows a controlled and intelligent approach to the emergency and a genuine sympathy for his men. Where does he show his intelligence and control? Where does he show his sympathy?

3. If Corey had been in charge, how would his behavior have differed from Donlin's? (Be specific in suggesting what Corey would have done.)

4. This play is highlighted by irony. It is ironic that three men think they are facing death on a distant asteroid when, in reality, they are outside Reno, Nevada. It is ironic that Corey, in his struggle to survive, kills the one man who has found the answer for all of them. When you look back at the play, knowing the ending, some of the speeches seem strangely inappropriate or ironic. See if you can find at least one good example.

5. Unlike "Flight into Danger," where the characters face a real danger and survive, the characters in "I Shot an Arrow" face an imagined danger and, with one exception, they perish. How do you explain the difference? What do both plays have to say about people facing danger?

Building Vocabulary

The following sentences are based on the play. Decide which of the words following the sentences best fits each blank. Write your answers on a separate sheet of paper.

1. The rocket blasted clear of the pad with an _____ roar.

2. Donlin recorded that the cause of his ship's _____ and ultimate crash was unknown.

3. There was an almost incredible silence, a complete _____ of noise.

4. When Donlin questioned him about Pierson, Corey grew _____ .

5. Donlin hurried to the _____ body of Pierson lying face forward on the sand.

6. There was only one way to explain Corey's behavior; he was _____ .

prostrate	prototype	demented
wary	cessation	infinity
malfunction	awesome	

Writing Projects

1. The author describes the desert in which the men crash as "barren," "rocky" and "blistering." The mountains in the background, he says, are "pure bed rock—jagged shapes from another world." Notice how all the adjectives help create the sense of a hostile, destructive environment.

   In one paragraph, write a **description** of an outdoor scene that you found either frightening or pleasant. (*For help with this assignment see Writing Manual, p. 203.*)

2. Sometimes we can see two dissimilar characters more clearly by **contrasting** them with one another. Use this technique with Colonel Donlin and Corey. List the specific points on which these two characters differ. One point of difference, for example, is their attitude toward the dying Hudak. List three points of difference, arrange them in the order in which they occur in the play, and then use these points to develop a paragraph or two contrasting the two men. (*For help with this assignment see Writing Manual, p. 207.*)

The Dogs of War

Marjorie R. Watson

THIS PLAY seems to have an historical setting, but actually the playwright has created an imaginary country. Before you read very far, you will realize that this country is somewhere in Eastern Europe, and the period is a long time ago, certainly before the Russian Revolution in 1917.

The title does not refer to actual dogs but to a certain view of war. In this view, war is seen as the unleashing of vicious dogs that battle one another.

The country in the play battles serious natural and political problems. A terrible plague has so weakened the tiny province that a strong-armed dictator has been able to invade it. The future of this country is the story of the play.

Vocabulary Preview

ABATED (uh-BAY-tud) reduced; lessened in degree
   After he took the medicine, the pain *abated*.
GROVEL (GROV-ul) to cringe or crawl in fearful respect
   It hurt his pride to *grovel* before his enemies.
PERILOUS (PER-uh-lus) dangerous; hazardous
   They were warned that the journey was *perilous*.

SANCTUARY (SANK-choo-air-ee) a sacred place; a place of refuge and protection

No harm could come to the animals in this *sanctuary*.

HAMPER (HAM-pur) to impede; to interfere with

The waves weren't big enough to *hamper* the swimmer.

REGICIDE (REJ-uh-syd) the killing of a king; one who kills a king

After the *regicide*, the queen took control of the country.

LOOTING (LOOT-ing) robbing or taking away by force, as in war

The soldiers were punished for *looting* after the battle.

TEDIOUS (TEE-dee-us) tiresome and dull

He found that copying the long list was *tedious* work.

Another Word You Will Need to Know

RAVAGE (RAV-uj) destroy

Characters

A Nun
Anton Ivanovich, a young man
Marya Morevna, his wife
Pavel Karpovich, a foreign invader
Soldiers

Setting

A convent

The Dogs of War

A bell is heard tolling, but ceases as the Curtain rises. A nun is standing with her head bowed and her hands folded in prayer.

She makes the sign of the cross, sighs, and moves down and begins to examine some articles in a basket. There is a sound of knocking, and she goes to the door and calls, as if to another door down a passage.

NUN.   Enter, friend. Our door is open to all who choose to lift the latch.

(*She comes back into the room, and Anton enters. He is a young man whose bearing and speech do not match his peasant clothes. He is tired and travel-stained.*)

ANTON.   Peace be with you, little mother. May we come in and rest here awhile?

NUN.   Assuredly, my son. You may sup and sleep here if you wish.

ANTON.   Marya! Marya, where are you?

(*Marya appears in the doorway. She is exhausted and can scarcely drag one foot after the other. She, too, is wearing peasant costume, and has a shawl over her head and tied under her chin.*)

MARYA.   My head feels like a bubble that will burst at any moment, but I am afraid my feet are made of clay.

(*The nun helps her to a seat.*)

NUN.   Have you come far?

ANTON.   From Tanilof.

NUN.   Not so very far.

MARYA.   But the roads are so rough and the hills so steep.

ANTON.   We live in the valley, and my wife isn't used to mountain roads.

NUN.   And her shoes are so thin. The poor child's feet must be blistered and cut to pieces.

(*This remark perturbs Anton and Marya, who exchange glances.*)

ANTON.   Yes, it was stupid to wear them. I told her so. They are a cast-off pair that our mistress gave her, and not suited to a girl of Marya's station. I told her so, but she would wear them.

MARYA.   They are quite ruined now. The stones have cut right through the soles. I shall have to buy some more before we go on.

NUN. There is no place here where you can buy shoes. Where are you going?

ANTON. To Russia.

NUN. To Russia! And you have no other shoes, no change of clothes?

ANTON. A man with a cart is bringing our luggage after us.

NUN. It is a pity he couldn't have brought you as well.

ANTON. He was to have done that, but somehow we missed him.

NUN. I see. And you are walking to Russia?

ANTON. I—we—only until the plague has abated.

NUN. But how will you live in Russia?

ANTON. We have heard there is plenty of work to be had just over the border.

NUN. What kind of work are you seeking?

ANTON. Oh . . . work on the land.

NUN. And your wife?

ANTON. She works in the fields, too.

NUN. Ah, that is hard work.

(*Marya feels the nun's eyes on her hands and tries to hide them.*)

And when the plague has passed, will your old master take you back again?

ANTON. He's dead. It was the plague. It's everywhere. Why was the convent bell tolling?

NUN. For the souls of those whom the plague has taken.

ANTON. Is the plague here, too?

NUN. No. Up here in the hills we are out of its reach, but when a country is stricken as this one is, there must be souls passing on every hour, and so, as the clock strikes, we toll the bell and pray.

ANTON. What good can that do? God will not listen to your bell or your prayers.

NUN. The sisters of the convent have gone down into the towns to nurse the sick, and only three of us have remained here lest travellers come seeking help and refuge.

ANTON. God's asleep that he lets this curse come upon us now. Wasn't it enough that the foul upstart, Pavel Karpovich, should invade the country, without the plague coming to ravage our troops?

NUN. Perhaps God is not asleep, my son. The plague is defeating Pavel Karpovich as our little army could never have. If the reports are true, he is afraid of the plague and has retreated to the frontier again.

ANTON. The reports are true. But what of that? He is crouching there like a cat over a mousehole. When the plague has burnt itself out, seared the people's spirit, and halved our troops, he will march back, and there will be no one to withstand him.

NUN. The King is an old, sick man with a few years left to him, but he has a grandson, an inexperienced youth, who, if he loves his country as much as the people believe he does, will go far. Besides, he has a Russian wife.

ANTON. Yes, and—but what of that?

NUN. Marya Morevna is the Czar's niece.

ANTON. Then you, too, think he will send soldiers to help us?

NUN. It is quite possible, especially if his niece were to plead with him.

(*Marya and Anton exchange glances. The nun smiles.*)

We must have patience and hope, and pray the good God to soften the Czar's heart towards us. (*She picks up the basket and moves it to a side table.*) And in the meantime we must fight the plague. These things are offerings from people who have not been stricken by the plague. They are to be sold and the money used to help the sick. I think this casket is of great value if only we can find someone to buy it.

(*She opens the casket and gives a little gasp of surprise, which makes Anton look in it. He takes out a dagger.*)

ANTON. Did this knife startle you? I suppose you don't often see such things as this. It is a very fine piece of work. The blade is beautifully chased.

NUN. No, it was not that which startled me. I saw twenty years at one glance in this mirror. (*She takes out an ornamented hand mirror.*) There are no mirrors in this convent and I have not seen my own face for twenty years. (*With a sigh she puts the mirror back. Anton sheathes the dagger and puts it into the casket. The nun notices Marya seems drowsy, and puts the casket down on the bench away from the basket and goes to her.*) You shall sleep here tonight.

ANTON. No. We must go on.

NUN. I will fetch you food and drink, and then when you have eaten we will talk of what must be and what can be done.

(*She goes out.*)

ANTON. I think we can trust her. You see, even she thinks the Czar will send soldiers to help us. I think I shall take her into my confidence when she comes back.

MARYA. I think she already knows all we can tell her.

ANTON. She may perhaps have guessed we aren't peasants, because she noticed your shoes. They were a bad mistake.

MARYA. I didn't know we should have to walk.

ANTON. Nor should we if that fool Stefan had met us as he was told.

MARYA. But, Anton, perhaps he couldn't come. Perhaps the plague has stricken him.

ANTON. Or perhaps he is lying in a ditch with a knife in his back.

MARYA. Oh, Anton!

ANTON. Every possible misfortune has dogged us.

MARYA. I've been stupid. I shouldn't have worn these shoes even to ride in a cart, they so obviously don't belong to a peasant girl. But I quite forgot to change them. Perhaps I shouldn't have been so tired if I had worn thicker shoes.

ANTON. Never mind, only one person has noticed them so far, and I managed an excuse.

MARYA. I don't think she believed you.

ANTON. Well, I am sure she is to be trusted, and perhaps one of the sisters in the convent can lend you a thicker pair.

MARYA. Anton, must we go on tonight?

ANTON. Of course. You know we must. Already we are hours behind time. Pray God the coach is still there and they haven't given up all hope of our coming.

MARYA. Anton—I don't think I can go on tonight.

ANTON. Pull yourself together. We must go on. For all we know, Pavel Karpovich may be following us. There is no plague here, so he won't be afraid to come. We really shouldn't have stopped, but I thought you might feel better if you had a rest and some food. If the coach goes, how are we to reach St. Petersburg? Don't you see? Can't you understand? I suppose you can't be expected to feel as I do. It isn't your country. You haven't looked at the pine woods and thunder clouds hanging dark on the side of the mountains, or ridden through the country when the meadows are heavy with the smell of flowers, or watched the sun setting behind the city spires and felt you were part of it all—as much a part as a tree in the forest, a flower in the field, or a stone in the steeple. And now Pavel Karpovich—the plague rot him body and soul!—is waiting to snatch it away and make it a corner of his own state, a settlement for his surplus population. I have got to stop him. The Czar must help us, if I have to grovel at his feet for it. Surely you understand? Haven't you ever felt that way for your own country—for Russia?

MARYA.   No. Perhaps because I have never had cause. You must remember I was brought up in a convent and saw very little of my own country. As soon as I was old enough I was married to the prince of a tiny country to which no one attached any importance. I was told I was no longer a Russian. By my marriage I had become one of my husband's race; I owed my love to a country I had not then seen.

ANTON.   Does my country mean nothing to you? What do my people mean?

MARYA.   You.

ANTON.   The towns and the forests and the mountains?

MARYA.   You. You are all I have in the whole world.

ANTON.   Marya, you make me feel ashamed. I love you with all my heart, with all my soul—

MARYA.   But you love your country more.

ANTON.   Not more.

MARYA.   Yes, you do, Anton. I'm not jealous. If ever you have to choose between me and your country, let me go. I shall understand.

ANTON.   No, I couldn't do that.

MARYA.   You would forget me in time and be happy again, but you would never forget your country. I think you would die in exile.

ANTON.   Let us not talk of such things. All may be well yet. We'll make the Czar help us. But why should I drag you to St. Petersburg? This isn't your country, they aren't your people.

MARYA.   "Whither thou goest, I will go; where thou lodgest, I will lodge; thy people shall be my people, and thy God my God."

ANTON.   Marya!

(*He is about to take her in his arms when the nun returns, and he draws away.*)

NUN.   You must be very hungry.

MARYA.   No, only thirsty. I couldn't eat. I am not hungry.

(*The nun gives her wine, and Anton passes her food, which she does not take.*)

ANTON.   But you must eat.

NUN.   Don't worry her. It would do her little good while she is so tired.

ANTON.   I am as hungry as a wolf. (*He starts to eat, but stops to talk.*) Little mother, we want to share our secret with you. We aren't peasants. (*He sees her smile.*) Perhaps you guessed that much. I am Anton Ivanovich, and this is my wife, Marya Morevna. We are going to Russia to implore the Czar to help us against Pavel Karpovich.

NUN.   But, Your Highness, it seems a very perilous journey for two such young people to make alone. Could you not write?

ANTON.   The King has written, but no answer has come. Messengers have been sent, but they have not returned. Either the Czar will not listen, or Pavel Karpovich is too clever for us.

NUN.   And you think you can succeed where others have failed?

ANTON.   We kept our departure very secret, and we are disguised.

(*This makes the nun smile, and he starts to eat again.*)

MARYA.   We came by coach to Tanilof—at least just outside—we didn't dare to go into the town for fear of the plague. There we changed our clothes, and walked half a mile down the road to a place where a man, whom we thought we could trust, was to have met us with a wagon and driven us to the Russian frontier, where friends are waiting for us with a coach and proper clothes. The man never came, and we don't know whether it was the plague or Pavel Karpovich that stopped him.

ANTON.   It's all my fault we are here. I wouldn't go back. Marya isn't used to walking, and I didn't realize how far it would be. I kept telling her it was just a little farther, and we kept on going a little farther and just a little farther until we came here.

MARYA.   Without me you would have reached the frontier by now. I suppose a peasant girl would not have noticed the distance.

ANTON.   It all seemed so easy when I first thought it out. The Czar used to be fond of Marya, and I thought if he saw her he might be more easily moved. Now I am afraid Pavel Karpovich must know of our plans. If he does, he will follow us. You see, we must go on.

NUN.   I very much doubt if you could walk much farther yourself, let alone your wife, but there is a man who lives at the farmstead down the road, and who has a horse. It is not a very good horse I am afraid, but it is the only one for many a mile and (*looking at his clothes with a smile*) after all, a peasant shouldn't ride too good a horse. The man is kindhearted and will do anything a sister from this convent asks of him. I will send across to him. You must go on and make your friends wait. Tomorrow, when she has rested, I will find some means of sending your wife to you.

ANTON.   I can't leave her behind. If our wagoner was killed by Pavel Karpovich's men, it means he probably knows where we are and is following us.

NUN.   Then you will be safer apart, and less easily recognized. You need not fear for your wife. She is in sanctuary here.

MARYA. She is right, Anton. I should only be a drag on you.

ANTON. What's that?

NUN. I heard nothing.

ANTON. Listen!

(*The sound of hoofs can be heard very faintly, but grows louder during the following dialogue.*)

That will be Pavel Karpovich and his men!

NUN. Come away from that window! You must go at once! Leave by the door at the side of the convent and cut across that field. Go to the homestead and say I sent you. Ask for the horse, and make straight for the frontier as fast as you can.

MARYA. Anton, I am coming with you!

ANTON. Quickly then!

(*Marya runs after him, but sways, and is saved from falling by the nun.*)

ANTON. Marya!

NUN. You see, she cannot go! She is safer here than with you. My child, you would only hamper him. He must go on alone.

MARYA. Oh, Anton, I have failed you again!

ANTON. I'm not going.

MARYA. Anton!

(*He opens the casket and takes out the dagger.*)

ANTON. I shall kill Pavel Karpovich. I see it all quite clearly now. God has delivered him into my hands. When Pavel Karpovich is dead there will be peace between his land and mine. There was always peace until he killed his king and made himself dictator. This knife will bring peace again to two countries.

(*The nun tries to get the knife away from him, but he will not let go.*)

NUN. No! Give me that knife. You shall not commit murder here. How do you know you will succeed? He is a strong man, and even if you kill him he will not be alone. He may be a regicide and a traitor, but his men love him. They would tear you limb from limb in revenge.

ANTON. But there would be peace in the land.

MARYA. Go, Anton! Go, for my sake! The King is old and sick, the plague has taken most of his councillors. The people look to you to lead them now. Who will they have if you fail them?

ANTON. They will have less need of me when Pavel Karpovich is dead.

NUN. And your wife? His troops are wild men, but their love for their leader is almost worship. When they had lynched you, what would they do to your wife?

(*This slackens Anton's grip on the knife, and she takes it from him and puts it back in the casket.*)

We don't know yet whether he is with his men. You might surrender yourself to them for nothing.

MARYA. Go, Anton! This delay is only ruining our chances of reaching Russia. Go, go—for your country's sake, go!

NUN. There lies the road to Russia. Go with God, and may He soften the Czar's heart towards our country.

(*Anton is about to run to Marya, but the nun catches him by the arms. There is knocking on the outer door.*)

You have no time. Go quickly.

(*She hurries him out of the room and is heard talking off.*)

Who knocks?

(*Voice off.*) Open, in the name of Pavel Karpovich.

NUN. Our door is never locked. All who will may enter.

(*She returns, and a second later Pavel Karpovich and two or three soldiers enter. He is an educated and better-dressed edition of his own Cossack-looking men. He glances round the room, and his eyes stay on Marya.*)

PAVEL. Greetings, little mother.

NUN. Peace be with you. (*She slightly stresses the word "peace."*)

PAVEL. Amen. Have you had travelers call tonight?

NUN. We have no guest save this child, who has taken refuge here from the plague.

PAVEL. From the plague? (*He puts his hand under Marya's chin and tilts her face up, then looks her all over.*) It would be a pity for the plague to nip so sweet a bud.

(*To the women's horror he goes straight to the window.*)

NUN. May I offer you some refreshment?

PAVEL. We have supped, thank you. Borinka!

(*His lieutenant goes to him, and they look out of the window together so that the women cannot see their faces. All the time they are talking, PAVEL is watching something outside the window, and occasionally grins at BORINKA.*)

What a wonderful night! The moonlight is so strong that you can see right across the field as far as the homestead. Do you see, Borinka?

NUN. At least let me offer you some wine.

PAVEL. Thank you, no. You are safer up here in the hills where the air is fresh and clean. I hear your preachers have been calling on God to blast me, but I think this plague shows He is on my side.

NUN. No. The plague is helping us. Has it not driven you back almost to where you started?

PAVEL. Temporarily, but it is going to give me a great, bloodless victory. Of course, that will disappoint Borinka here and his ruffians, but the plague is not leaving you any troops. All we shall have to do is to march to the capital and take possession of it. Then there will be one good, strong state instead of two stupid little kingdoms.

NUN. Do you think God will let you do all this unscathed?

PAVEL. God has sent the plague to you, not to me.

MARYA. The other countries will not let you do this.

PAVEL. No one in Europe ever thinks twice of this little corner of the earth. We shall have grown big and powerful before anyone realizes there is anything to fear.

MARYA. But Russia? She remembered us well enough to send a child of hers to be our princess.

PAVEL. Oh, Russia, Russia!

(He bursts out laughing and Borinka joins in.)

I hear there are other misfortunes abroad besides the plague. I heard to-day there was a man called Stefan, who had a horse and wagon, and he was to have gone to a place near Tanilof to pick up two peasants, a man and a woman, but, unfortunately, poor Stefan met with an accident. Didn't he, Borinka? *(Borinka grins.)* But look, Anton Ivanovich has reached the homestead at last. The field was heavy going, but he has arrived safely. I suppose he is going to try to borrow a horse to take him to Russia—to Russia, Borinka.

(They laugh again.)

MARYA. What do you want? Why did you let him go so far if you only wanted to seize him in the end? Why must you play with him like a cat with a mouse?

(The nun signs to her to be quiet, but it is too late.)

PAVEL. Calm yourself, dear lady. I have no intention of taking him prisoner now he has so kindly left behind his charming princess, Marya Morevna. I may be a son of the people, but I am not such a boor that I cannot tell a princess from a peasant girl.

NUN. Her Highness has sought sanctuary here. No one can touch her against her will.

PAVEL. I have no desire to touch her against her will. Leave that box alone, Borinka. This is a convent and there is to be no looting.

(*Borinka has been examining the casket, but quickly slips the dagger back on hearing Pavel's command.*)

MARYA. I am a princess of the house of Russia.

PAVEL. I am afraid Anton Ivanovich is having a tedious journey to no purpose. The royal house of Russia is divided against itself. The Czar has been assassinated. The king is dead, long live the king! The new Czar won't be interested in you and Anton Ivanovich, and it will take all the soldiers he has to keep him on his throne.

(*Marya sinks to the seat in a daze.*)

NUN. They that take the sword shall perish by the sword.

PAVEL. At the moment it is your soldiers who are perishing, and by the plague. You can't blame me for that.

NUN. You shall not pass through this untouched.

PAVEL. So far we haven't a single case. I believe one of the symptoms of the plague is a black swelling at the base of the throat. (*He feels his throat.*)

NUN. That is so.

PAVEL. My men are examined every day, and not one has shown any sign of swelling.

NUN. I cannot tell how He will strike, but God will punish you.

PAVEL. And why? You who claim to be of God's household should not be bound by the ties of patriotism. You should be able to see farther than most people. Who gave your fathers this particular country? They took it while they were wild and uncivilized. If that was God's doing then, it is His will I take it now. I am going to build a great state out of two petty provinces, and there is no one who can stop me.

MARYA. Why did you have Stefan killed and hinder us in our journey if you knew we could do nothing to deter you?

PAVEL. Out of curiosity. Soon after I became dictator I asked the Czar of Russia to give me his niece for my wife, but it happened the king of this country was seeking her for his grandson. I had a desire to see the woman who chose to stagnate here with a brainless stripling rather than marry a man who had made for himself all that the other had inherited.

MARYA.   I was only a pawn. It was Russia's alliance you both wanted, not me.

PAVEL.   And now Russia's friendship is not worth a tinker's curse. Your value now lies in yourself alone. Knowing that, I was curious to see you.

MARYA.   I knew neither you nor Anton Ivanovich when I made that choice.

PAVEL.   You condemned me unseen. I was told you called me many hard names. Is that true?

MARYA.   Yes—regicide, traitor . . . guttersnipe!

PAVEL.   Do you still want to call me by these names?

(*He goes very close to her, and she lowers her eyes. He smiles and turns away to Borinka. During the following lines Marya puts her hand to her head as if overcome by faintness. She begins to unfasten the shawl about her head, and turns up stage as she does so. She stops quite still and lets the shawl slip back as she sees the casket. She glances at Pavel and moves towards the seat. Pavel and Borinka go on talking and pretend not to see her. She opens the casket, and at the same time the nun takes a step forward. Together they look into the casket, and then the nun raises her eyes to Marya's and they stand looking at each other. With a sudden movement the nun shuts the casket. Marya snatches up her shawl, ties it about her head again, and turns away from the bench. Her hands are trembling but her face is set.*)

Take your men back to the village for the night, and wait until I come. No, no, make no attempt to follow Anton Ivanovich. He may go to Russia if he chooses. He will be well out of the way there. (*His voice fades so that his words are not heard, but begins to grow louder as Marya turns round.*) You can take this, Borinka. We should not wear weapons in this house. (*He gives his sword to Borinka.*) When I have talked with Marya Morevna I will follow you. You see, madam, I am unarmed. Are you afraid to be left alone with me?

NUN.   Madam!

MARYA.   Leave us!

NUN.   No!

MARYA.   Leave us!

NUN.   This convent is sanctuary.

PAVEL.   It is Marya Morevna who bids you go, not I.

NUN.   Marya! Marya Morevna!

(*Pavel signs to his men, who hurry the nun out. Marya is staring before her, and does not see Borinka take the dagger out of the casket, show it to Pavel, and take it away with him.*)

PAVEL. Won't you sit down? What is this war to you, who belong neither to his race nor to mine?

MARYA. You are talking of people and cities, of the hills and fields of two countries of which I know nothing. For me this is a war between two men.

PAVEL. One you married, and the other you might have married. If you had to choose again, would your answer be the same?

MARYA. Women are but women, even in Russian courts.

PAVEL. You have not answered me. What has your little princeling ever done for his country that men should make themselves targets for my soldiers? Why should they die to keep him and his senile old grandfather in their dusty, unsanitary old palace? Why, he hasn't wits enough to see that he could kill the plague forever by draining the swamps! If his people were anything but half imbecilic peasants and myopic old aristocrats they would have turned the old fool and his silly brat out long ago.

MARYA. Or killed them as you killed your king.

PAVEL. That was a regrettable necessity. I had to do it for the country's peace. Petty royalist rebellions and plots were interfering with our progress.

MARYA. Do you intend to kill Anton Ivanovich?

PAVEL. That may not be necessary, especially if he stays in Russia, which he will do if he is wise. This plague will not leave the people strength or spirit to rally around him, and killing a man often makes the multitude mistake him for a hero and a martyr.

MARYA. How much of all this is for your country and how much for yourself?

PAVEL. My country has never been happier nor richer than it is now. Trade is flourishing and the people are prosperous. True, I have pulled down their old palaces and houses, but I have replaced them with fine new streets where the air and the sun keep out the plague. Offer the people their kings again, and I know what their answer would be. What I have done for my country I can do for this.

MARYA. What is this country to you that you should make it richer and happier?

PAVEL. Nothing. The wealth and happiness it gains will be incidental. The people of my country have outgrown their land, while the population of yours is continually depleted by plague. The solution is obvious, and when I have bound the two in one we shall have a state strong enough to shake Europe.

MARYA.   Has your ambition no horizon?

PAVEL.   It is as vast as—

MARYA.   Love.

PAVEL.   Marya Morevna, you might have been queen of all the world.

MARYA.   What is a crown to a woman in love?

(*Pavel looks at the casket and smiles to himself.*)

PAVEL.   Marya Morevna, would your choice still be the same?

(*For answer her hands creep up and round his neck. He seizes her in his arms and kisses her.*)

And Anton Ivanovich has gone to Russia! Marya, you can still be queen of all the world if you choose.

(*She kisses him, and he glances at the casket.*)

Why are you doing this, Marya Morevna?

MARYA.   Have you no faith in love?

PAVEL.   No, but I believe in ambition. Marya, are you ambitious too?

MARYA.   No. I am in love.

PAVEL.   But not with me.

MARYA.   Now Russia has failed him, Anton Ivanovich will have no need of me.

PAVEL.   You little wanton! Are you selling yourself to the highest bidder?

MARYA.   What does that matter to you, who care only for results and not motives?

PAVEL.   So now he has no prospects of a crown you are going to desert Anton Ivanovich. Will you come with me?

MARYA.   I will stay with you as long as I live.

PAVEL.   I don't promise to keep you that long.

(*She puts her hands on his shoulders.*)

MARYA.   Pavel Karpovich!

(*He takes her in his arms and kisses her again.*)

PAVEL.   Marya, the dagger is no longer in that casket.

MARYA.   What should I want with a dagger?

(*This surprises him.*)

PAVEL.   Why—that woman thought you were going to try to kill me. I saw it in her face.

MARYA.   Did you think so, too?

PAVEL.   Yes. Marya, your first intention was to kill me, wasn't it?

MARYA.   Yes.

PAVEL.   And with that dagger?

MARYA.   No.

PAVEL.   Then what did you see in that casket?

MARYA.   A mirror.

PAVEL.   A mirror?

MARYA.   And in that mirror I saw death.

PAVEL.   What's this? Some superstitious nonsense? Whose death?

MARYA.   Yours and mine. I don't need a dagger, Pavel Karpovich.

PAVEL.   What do you mean? What are you talking about? Marya! Marya Morevna! Answer me!

(*He shakes her, but she is half fainting by this time.*)

MARYA.   It's so hot. I am stifling!

(*She tears at the shawl and it falls off. Pavel gives a gasp of horror and lets go of her. She sinks onto the floor, half sitting, half lying against the bench, with her head back on the seat so that her throat is exposed. Pavel stands rooted to the ground by horror, gazing at the black swelling of the plague. The convent bell begins to toll.*)

THE END

Looking into the Plot

1. Arrange these incidents in the order in which they occur in the story:
   (a) Marya kisses Pavel Karpovich.
   (b) Anton and Marya wait in vain for Stefan to meet them.
   (c) Marya asks to be alone with Pavel.
   (d) The Nun realizes that Marya and Anton are not peasants.
   (e) Marya sees evidence of plague reflected in a mirror.
   (f) Marya and Anton say goodbye.
   (g) Marya and Anton decide to go to Russia.
2. What help can Marya and Anton hope to get in Marya's native land? Why?
3. What evidence is there that Marya is seriously ill? List the hints that the author gives from Marya's entrance on.
4. At what moment does Marya discover she has the power to destroy Pavel? Look at the stage directions carefully. When does the author indicate that Marya has made a decision?
5. Why isn't Marya upset when Pavel tells her the dagger is no longer in the casket?
6. When does the reader learn the symptoms of the plague? Why are they important to know?

Thinking It Through

1. *Dramatic irony* is a device a playwright uses to increase the tension of a play. A character says something which means much more than he or she realizes. Sometimes the audience picks up on this immediately; sometimes, not till much later.

   Knowing that her own exhaustion will slow them up and put Anton's life in danger, Marya says, "Oh, Anton, I have failed you again." In view of the ending of the play, what is ironic about her words?
2. The goals of Anton, Marya and Pavel are clearly expressed. Which of the three is moved primarily by love? By ambition? By patriotism? Quote words of all three that show these goals.
3. Toward the end of the play, Marya says to Pavel, "Women are but

women, even in Russian courts." Do you think she really accepts this view of women? If not, whose view is she stating, and why?

Building Vocabulary

The following sentences are based on the play. Decide which of the words following the sentences best fits each blank. Write your answers on a separate sheet of paper.

1. We will stay away until the plague has _____ .

2. The Czar must give us help, even if I have to _____ at his feet for it.

3. It is a very _____ journey for two young people to make alone.

4. Don't fear for your wife; she is in _____ here.

5. Your weakness would only _____ him on his journey.

sanctuary	perilous	grovel
abated	hamper	regicide
tedious	looting	

Writing Projects

1. One important character in the play, the Nun, is present for most, but not all, of the action. She is a wise woman who can see into the nature of other characters. She is a good woman who lives to help others and to serve God.

   Write an account of the story of Anton, Marya and Pavel as the Nun would tell it. Begin with the arrival of Anton and Marya and end with the last thing the Nun hears of them. Keep in mind that you are writing from the Nun's **point of view**. She sees only some of the action; the rest she has to learn about or imagine. (*For help with this assignment see Writing Manual, p. 202.*)

2. Imagine that Anton has returned to his country. As its new ruler he would like to declare Marya's birthday a national holiday. Write the brief speech he might make to his people explaining why his dead wife is deserving of this honor. Find at least two **reasons**. (*For help with this assignment see Writing Manual, p. 205.*)

TRIFLES

Trifles

Susan Glaspell

THIS PLAY is called "Trifles"—a word signifying items of little importance or value. Normally we pay no attention to trifles, yet it is trifles in this play that help solve a baffling crime. Strangely, the official detectives, who should know better, overlook these seemingly unimportant clues, leaving it up to amateurs to find them.

Strange, also, is the fact that the two most important characters in the play never appear on the stage. Their presence is felt throughout, however, and by the final curtain the audience knows much about them.

"Trifles" has been a favorite with audiences and readers for over fifty years. We are sure that you too will enjoy this unusual story. Keep your senses alert as you join five people in an old farmhouse searching for the motive to fit a most extraordinary crime.

Vocabulary Preview

CRAFTY (KRAF-tee) skillful in underhanded or evil schemes
The *crafty* thief found a way to open the safe without disturbing the owners.

ABASHED (uh-BASHT) embarrassed; ashamed

The children looked *abashed* when the officer scolded them.

REPROACH (ri-PROHCH) to find fault with; to blame

We were ready to *reproach* the man, but he apologized and promised not to trouble us again.

COVERT (KOH-vurt) concealed; secret

The men moved in a *covert* way toward the enemy camp.

FACETIOUSLY (fah-SEE-shus-lee) in a light, humorous manner

He *facetiously* introduced us to his pet dog, cat and parakeet.

Other Words You Will Need to Know

CLOSE (KLOHS) stingy; unwilling to spend money

RED-UP (RED UP) (country expression) neat and tidy

Characters

Sheriff Peters
County Attorney Henderson
Mr. Hale, a farmer
Mrs. Peters, the sheriff's wife
Mrs. Hale

Trifles

SCENE:

The kitchen in the now abandoned farmhouse of John Wright, a gloomy kitchen, and left without having been put in order—the walls covered with a faded wall paper. Down Right is a door leading to the parlor. On the Right wall above this door is a built-in kitchen cupboard with shelves in the upper portion and drawers below. In the rear wall at Right, up two steps is a door opening onto stairs leading to the second floor. In the rear wall at Left is a door to the shed and from there to the outside. Between these two doors is an old-fashioned black iron stove. Running along the Left wall from the shed door is an old iron sink and sink shelf, in which is set a hand pump. Downstage of the sink is an uncurtained window. Near the window is an old wooden rocker. Center stage is an unpainted wooden kitchen table with straight chairs on either side. There is a small chair Down Right. Unwashed pans under the sink, a loaf of bread outside the breadbox, a dish towel on the table—other signs of uncompleted work. At the rear the shed door opens and the Sheriff comes in followed by the County Attorney and Hale. The Sheriff and Hale are men in middle life, the County Attorney is a young man; all are much bundled up and go at once to the stove. They are followed by the two women—the Sheriff's wife, Mrs. Peters, first; she is a slight wiry woman, a thin nervous face. Mrs. Hale is larger and would ordinarily be called more comfortable looking, but she is disturbed now and looks fearfully about as she enters. The women have come in slowly, and stand close together near the door.

COUNTY ATTORNEY. (*At stove rubbing his hands.*) This feels good. Come up to the fire, ladies.

MRS. PETERS. (*After taking a step forward.*) I'm not—cold.

SHERIFF. (*Unbuttoning his overcoat and stepping away from the stove to right of table as if to mark the beginning of official business.*) Now, Mr. Hale, before we move things about, you explain to Mr. Henderson just what you saw when you came here yesterday morning.

COUNTY ATTORNEY. (*Crossing down to left of the table.*) By the way, has anything been moved? Are things just as you left them yesterday?

SHERIFF. (*Looking about.*) It's just the same. When it dropped below zero last night I thought I'd better send Frank out this morning to make a fire for us—(*sits right of center table*) no use getting pneumonia with a big case on, but I'd told him not to touch anything except the stove—and you know Frank.

COUNTY ATTORNEY. Somebody should have been left here yesterday.

SHERIFF. Oh—yesterday. When I had to send Frank to Morris Center for that man who went crazy—I want you to know I had my hands full yesterday. I knew you could get back from Omaha by today and as long as I went over everything here myself—

COUNTY ATTORNEY. Well, Mr. Hale, tell just what happened when you came here yesterday morning.

HALE. Harry and I had started to town with a load of potatoes. We came along the road from my place and as I got here I said, "I'm going to see if I can't get John Wright to go in with me on a party telephone." I spoke to Wright about it once before and he put me off, saying folks talked too much anyway, and all he asked was peace and quiet—I guess you know about how much he talked himself; but I thought maybe if I went to the house and talked about it before his wife, though I said to Harry that I didn't know as what his wife wanted made much difference to John—

COUNTY ATTORNEY. Let's talk about that later, Mr. Hale. I do want to talk about that, but tell now just what happened when you got to the house.

HALE. I didn't hear or see anything; I knocked at the door, and still it was all quiet inside. I knew they must be up, it was past eight o'clock. So I knocked again, and I thought I heard somebody say, "Come in." I wasn't sure, I'm not sure yet, but I opened the door—this door (*indicating the door by which the two women are still standing*) and there in that rocker—(*pointing to it*) sat Mrs. Wright. (*They all look at the rocker.*)

COUNTY ATTORNEY. What—was she doing?

HALE. She was rockin' back and forth. She had her apron in her hand and was kind of—pleating it.

COUNTY ATTORNEY. And how did she—look?

HALE. Well, she looked queer.

COUNTY ATTORNEY. How do you mean—queer?

HALE. Well, as if she didn't know what she was going to do next. And kind of done up.

COUNTY ATTORNEY. (*Takes out notebook and pencil and sits left of center table.*) How did she seem to feel about your coming?

HALE. Why, I don't think she minded—one way or other. She didn't pay much attention. I said, "How do, Mrs. Wright, it's cold, ain't it?" And she said, "Is it?"—and went on kind of pleating at her apron. Well, I was surprised; she didn't ask me to come up to the stove, or to set down, but just sat there, not even looking at me, so I said, "I want to see John." And then she—laughed. I guess you would call it a laugh. I thought of Harry and the team outside, so I said a little sharp: "Can't I see John?" "No," she says, kind o' dull like. "Ain't he home?" says I. "Yes," says she, "he's home." "Then why can't I see him?" I asked her, out of patience. " 'Cause he's dead," says she. "Dead?" says I. She just nodded her head, not getting a bit excited, but rockin' back and forth. "Why—where is he?" says I, not knowing what to say. She just pointed upstairs—like that. (*Himself pointing to the room above.*) I started for the stairs, with the idea of going up there. I walked from there to here—then I says, "Why, what did he die of?" "He died of a rope 'round his neck," says she, and just went on pleatin' at her apron. Well, I went out and called Harry. I thought I might—need help. We went upstairs and there he was lyin'—

COUNTY ATTORNEY. I think I'd rather have you go into that upstairs, where you can point it all out. Just go on now with the rest of the story.

HALE. Well, my first thought was to get that rope off. It looked... (*stops, his face twitches*) ...but Harry, he went up to him, and he said, "No, he's dead all right, and we'd better not touch anything." So we went back downstairs. She was still sitting that same way. "Has anyone been notified?" I asked. "No," says she, unconcerned. "Who did this, Mrs. Wright?" said Harry. He said it business-like—and she stopped pleatin' of her apron. "I don't know," she says. "You don't *know?*" says Harry. "No," says she. "Weren't you sleepin' in the bed with him?" says Harry. "Yes," says she, "but I was on the inside." "Somebody slipped a rope 'round his neck and strangled him and you didn't wake up?" says Harry. "I didn't wake up," she said after him. We must 'a' looked as if we didn't see how that could be, for after a minute she said, "I sleep sound." Harry was going to ask her more questions but I said maybe we ought to let her tell her story to the coroner, or the sheriff, so Harry went fast as he could to Rivers' place, where there's a telephone.

COUNTY ATTORNEY. And what did Mrs. Wright do when she knew that you had gone for the coroner?

HALE. She moved from the rocker to that chair over there (*pointing to a small chair in the corner*) and just sat there with her hands held together and looking down. I got a feeling that I ought to make some conversation, so I said I had come in to see if John wanted to put in a telephone, and at that she started to laugh, and then she stopped and looked at me—scared. (*The* County Attorney, *who has had his notebook out, makes a note.*) I dunno, maybe it wasn't scared. I wouldn't like to say it was. Soon Harry got back, and then Dr. Lloyd came, and you, Mr. Peters, and so I guess that's all I know that you don't.

COUNTY ATTORNEY. (*Rising and looking around.*) I guess we'll go upstairs first—and then out to the barn and around there. (*To the sheriff.*) You're convinced that there was nothing important here—nothing that would point to any motive?

SHERIFF. Nothing here but kitchen things. (*The County Attorney, after again looking around the kitchen, opens the door of a cupboard closet in Right wall. He brings a small chair from Right—gets up on it and looks on a shelf. Pulls his hand away, sticky.*).

COUNTY ATTORNEY. Here's a nice mess. (*The women draw nearer.*)

MRS. PETERS. (*To the other woman.*) Oh, her fruit; it did freeze. (*To the Lawyer.*) She worried about that when it turned so cold. She said the fire'd go out and her jars would break.

SHERIFF. (*Rises.*) Well, can you beat the women! Held for murder and worryin' about her preserves.

COUNTY ATTORNEY. (*Getting down from the chair.*) I guess before we're through she may have something more serious than preserves to worry about.

HALE. Well, women are used to worrying over trifles. (*The two women move a little closer together.*)

COUNTY ATTORNEY. (*With the gallantry of a young politician.*) And yet, for all their worries, what would we do without the ladies? (*The women do not unbend. He goes below the center table to the sink, takes a dipperful of water from the pail and pouring it into a basin, washes his hands. While he is doing this the Sheriff and Hale cross to cupboard, which they inspect. The County Attorney starts to wipe his hands on the roller towel, turns it for a cleaner place.*) Dirty towels! (*Kicks his foot against the pans under the sink.*) Not much of a housekeeper, would you say, ladies?

MRS. HALE. (*Stiffly.*) There's a great deal of work to be done on a farm.

COUNTY ATTORNEY. To be sure. And yet (*with a little bow to her*) I know there are some Dickson County farmhouses which do not have such roller towels. (*He gives a pull to expose its full length again.*)

MRS. HALE. Those towels get dirty awful quick. Men's hands aren't always as clean as they might be.

COUNTY ATTORNEY. Ah, loyal to your sex, I see. But you and Mrs. Wright were neighbors. I suppose you were friends too.

MRS. HALE. (*Shaking her head.*) I've not seen much of her of late years. I've not been in this house—it's more than a year.

COUNTY ATTORNEY. (*Crossing to the women.*) And why was that? You didn't like her?

MRS. HALE. I liked her well enough. Farmers' wives have their hands full, Mr. Henderson. And then—

COUNTY ATTORNEY. Yes—?

MRS. HALE. (*Looking about.*) It never seemed a very cheerful place.

COUNTY ATTORNEY. No— it's not cheerful. I shouldn't say she had the homemaking instinct.

MRS. HALE. Well, I don't know as Wright had, either.

COUNTY ATTORNEY. You mean that they didn't get on very well?

MRS. HALE. No, I don't mean anything. But I don't think a place'd be any cheerfuller for John Wright's being in it.

COUNTY ATTORNEY. I'd like to talk more of that a little later. I want to get a look at things upstairs now. (*He goes past the women to where steps lead to a stair door.*)

SHERIFF. I suppose anything Mrs. Peters does'll be all right. She was to take in some clothes for her, you know, and a few little things. We left in such a hurry yesterday.

COUNTY ATTORNEY. Yes, but I would like to see what you take, Mrs. Peters, and keep an eye out for anything that might be of use to us.

MRS. PETERS. Yes, Mr. Henderson. (*The men leave by door to stairs. The women listen to the men's steps on the stairs, then look about the kitchen.*)

MRS. HALE. (*Crossing to the sink.*) I'd hate to have men coming into my kitchen, snooping around and criticizing. (*She arranges the pans under sink which the Lawyer had shoved out of place.*)

MRS. PETERS. Of course it's no more than their duty. (*Crosses to cupboard.*)

MRS. HALE. Duty's all right, but I guess that deputy sheriff that came out to make the fire might have got a little of this on. (*Gives the roller towel a pull.*) Wish I'd thought of that sooner. Seems mean to talk about her for not having things slicked up when she had to come away in such a hurry. (*Crosses to Mrs. Peters at cupboard.*)

MRS. PETERS. (*Who has been looking through the cupboard, lifts one end of a towel that covers a pan.*) She had bread set. (*Stands still.*)

MRS. HALE. (*Eyes fixed on a loaf of bread beside the breadbox, which is on a low shelf of the cupboard.*) She was going to put this in there. (*Picks up loaf, then abruptly drops it. In a manner of returning to familiar things.*) It's a shame about her fruit. I wonder if it's all gone. (*Gets up on the chair and looks.*) I think there's some here that's all right, Mrs. Peters. Yes—here; (*holding it toward the window*) this is cherries, too. (*Looking again.*) I declare I believe that's the only one. (*Gets down, jar in her hand. Goes to the sink and wipes it off on the outside.*) She'll feel awful bad after all her hard work in the hot weather. I remember the afternoon I put up my cherries last summer. (*She puts the jar on the big kitchen table, center of the room. With a sigh, is about to sit down in the rocking chair. Before she is seated realizes what chair it is; with a slow look at it, steps back. The chair which she has touched rocks back and forth. Mrs. Peters moves to center table and they both watch the chair rock for a moment or two.*)

MRS. PETERS. (*Shaking off the mood which the empty rocking chair has evoked. Now in a businesslike manner she speaks.*) Well, I must get those things from the front room closet. (*She goes to the door at the Right, but, after looking into the other room, steps back.*) You coming with me, Mrs. Hale? You could help me carry them. (*They go in the other room; reappear, Mrs. Peters carrying a dress, petticoat and skirt, Mrs. Hale following with a pair of shoes.*) My, it's cold in there. (*She puts the clothes on the big table, and hurries to the stove.*)

MRS. HALE. (*Right of center table examining the skirt.*) Wright was close. I think maybe that's why she kept so much to herself. She didn't even belong to the Ladies' Aid. I suppose she felt she couldn't do her part, and then you don't enjoy things when you feel shabby. I heard she used to wear pretty clothes and be lively, when she was Minnie Foster, one of the town girls singing in the choir. But that—oh, that was thirty years ago. This all you was to take in?

MRS. PETERS. She said she wanted an apron. Funny thing to want, for there isn't much to get you dirty in jail, goodness knows. But I suppose just to make her feel more natural. (*Crosses to cupboard.*) She said they was in the top drawer of this cupboard. Yes, here. And then her little shawl that always hung behind the door. (*Opens stair door and looks.*) Yes, here it is. (*Quickly shuts door leading upstairs.*)

MRS. HALE. (*Abruptly moving toward her.*) Mrs. Peters?

MRS. PETERS. Yes, Mrs. Hale?

MRS. HALE. Do you think she did it?

MRS PETERS. (*In a frightened voice.*) Oh, I don't know.

MRS. HALE. Well, I don't think she did. Asking for an apron and her little shawl. Worrying about her fruit.

MRS. PETERS. (*Starts to speak, glances up, where footsteps are heard in the room above. In a low voice.*) Mr. Peters says it looks bad for her. Mr. Henderson is awful sarcastic in a speech and he'll make fun of her sayin' she didn't wake up.

MRS. HALE. Well, I guess John Wright didn't wake when they was slipping that rope under his neck.

MRS. PETERS. (*Crossing slowly to table and placing shawl and apron on table with other clothing.*) No, it's strange. It must have been done awful crafty and still. They say it was such a—funny way to kill a man, rigging it all up like that.

MRS. HALE. That's just what Mr. Hale said. There was a gun in the house. He says that's what he can't understand.

MRS. PETERS. Mr. Henderson said coming out that what was needed for the case was a motive; something to show anger, or—sudden feeling.

MRS. HALE. (*Who is standing by the table.*) Well, I don't see any signs of anger around here. (*She puts her hand on the dish towel which lies on the table, stands looking down at table, one-half of which is clean, the other half messy.*) It's wiped to here. (*Makes a move as if to finish work, then turns and looks at loaf of bread outside the breadbox. Drops towel. In that voice of coming back to familiar things.*) Wonder how they are finding things upstairs. I hope she had it a little more red-up up there. You know, it seems kind of *sneaking.* Locking her up in town and then coming out here and trying to get her own house to turn against her!

MRS. PETERS. But, Mrs. Hale, the law is the law.

MRS. HALE. I s'pose 'tis. (*Unbuttoning her coat.*) Better loosen up your things, Mrs. Peters. You won't feel them when you go out. (*Mrs. Peters takes off her fur tippet, goes to hang it on chair back left of table, stands looking at the work basket on floor near window.*)

MRS. PETERS. She was piecing a quilt. (*She brings the large sewing basket to the center table and they look at the bright pieces.*)

MRS. HALE. It's a log cabin pattern. Pretty, isn't it? I wonder if she was goin' to quilt it or just knot it? (*Footsteps have been heard coming down the stairs. The Sheriff enters followed by Hale and the County Attorney.*)

SHERIFF. They wonder if she was going to quilt it or just knot it! (*The men laugh, the women look abashed.*)

COUNTY ATTORNEY. (*Rubbing his hands over the stove.*) Frank's fire didn't do much up there, did it? Well, let's go out to the barn and get that cleared up. (*The men go outside.*)

MRS. HALE. (*Resentfully.*) I don't know as there's anything so strange, our takin' up our time with little things while we're waiting for them to get the evidence. (*She sits in chair right of table smoothing out a block with decision.*) I don't see as it's anything to laugh about.

MRS. PETERS. (*Apologetically.*) Of course they've got awful important things on their minds. (*Pulls up a chair and joins Mrs. Hale at the table.*)

MRS. HALE. (*Examining another block.*) Mrs. Peters, look at this one. Here, this is the one she was working on, and look at the sewing! All the rest of it has been so nice and even. And look at this! It's all over the place! Why, it looks as if she didn't know what she was about! (*After she has said this they look at each other, then start to glance back at the door. After an instant Mrs. Hale has pulled at a knot and ripped the sewing.*)

MRS. PETERS. Oh, what are you doing, Mrs. Hale?

MRS. HALE. (*Mildly.*) Just pulling out a stitch or two that's not sewed very good. (*Threading a needle.*) Bad sewing always made me fidgety.

MRS. PETERS. (*With a glance at the door, nervously.*) I don't think we ought to touch things.

MRS. HALE. I'll just finish up this end. (*Suddenly stopping and leaning forward.*) Mrs. Peters?

MRS. PETERS. Yes, Mrs. Hale?

MRS. HALE. What do you suppose she was so nervous about?

MRS. PETERS. Oh—I don't know. I don't know as she was nervous. I sometimes sew awful queer when I'm just tired. (*Mrs. Hale starts to say something, looks at Mrs. Peters, then goes on sewing.*) Well, I must get these things wrapped up. They may be through sooner than we think. (*Putting apron and other things together.*) I wonder where I can find a piece of paper, and string. (*Rises.*)

MRS. HALE. In that cupboard, maybe.

MRS. PETERS. (*Looking in cupboard.*) Why, here's a bird cage. (*Holds it up.*) Did she have a bird, Mrs. Hale?

MRS. HALE. Why, I don't know whether she did or not—I've not been here for so long. There was a man around last year selling canaries cheap, but I don't know as she took one; maybe she did. She used to sing real pretty herself.

MRS. PETERS. (*Glancing around.*) Seems funny to think of a bird here. But she must have had one, or why would she have a cage? I wonder what happened to it?

MRS. HALE. I s'pose maybe the cat got it.

MRS. PETERS. No, she didn't have a cat. She's got that feeling some people have about cats— being afraid of them. My cat got in her room and she was real upset and asked me to take it out.

MRS. HALE. My sister Bessie was like that. Queer, ain't it?

MRS. PETERS. (*Examining the cage.*) Why, look at this door. It's broke. One hinge is pulled apart. (*Takes a step down to Mrs. Hale's right.*)

MRS. HALE. (*Looking too.*) Looks as if someone must have been rough with it.

MRS. PETERS. Why, yes. (*She brings the cage forward and puts it on the table.*)

MRS. HALE. (*Glancing toward door.*) I wish if they're going to find any evidence they'd be about it. I don't like this place.

MRS. PETERS. But I'm awful glad you came with me, Mrs. Hale. It would be lonesome for me sitting here alone.

MRS. HALE. It would, wouldn't it? (*Dropping her sewing.*) But I tell you what I do wish, Mrs. Peters. I wish I had come over sometimes when *she* was here. I—(*looking around the room*)—wish I had.

MRS. PETERS. But of course you were awful busy, Mrs. Hale—your house and your children.

MRS. HALE. I could've come. I stayed away because it weren't cheerful—and that's why I ought to have come. I—(*looking out window*)—I've never liked this place. Maybe because it's down in a hollow and you don't see the road. I dunno what it is, but it's a lonesome place and always was. I wish I had come over to see Minnie Foster sometimes. I can see now— (*Shakes her head.*)

MRS. PETERS. Well, you mustn't reproach yourself, Mrs. Hale. Somehow we just don't see how it is with other folks until—something turns up.

MRS. HALE. Not having children makes less work—but it makes a quiet house, and Wright out to work all day, and no company when he did come in. (*Turning from window.*) Did you know John Wright, Mrs. Peters?

MRS. PETERS. Not to know him; I've seen him in town. They say he was a good man.

MRS. HALE. Yes—good; he kept his word as well as most, I guess, and paid his debts. But he was a hard man, Mrs. Peters. Just to pass the time of day with him—(*Shivers.*) Like a raw wind that gets to the bone. (*Pauses, her eye falling on the cage.*) I should think she would 'a'wanted a bird. But what do you suppose went with it?

MRS. PETERS. I don't know, unless it got sick and died. (*She reaches over and swings the broken door, swings it again, both women watch it.*)

MRS. HALE. You weren't raised around here, were you? (*Mrs. Peters shakes her head.*) You didn't know—her?

MRS. PETERS. Not till they brought her yesterday.

MRS. HALE. She—come to think of it, she was kind of like a bird herself—real sweet and pretty, but kind of timid and—fluttery. How—she—did—change. (*Silence; then as if struck by a happy thought and relieved to get back to everyday things. Crosses to cupboard, replaces small chair used to stand on to its original place.*) Tell you what, Mrs. Peters, why don't you take the quilt in with you? It might take up her mind.

MRS. PETERS. Why, I think that's a real nice idea, Mrs. Hale. There couldn't possibly be any objection to it, could there? Now, just what would I take? I wonder if her patches are in here—and her things. (*They look in the sewing basket.*)

MRS. HALE. (*Crosses to right of table.*) Here's some red. I expect this has got sewing things in it. (*Brings out a fancy box.*) What a pretty box. Looks like something somebody would give you. Maybe her scissors are in here. (*Opens box. Suddenly puts her hand to her nose.*) Why—(*Mrs. Peters bends nearer, then turns her face away.*) There's something wrapped up in this piece of silk.

MRS. PETERS. Why, this isn't her scissors.

MRS. HALE. (*Lifting the silk.*) Oh, Mrs. Peters—it's—(*Mrs. Peters bends closer.*)

MRS PETERS. It's the bird.

MRS. HALE. But, Mrs. Peters—look at it! Its neck! Look at its neck! It's all—other side *to.*

MRS. PETERS. Somebody—wrung—its neck. (*Their eyes meet. A look of growing comprehension, of horror. Steps are heard outside. Mrs. Hale slips box under quilt pieces, and sinks into her chair. Enter Sheriff and County Attorney. Mrs. Peters stands looking out of window.*)

COUNTY ATTORNEY. (*As one turning from serious things to little pleasantries.*) Well, ladies, have you decided whether she was going to quilt it or knot it?

MRS. PETERS. We think she was going to—knot it. (*Sheriff crosses to stove, lifts stove lid and glances at fire, then stands warming hands at stove.*)

COUNTY ATTORNEY. Well, that's interesting, I'm sure. (*Seeing the bird cage.*) Has the bird flown?

MRS. HALE. (*Putting more quilt pieces over the box.*) We think the—cat got it.

COUNTY ATTORNEY. (*Preoccupied.*) Is there a cat? (*Mrs. Hale glances in a quick covert way at Mrs. Peters.*)

MRS. PETERS. (*Turning from window takes a step in.*) Well, not now. They're superstitious, you know. They leave.

COUNTY ATTORNEY. (*To Sheriff Peters, continuing an interrupted conversation.*) No sign at all of anyone having come from the outside. Their own rope. Now let's go up again and go over it piece by piece. (*They start upstairs.*) It would have to have been someone who knew just the— (*Mrs. Peters sits down left of table. The two women sit there not looking at one another, but as if peering into something and at the same time holding back. When they talk now it is in the manner of feeling their way over strange ground, as if afraid of what they are saying, but as if they cannot help saying it.*)

MRS. HALE. (*Hesitatively and in hushed voice.*) She liked the bird. She was going to bury it in that pretty box.

MRS. PETERS. (*In a whisper.*) When I was a girl—my kitten—there was a boy took a hatchet, and before my eyes—and before I could get there—(*Covers her face an instant.*) It they hadn't held me back I would have—(*catches herself, looks upstairs where steps are heard, falters weakly*)—hurt him.

MRS. HALE. (*With a slow look around her.*) I wonder how it would seem never to have any children around. (*Pause.*) No, Wright wouldn't like the bird—a thing that sang. She used to sing. He killed that, too.

MRS. PETERS. (*Moving uneasily.*) We don't know who killed the bird.

MRS. HALE. I knew John Wright.

MRS. PETERS. It was an awful thing was done in this house that night, Mrs. Hale. Killing a man while he slept, slipping a rope around his neck that choked the life out of him.

MRS. HALE. His neck. Choked the life out of him. (*Her hand goes out and rests on the bird cage.*)

MRS. PETERS. (*With rising voice.*) We don't know who killed him. We don't know.

MRS. HALE. (*Her own feeling not interrupted.*) If there'd been years and years of nothing, then a bird to sing to you, it would be awful—still, after the bird was still.

MRS. PETERS. (*Something within her speaking.*) I know what stillness is. When we homesteaded in Dakota, and my first baby died—after he was two years old, and me with no other then—

MRS. HALE. (*Moving.*) How soon do you suppose they'll be through looking for the evidence?

MRS. PETERS. I know what stillness is. (*Pulling herself back.*) The law has got to punish crime, Mrs. Hale.

MRS. HALE. (*Not as if answering that.*) I wish you'd seen Minnie Foster when she wore a white dress with blue ribbons and stood up there in the choir and sang. (*A look around the room.*) Oh, I *wish* I'd come over here once in a while! That was a crime! That was a crime! Who's going to punish that!

MRS. PETERS. (*Looking upstairs.*) We mustn't—take on.

MRS. HALE. I might have known she needed help! I know how things can be— for women. I tell you, it's queer, Mrs. Peters. We live close together and we live far apart. We all go through the same things—it's all just a dif- ferent kind of the same thing. (*Brushes her eyes, noticing the jar of fruit, reaches out for it.*) If I was you I wouldn't tell her her fruit was gone. Tell her it *ain't*. Tell her it's all right. Take this in to prove it to her. She—she may never know whether it was broken or not.

MRS. PETERS. (*Takes the jar, looks about for something to wrap it in; takes petticoat from the clothes brought from the other room, very ner- vously begins winding this around the jar. In a false voice.*) My, it's a good thing the men couldn't hear us. Wouldn't they just laugh! Getting all stirred up over a little thing like a—dead canary. As if that could have anything to do with—with—wouldn't they *laugh!* (*The men are heard coming downstairs.*)

MRS. HALE. (*Under her breath.*) Maybe they would—maybe they wouldn't.

COUNTY ATTORNEY. No, Peters, it's all perfectly clear except a reason for doing it. But you know juries when it comes to women. If there was some definite thing. (*Crosses slowly to above table. Mrs. Hale and Mrs. Peters remain seated at either side of table.*) Something to show—something to make a story about—a thing that would connect up with this strange way of doing it—(*The women's eyes meet for an instant. Enter Hale from outer door.*)

HALE. (*Remaining by door.*) Well, I've got the team around. Pretty cold out there.

COUNTY ATTORNEY. I'm going to stay awhile by myself. (*To the Sheriff.*) You can send Frank out for me, can't you? I want to go over everything. I'm not satisfied that we can't do better.

SHERIFF. Do you want to see what Mrs. Peters is going to take in? (*The Lawyer picks up the apron, laughs.*)

COUNTY ATTORNEY. Oh, I guess they're not very dangerous things the ladies have picked out. (*Moves a few things about, disturbing the quilt pieces which cover the box. Steps back.*) No, Mrs. Peters doesn't need supervising. For that matter a sheriff's wife is married to the law. Ever think of it that way, Mrs. Peters?

MRS. PETERS. Not—just that way

SHERIFF. (*Chuckling.*) Married to the law (*Moves to the other room.*) I just want you to come in here a minute, George. We ought to take a look at these windows.

COUNTY ATTORNEY. (*Scoffingly.*) Oh, windows!

SHERIFF. We'll be right out, Mr. Hale. (*Hale goes outside. The Sheriff follows the County Attorney into the other room. Then Mrs. Hale rises, hands tight together, looking intensely at Mrs. Peters, whose eyes make a slow turn, finally meeting Mrs. Hale's. A moment Mrs. Hale holds her, then her own eyes point the way to where the box is concealed. Suddenly Mrs. Peters throws back quilt pieces and tries to put the box in the bag she is carrying. It is too big. She opens box, starts to take bird out, cannot touch it, goes to pieces, stands there helpless. Sound of a knob turning in the other room. Mrs. Hale snatches the box and puts it in the pocket of her big coat. Enter the County Attorney and Sheriff, who remains Down Right.*)

COUNTY ATTORNEY. (*Crosses to door facetiously.*) Well, Henry, at least we found out that she was not going to quilt it. She was going to—what is it you call it, ladies?

MRS. HALE. (*Standing facing front, her hand against her pocket.*) We call it— knot it, Mr. Henderson.

CURTAIN

Looking into the Plot

1. Arrange these incidents in the order in which they probably occurred:
   (a) Mrs. Hale hides a fancy box in her coat pocket.
   (b) Minnie Foster sings in the church choir.
   (c) Mrs. Wright buys a canary.
   (d) Mr. Hale stops by the Wright farmhouse to see if Mr. Wright will share a party telephone with him.
   (e) The county attorney comments on Mrs. Wright's dirty kitchen towel.
   (f) The canary is killed.

   (g) Mrs. Peters finds a bird cage.

   (h) Mr. Wright is killed.

2. Why have Mr. and Mrs. Hale come to the Wright farmhouse with the sheriff and the county attorney? Why is Mrs. Peters there?

3. While the men busy themselves in other parts of the house, Mrs. Hale and Mrs. Peters stay in the kitchen. What are three important pieces of evidence that they discover there? What makes these trifles important?

4. What truth do both women begin to understand when they find the dead bird? Do they discuss it? If not, how does the author make their understanding clear to the audience? (Look back at the stage directions.)

5. After they find the dead bird, both women deliberately withhold this evidence from the county attorney. Have they agreed to do this? If not, how do they communicate their purposes to one another? (Look back at the stage directions.)

6. Without actually saying so, the two women make a case for the defense of Mrs. Wright. What ideas and what personal experiences do they share? How do these ideas and experiences help to "defend" Mrs. Wright?

7. What final silent agreement do Mrs. Hale and Mrs. Peters come to at the end of the play? How does the presence of the bird create a last-minute suspense.

Thinking It Through

1. What does Mrs. Hale discover about the kind of life Mrs. Wright led? How does this make her feel? Use three adjectives to describe Mrs. Hale.

2. The county attorney suggests that Mrs. Peters, as wife of the sheriff, should feel a special obligation to serve the interests of the law. Where does she show an awareness of this obligation? Why does she ultimately put sympathy for Mrs. Wright above loyalty to the law? Use three adjectives to describe Mrs. Peters's character.

3. Mr. Wright is described as a good man who was honest and paid his debts. What important human qualities did he lack? How does Mrs. Hale describe his effect on others? In what sense was he a destructive man?

4. Mrs. Wright seems to be a ghostly presence throughout the play. Find places where the ladies are nervously aware of her. In what way is the caged bird an ideal image for Mrs. Wright? What parallel do you find between the bird's fate and Mrs. Wright's life?

5. It is the women and not the men who find those "trifles" that are vitally important evidence. How is this partly a result of the way men treat women in this play? What does the author seem to be saying about the danger of

judging individuals only in terms of the groups they belong to (i.e., women, minorities)?

6. This play has sometimes been titled "A Jury of Her Peers." (Peers are equals.) What makes this a good title? Which of the titles do you like better? Why?

Building Vocabulary

The following sentences are based on the play. Decide which of the words following the sentences best fits each blank. Write your answers on a separate sheet of paper.

1. "It wasn't your fault and you mustn't _____ yourself," Mrs. Peters said to Mrs. Hale.

2. The murderer must have been clever and _____ to accomplish such a crime.

3. The ladies looked _____ when the county attorney _____ praised their attention to detail.

4. Mrs. Hale and Mrs. Peters exchanged _____ glances.

> crafty   covert   facetiously
> abashed   reproach

Writing Projects

1. Minnie Foster Wright's married life was lonely and cheerless. Write a paragraph that supports this statement, using three specific **factual details** of the play. Make sure the details are arranged in order of importance and linked with transitions. (*For help with this assignment see Writing Manual, p. 206.*)

2. The stage set of "Trifles" is a simple country kitchen. This is the room where Mrs. Wright has spent much of her time cooking, baking bread, canning fruits and just sitting in her rocking chair, sewing. The details of this room help to present Mrs. Wright and her life to the audience.

Choose a room that expresses the character of a person you know, and write a **description** of it. It might be your grandmother's kitchen, the bedroom of a brother, sister or best friend, or your own room. Use the description of the Wright kitchen as a model. (*For help with this assignment see Writing Manual, p. 203.*)

THE
MONKEY'S PAW

The Monkey's Paw

Louis N. Parker
Adapted from the short story
by W. W. Jacobs

THE MONKEY'S PAW is one of the most famous and enduring short stories ever written. When you read it as a play you will understand why.

In this tale of good, simple folk, we encounter the hopes and fears and tragedies of all people. The hopes are the fairy-tale hopes that persist in all generations, here represented by a magic token that will grant three wishes. The fears and tragedies closely follow the granting of the wishes. Must it be so? See what this play seems to say.

Vocabulary Preview

PERVADE (pur-VAYD) to spread throughout
    The odor of the burning candles *pervaded* the room.
INVOLUNTARY (in-VOL-un-tair-ee) not done of one's own free will
    The sight was so frightening that an *involuntary* scream escaped from her lips.
DISTRACT (dis-TRAKT) to draw the mind away in another direction
    The loud radio *distracted* him from the book he was reading.

PENSIVE (PEN-siv) thinking deeply, often of sad things.

In a *pensive* mood, he sat by the river, remembering the bittersweet moments of his childhood.

Other Words You Will Need to Know

FAKIR (fuh-KEER) a Muslim or Hindu beggar who performs magical acts
SPELL   a word giving magical power
INFERNAL (in-FUR-nul) devilish, inhuman

Characters

Mr. White
Mrs. White
Herbert
Sergeant-Major Morris
Mr. Sampson

Setting

The living room of an old-fashioned cottage on the outskirts of Fulham, England. In the corner Upstage a deep window; further Down, three or four steps lead up to a door. Still further Down a dresser, with plates, glasses, etc. Up Left an alcove with the street door fully visible. On the inside of the street door, a wire letter box. In the Center, a round table. Against the Upstage wall, an old-fashioned piano. A comfortable arm-chair on each side of the fireplace. On the mantelpiece a clock, old china figures, etc. An air of comfort pervades the room.

The Monkey's Paw

SCENE I

At the rise of the curtain, Mrs. White, a pleasant-looking old woman, is seated in the armchair below the fire, attending to a kettle which is steaming on the fire, and keeping a laughing eye on Mr. White and Herbert. These two are seated at the table nearest the fire with a chessboard between them. Mr. White is evidently losing. His hair is ruffled; his spectacles are high up on his forehead. Herbert, a fine young fellow, is looking with satisfaction at the move he has just made. Mr. White makes several attempts to move, but thinks better of them. There is a shaded lamp on the table. The door is tightly shut. The curtains of the window are drawn; but every now and then the wind is heard whistling outside.

MR. WHITE. (*Moving at last, and triumphant.*) There, Herbert, my boy! Got you, I think.

HERBERT. Oh, you're a deep one, Dad, aren't you?

MRS. WHITE. Mean to say he's beaten you at last?

HERBERT. Certainly not! Why he's overlooked —

MR. WHITE. (*Very excited.*) I see it! Lemme have that back!

HERBERT. Not much. Rules of the game!

MR. WHITE. (*Disgusted.*) I don't hold with them scientific rules. You turn what ought to be an innocent relaxation —

MRS. WHITE. Don't talk so much, Father. You put him off.

HERBERT. (*Laughing.*) Not he!

MR. WHITE. (*Trying to distract his attention.*) Listen to the wind.

HERBERT. (*Drily.*) Ah! I'm listening. Check.

MR. WHITE. (*Still trying to distract him.*) I should hardly think Sergeant-Major Morris'd come tonight.

HERBERT. Mate. (*Rises.*)

MR. WHITE. (*With an outbreak of disgust and sweeping the chessmen off the board.*) That's the worst of living so far out. Your friends can't come for a quiet chat, and you addle your brains over a confounded —

HERBERT. Now, Father! Morris'll turn up all right.

MR. WHITE. (*Still in a temper.*) Lover's Lane, Fulham! Ho! Of all the beastly, slushy, out-of-the-way places to live in! Pathway's a swamp and the road's a torrent. What's the County Council thinking of, that's what I want to know? Because this is the only house in the road it doesn't matter if nobody can get near it, I s'pose.

MRS. WHITE.   Never mind, dear. Perhaps you'll win tomorrow.

MR. WHITE.   Perhaps I'll—perhaps I'll—! What d'you mean? (*Bursts out laughing.*) There! You always know what's going on inside of me, don't you, Mother?

MRS. WHITE.   Ought to, after thirty years, John. (*She goes to dresser, and busies herself wiping tumblers on tray there.*)

HERBERT.   (*Rises, goes to fireplace and lights pipe.*) And it's not such a bad place, Dad, after all. One of the few old-fashioned houses left near London. None o' your stucco villas. Homelike, I call it. And so do you, or you wouldn't have bought it.

MR. WHITE.   (*Growling.*) Nice job I made of that too! With two hundred pounds owing on it.

HERBERT.   Why, I shall work that off in no time, Dad. Matter of three years with the increase promised me.

MR. WHITE.   If you don't get married.

HERBERT.   Not me. Not that sort.

MRS. WHITE.   I wish you would, Herbert. A good, steady lad—

(*She brings the tray with a bottle of whisky, glasses, a lemon, spoons, cake, and a knife to the table.*)

HERBERT.   Lots of time, Mother. Sufficient for the day—as the saying goes. Just now my dynamos don't leave me any time for love-making. Jealous they are, I tell you!

MR. WHITE.   (*Chuckling.*) I lay awake at night often, and think: If Herbert took a nap, and let his what-d'you-call-ums—dynamos, run down, all Fulham would be in darkness. What a joke!

HERBERT.   Joke! And me fired! Pretty idea of a joke you've got, I don't think.

(*Knock at outer door.*)

MRS. WHITE.   Listen!

(*Knock repeated, louder.*)

MR. WHITE.   (*Going toward door.*) That's him. That's the Sergeant-Major. (*He unlocks door.*)

HERBERT.   (*Removes chessboard.*) Wonder what yarn he's got for us tonight.

MRS. WHITE.   Don't let the door slam, John!

(*Mr. White opens the door a little, struggling with it. Wind. Sergeant-Major Morris, a veteran with a distinct military appearance—left arm*) gone — is seen to enter. Mr. White helps him off with his coat, which he hangs up in the outer hall.)

MR. WHITE.   Slip in quick! It's as much as I can do to hold it against the wind.

SERGEANT.   Awful! Awful! (Busy taking off hs cloak.) And a mile up the road by the cemetery — it's worse. Enough to blow the hair off your head.

MR. WHITE.   Give me your stick.

SERGEANT.   If it wasn't I knew what a welcome I'd get —

MR. WHITE.   (Preceding him into the room.) Sergeant-Major Morris!

MRS. WHITE.   Tut! tut! So cold you must be! Come to the fire.

SERGEANT.   How are you, ma'am? (To Herbert.) How's yourself, Laddie? Not on duty yet, eh? Day week, eh?

HERBERT.   No, sir. Night week. But there's half an hour yet.

SERGEANT.   (Sitting in the armchair above the fire, which Mrs. White is motioning him toward.) Thank you kindly, ma'am. That's good! That's a sight better than the trenches at Chitral. That's better than sitting in a puddle with the rain pouring down in buckets, and the natives taking pot shots at you.

MRS. WHITE.   Didn't you have no umbrellas? (She stirs the fire.)

SERGEANT.   Umbrell — ? Ho! ho! That's good! Eh, White? That's good. Did you hear what she said? Umbrellas! And goloshes! and hot water bottles! Oh, yes! No offense, ma'am, but it's easy to see you was never a soldier.

HERBERT.   (Rather hurt.) Mother spoke out of kindness, sir.

SERGEANT.   And well I know it; and no offense intended. No, ma'am, hardship, hardship is the soldier's lot. Starvation, fever, and get yourself shot.

MRS. WHITE.   You don't look to've taken much harm — except — (Indicates his empty sleeve. She takes kettle to table.)

SERGEANT.   (Showing a medal hidden under his coat.) And that I got this for. No, ma'am. Tough. Thomas Morris is tough.

MR. WHITE.   (Holding a glass under the Sergeant's nose.) Put your nose into this.

SERGEANT.   Whisky? And hot? And sugar? And a slice of lemon? No. I said I'd never, but seeing the sort of night. Well! (Waving the glass at them.) Here's another thousand a year!

MR. WHITE.   (Also with a glass.) Same to you, and many of them.

SERGEANT.   (To Herbert, who has no glass.) What? Not you?

HERBERT.   (Laughing.) Oh! it isn't for want of being sociable. But my work don't go with it. Not if it was ever so little. I've got to keep a cool head, a steady eye, and a still hand. The fly wheel might gobble me up.

MRS. WHITE. Don't, Herbert.

HERBERT. (*Laughing.*) No fear, Mother.

SERGEANT. Ah! you electricians! Sort of magicians, you are. Light! says you, and light it is. And, power! says you, and the trams go whizzing. And, knowledge! says you, and words go humming to the ends of the world. It fair beats me, and I've seen a bit in my time, too.

HERBERT. (*Nudges his father.*) Your Indian magic? All a fake, governor. The fakir's fake.

SERGEANT. Fake, you call it? I tell you, I've *seen* it.

HERBERT. Oh, come, now! Such as what? Come, now!

SERGEANT. I've seen a fellow with no more clothes on than a baby, if you know what I mean, take an empty basket — empty, mind! as empty as — as this here glass —

MR. WHITE. Hand it over, Morris. (*Hands it to Herbert, who goes quickly above table and fills it.*)

SERGEANT. Which was not my intentions, but used for illustration.

HERBERT. (*While mixing.*) Oh, *I've* seen the basket trick! and I've read how it was done. Why, I could do it myself, with a bit of practice. Ladle out something stronger. (*Brings him the glass.*)

SERGEANT. Stronger? What do you say to an old fakir chucking a rope up in the air, in the *air*, mind you! — and swarming up it, as if it was hooked on, and vanishing clean out of sight? I've seen *that*.

Herbert goes to table, plunges a knife into a piece of cake and offers it to the Sergeant with exaggerated politeness.

SERGEANT. (*Eyeing it with disgust.*) Cake? What for?

HERBERT. That yarn takes it.

(*Mr. and Mrs. White delighted.*)

SERGEANT. Mean to say you doubt my word?

MRS. WHITE. No, no! He's only teasing you. You shouldn't, Herbert.

MR. WHITE. Herbert always was one for a bit of fun!

SERGEANT. But it's true. Why, if I chose, I could tell you things — But there! you don't get no more yarns out of me.

MR. WHITE. Nonsense, old friend. You're not going to get sticky about a bit of fun. What was that you started telling me the other day about a monkey's paw, or something? (*Nudges Herbert and winks at Mrs. White.*)

SERGEANT. (*Gravely.*) Nothing. Leastways, nothing worth hearing.

MRS. WHITE. (*With astonished curiosity.*) Monkey's *paw* —?

MR. WHITE. Ah — you was telling me —

SERGEANT. Nothing. Don't go on about it. (*Puts his empty glass to his lips, then stares at it.*) What? Empty again? There! When I begin thinking of the paw, it makes me that absent-minded.

MR. WHITE. (*Rises and fills glass.*) You said you always carried it on you.

SERGEANT. So I do, for fear of what might happen. (*Sunk in thought.*) Ay; — ay!

MR. WHITE. (*Handing him his glass refilled.*) There.

MRS. WHITE. What's it for?_

SERGEANT. You wouldn't believe me, if I was to tell you.

HERBERT. *I* will, every word.

SERGEANT. Magic, then! Don't you laugh!

HERBERT. I'm not. Got it on you now?

SERGEANT. Of course.

HERBERT. Let's see it.

SERGEANT. Oh, it's nothing to look at. (*Hunting in his pocket.*) Just an ordinary little paw, dried to a mummy. (*Produces it and holds it toward Mrs. White.*) Here.

MRS. WHITE. (*Who has leaned forward eagerly to see it, starts back with a little cry of disgust.*) Oh!

HERBERT. Give us a look. (*Morris passes the paw to Mr. White, from whom Herbert takes it.*) Why, it's all dried up!

SERGEANT. I said so.

(*Wind.*)

MRS. WHITE. (*With a slight shudder.*) Listen to the wind!

MR. WHITE. (*Taking the paw from Herbert.*) And what might there be special about it?

SERGEANT. (*Impressively.*) That there paw has had a spell put upon it!

MR. WHITE. No! (*In great alarm he thrusts the paw back into Morris's hand.*)

SERGEANT. (*Pensively, holding the paw in the palm of his hand.*) Ah! By an old fakir. He was a very holy man. He'd sat all doubled up in one spot for fifteen years; thinking of things. And he wanted to show that fate ruled people. That everything was cut and dried from the beginning, as you might say. That there wasn't no getting away from it. And that, if you tried to, you caught it hot. (*Pauses solemnly.*) So he put a spell on this bit of a paw. It might have been anything else, but he took the first thing that came handy. Ah! He put a spell on it, and made it so that three people (*looking at them with deep meaning*) could each have three wishes. (*All but Mrs. White laugh rather nervously.*)

MRS. WHITE.   Ssh! Don't!

SERGEANT.   (*More gravely.*) But, but mark you, though the wishes were granted, those three people would have cause to wish they *hadn't* been.

MR. WHITE.   But how *could* the wishes be granted?

SERGEANT.   He didn't say. It would all happen so natural, you might think it a coincidence if so disposed.

HERBERT.   Why haven't you tried it, sir?

SERGEANT.   (*Gravely, after a pause.*) I have.

HERBERT.   (*Eagerly.*) You've had your three wishes?

SERGEANT.   (*Gravely.*) Yes.

MRS. WHITE.   Were they granted?

SERGEANT.   (*Staring at the fire.*) They were.

(*A pause.*)

MR. WHITE.   Has anybody else wished?

SERGEANT.   Yes. The first owner had his three wishes. (*Lost in recollection.*) Yes, oh yes, he had his three wishes all right. I don't know what his first two were, (*very impressively*) but the third was for death. (*All shudder.*) That's how I got the paw.

(*A pause.*)

HERBERT.   (*Cheerfully.*) Well! Seems to me you've only got to wish for things that *can't* have any bad luck about them—.

SERGEANT.   (*Shaking his head.*) Ah!

MR. WHITE.   (*Tentatively.*) Morris, if you've had your three wishes, it's no good to you, now. What do you keep it for?

SERGEANT.   (*Still holding the paw; looking at it.*) Fancy, I suppose. I did have some idea of selling it, but I don't think I will. It's done enough mischief already. Besides, people won't buy. Some of them think it's a fairy tale. And some want to try it first, and pay after.

(*Nervous laugh from the others.*)

MRS. WHITE.   If you could have another three wishes, would you?

SERGEANT.   (*Slowly, weighing the paw in his hand and looking at it.*) I don't know—I don't know. (*Suddenly, with violence, flinging it in the fire.*) No! I'm damned if I would!

(*Movement from all.*)

MR. WHITE.   (*Rises and quickly snatches it out of the fire.*) What are you doing?

SERGEANT.   (*Rising and following him and trying to prevent him.*) Let it burn! Let the infernal thing burn!

MRS. WHITE.   (*Rises.*) Let it burn, Father!

MR. WHITE.   (*Wiping it on his coat sleeve.*) No. If you don't want it, give it to me.

SERGEANT.   (*Violently.*) I won't! I won't! My hands are clear of it. I threw it on the fire. If you keep it, don't blame me, whatever happens. Here! Pitch it back again.

MR. WHITE.   (*Stubbornly.*) I'm going to keep it. What do you say, Herbert?

HERBERT.   (*Laughing.*) I say, keep it if you want to. Stuff and nonsense, anyhow.

MR. WHITE.   (*Looking at the paw thoughtfully.*) Stuff and nonsense. Yes, I wonder — (*casually*) I wish — (*He was going to say some ordinary thing, like "I wish I were certain."*)

SERGEANT.   (*Misunderstanding him; violently.*) Stop! Mind what you're doing. That's not the way.

MR. WHITE.   What is the way?

MRS. WHITE.   (*Moving away.*) Oh, don't have anything to do with it, John.

SERGEANT.   That's what I say, ma'am. But if I wasn't to tell him, he might go wishing something he didn't mean to. You hold it in your right hand, and wish aloud. But I warn you! I warn you!

MRS. WHITE.   Sounds like the Arabian Nights. Don't you think you might wish me four pair of hands?

MR. WHITE.   (*Laughing.*) Right you are, Mother! I wish —

SERGEANT.   (*Pulling his arm down.*) Stop it! If you must wish, wish for something sensible. Look here! I can't stand this. Gets on my nerves. Where's my coat? (*Goes into alcove.*)

(*Mr. White crosses to fireplace and carefully puts the paw on the mantelpiece. He is absorbed in it.*)

HERBERT.   I'm coming your way, to the works, in a minute. Won't you wait? (*Goes up, helps Morris with his coat.*)

SERGEANT.   (*Putting on his coat.*) No. I'm all shook up. I want fresh air. I don't want to be here when you wish. And wish you will as soon's my back's turned. I know. I know. But I've warned you, mind.

MR. WHITE.   (*Helping him into his coat.*) All right, Morris. Don't you fret about us. (*Gives him money.*) Here.

SERGEANT. (*Refusing it.*) No, I won't —

MR. WHITE. (*Forcing it into his hand.*) Yes, you will. (*Opens door.*)

SERGEANT. (*Turning to the room.*) Well, good night all. (*To White.*) Put it in the fire.

ALL. Good night.

(*Exit Sergeant. Mr. White closes door, comes toward fireplace, absorbed in the paw.*)

HERBERT. If there's no more in this than there is in his other stories, we shan't make much out of it.

MRS. WHITE. Did you give him anything for it, Father?

MR. WHITE. A trifle. He didn't want it, but I made him take it.

MRS. WHITE. There, now! You shouldn't. Throwing your money about.

MR. WHITE. (*Looking at the paw which he has picked up again.*) I wonder —

HERBERT. What?

MR. WHITE. I wonder whether we hadn't better chuck it in the fire?

HERBERT. (*Laughing.*) Likely! Why, we're all going to be rich and famous and happy.

MRS. WHITE. Throw it on the fire, indeed, when you've given money for it! So like you, Father.

HERBERT. Wish to be an emperor, Father, to begin with. Then you can't be henpecked!

MRS. WHITE. (*Going for him in front of the table with a duster.*) You young —!

HERBERT. (*Running away from her.*) Steady with that duster, Mother!

MR. WHITE. Be quiet, there! (*Herbert catches Mrs. White in his arms and kisses her.*) I wonder — (*He has the paw in his hand.*) I don't know what to wish for, and that's a fact. (*He looks about him with a happy smile.*) I seem to've got it all, all I want.

HERBERT. (*With his hands on the old man's shoulders.*) Old Dad! If you'd only cleared the debt on the house, you'd be quite happy, wouldn't you? (*Laughing.*) Well, go ahead! Wish for the two hundred pounds; that'll just do it.

MR. WHITE. (*Half laughing.*) Shall I?

HERBERT. Go on! Here! I'll play slow music. (*Crosses to piano.*)

MRS. WHITE. Don't, John. Don't have nothing to do with it!

HERBERT. Now, Dad! (*Plays.*)

MR. WHITE. I will! (*Holds up the paw, as if half ashamed.*) I wish for two hundred pounds.

(*Crash on the piano. At the same instant Mr. White utters a cry and lets the paw drop.*)

MRS. WHITE. ⎫ What's the matter?
HERBERT. ⎭

MR. WHITE. (*Gazing with horror at the paw.*) It moved! As I wished, it twisted in my hand like a snake.

HERBERT. (*Picks up the paw.*) Nonsense, Dad. Why it's as stiff as a bone. (*Lays it on the mantelpiece.*)

MRS. WHITE. Must have been your fancy, Father.

HERBERT. (*Laughing.*) Well? (*Looking round the room.*) I don't see the money and I bet I never shall.

MR. WHITE. (*Relieved.*) Thank goodness, there's no harm done! But it gave me a shock.

HERBERT. Half past eleven. I must get along. I'm on at midnight. We've had quite a merry evening.

MRS. WHITE. I'm off to bed. Don't be late for breakfast, Herbert.

HERBERT. I shall walk home as usual. Does me good. I shall be with you about nine. Don't wait, though.

MRS. WHITE. You know your father never waits.

HERBERT. Good night, Mother. (*Kisses her. She lights candle on the dresser, goes up stairs and exits.*)

HERBERT. (*Coming to his father, who is sunk in thought.*) Good night, Dad. You'll find the cash tied up in the middle of the bed.

MR. WHITE. (*Staring, seizes Herbert's hand.*) It moved, Herbert.

HERBERT. Ah! And a monkey hanging by his tail from the bed post, watching you count the golden sovereigns.,

MR. WHITE. (*Accompanying him to the door.*) I wish you wouldn't joke, my boy.

HERBERT. All right, Dad. (*Opens door.*) 'Gad! What weather! Good night. (*Exit.*)

(*The old man shakes his head, closes the door, locks it, puts the chain up, slips the lower bolt, has some difficulty with the upper bolt.*)

MR. WHITE. This bolt's stiff again! I must get Herbert to look to it in the morning.

(*Comes into the room, puts out the lamp, crosses towards steps; but is irresistibly attracted towards fireplace. Sits down and stares into the fire. His expression changes; he sees something horrible.*)

MR. WHITE.   (*With an involuntary cry.*) Mother! Mother!

MRS. WHITE.   (*Appearing at the door at the top of the steps with candle.*) What's the matter? (*Comes down.*)

MR. WHITE.   (*Mastering himself. Rises.*) Nothing. I—haha!—I saw faces in the fire.

MRS. WHITE.   Come along.

(*She takes his arm and draws him towards the steps. He looks back frightened towards the fireplace as they reach the first step.*)

CURTAIN

SCENE II:

(*Bright sunshine. The table, which has been moved nearer the window, is laid for breakfast. Mrs. White busy about the table. Mr. White standing in the window. The inner door is open, showing the outer door.*)

MR. WHITE.   What a morning Herbert's got for walking home!

MRS. WHITE.   What's o'clock? (*Looks at clock on mantelpiece.*) Quarter to nine. I declare. He's off at eight. (*Crosses to fire.*)

MR. WHITE.   Takes him half an hour to change and wash. He's just by the cemetery now.

MRS. WHITE.   He'll be here in ten minutes.

MR. WHITE.   (*Coming to the table.*) What's for breakfast?

MRS. WHITE.   Sausages. (*At the mantelpiece.*) Why, if here isn't that dirty monkey's paw! (*Picks it up, looks at it with disgust, puts it back. Takes sausages in dish from before fire and places them on table.*) Silly thing! The idea of us listening to such nonsense!

MR. WHITE.   (*Goes up to window again.*) Ay—the Sergeant-Major and his yarns! I suppose all old soldiers are alike—

MRS. WHITE.   Come on, Father. Herbert hates us to wait.

(*They both sit and begin breakfast.*)

MRS. WHITE.   How could wishes be granted, nowadays?

MR. WHITE.   Ah! Been thinking about it all night, have you?

MRS. WHITE.   You kept me awake with your tossing and tumbling—

MR. WHITE.   Ay, I had a bad night.

MRS. WHITE.   It was the storm, I expect. How it blew!

MR. WHITE.   I didn't hear it. I was asleep and not asleep, if you know what I mean.

MRS. WHITE.   And all that rubbish about its making you unhappy if your wish *was* granted! How could two hundred pounds hurt you, eh, Father?

MR. WHITE.   Might drop on my head in a lump. Don't see any other way. And I'd try to bear that. Though, mind you, Morris said it would all happen so naturally that you might take it for a coincidence, if so disposed.

MRS. WHITE.   Well—it hasn't happened. That's all I know. And it isn't going to. (*A letter is seen to drop in the letter-box.*) And how you can sit there and talk about it— (*Sharp postman's knock; she jumps to her feet.*) What's that?

MR. WHITE.   Postman, o'course.

MRS. WHITE.   (*Seeing the letter from a distance; in an awed whisper.*) He's brought a letter, John!

MR. WHITE.   (*Laughing.*) What did you think he'd bring? Ton o'coals?

MRS. WHITE.   John—! John—! Suppose—?

MR. WHITE.   Suppose what?

MRS. WHITE.   Suppose it was two hundred pounds!

MR. WHITE.   (*Suppressing his excitement.*) Eh!— Here! Don't talk nonsense. Why don't you fetch it?

MRS. WHITE.   (*Crosses and takes letter out of the box.*) It's thick, John— (*feels it*)—and—and it's got something crisp inside it. (*Takes letter to White, Right Center*)

MR. WHITE.   Who—who's it for?

MRS. WHITE.   You.

MR. WHITE.   Hand it over, then. (*Feeling and examining it with ill-concealed excitement.*) The idea! What a superstitious old woman you are! Where are my specs?

MRS. WHITE.   Let me open it.

MR. WHITE.   Don't you touch it. Where are my specs?

MRS. WHITE.   Don't let sudden wealth sour your temper, John.

MR. WHITE.   *Will* you find my specs?

MRS. WHITE.   (*Taking them off mantelpiece.*) Here, John, here.

(*As he opens the letter.*)

Take care! Don't tear it!

MR. WHITE.   Tear what?

MRS. WHITE.   If it was banknotes, John!

MR. WHITE.   (*Taking a thick, formal document out of the envelope and a crisp-looking slip.*) You've gone dotty.—You've made me nervous. (*Reads.*)

"Sir,—Enclosed please find receipt for interest on the mortgage of £200 on your house, duly received."

(*They look at each other. Mr. White sits down to finish his breakfast silently. Mrs. White goes to the window.*)

MRS. WHITE.   That comes of listening to tipsy old soldiers.

MR. WHITE.   (*Pettish.*) What does?

MRS. WHITE.   You thought there was banknotes in it.

MR. WHITE.   (*Injured.*) I didn't! I said all along—

MRS. WHITE.   How Herbert will laugh, when I tell him!

MR. WHITE.   (*With gruff good-humor.*) You're not going to tell him. You're going to keep your mouth shut. That's what you're going to do. Why, I should never hear the last of it.

MRS. WHITE.   Serve you right. I shall tell him. You know you like his fun. See how he joked you last night when you said the paw moved.

(*She is looking through the window.*)

MR. WHITE.   So it did. It did move. That I'll swear to.

MRS. WHITE.   (*Abstractedly: she is watching something outside.*) You thought it did.

MR. WHITE.   I say it did. There was no thinking about it. You saw how it upset me, didn't you?

(*She doesn't answer.*)

Didn't you?—Why don't you listen? (*Turns round.*) What is it?

MRS. WHITE.   Nothing.

MR. WHITE.   (*Turns back to his breakfast.*) Do you see Herbert coming?

MRS. WHITE.   No.

MR. WHITE.   He's about due. What *is* it?

MRS. WHITE.   Nothing. Only a man. Looks like a gentleman. Leastways, he's in black, and he's got a top-hat on.

MR. WHITE.   What about him? (*He is not interested; goes on eating.*)

MRS. WHITE.   He stood at the garden-gate as if he wanted to come in. But he couldn't seem to make up his mind.

MR. WHITE.   Oh, go on! You're full o' fancies.

MRS. WHITE.   He's going—no; he's coming back.

MR. WHITE.   Don't let him see you peeping.

MRS. WHITE.   (*With increasing excitement.*) He's looking at the house. He's got his hand on the latch. No. He turns away again. (*Eagerly.*) John! He looks like a sort of a lawyer.

MR. WHITE.   What of it?

MRS. WHITE. Oh, you'll only laugh again. But suppose—suppose he's coming about the two hundred—

MR. WHITE. You're not to mention it again!—You're a foolish old woman.—Come and eat your breakfast. (*Eagerly.*) Where is he now?

MRS. WHITE. Gone down the road. He has turned back. He seems to've made up his mind. Here he comes!—Oh, John, and me all untidy!

(*Knock.*)

MR. WHITE. (*To Mrs. White who is hastily smoothing her hair, etc.*) What's it matter? He's made a mistake. Come to the wrong house. (*Crosses to fireplace.*)

(*Mrs. White opens the door. Mr. Sampson, dressed from head to foot in solemn black, with a top-hat, stands in the doorway.*)

SAMPSON. (*Outside.*) Is this Mr. White's?

MRS. WHITE. Come in, sir. Please step in.

(*She shows him into the room; he is awkward and nervous.*)

You must overlook our being so untidy; and the room all anyhow; and John in his garden-coat. (*To Mr. White, reproachfully.*) Oh, John.

SAMPSON. (*To Mr. White.*) Morning. My name is Sampson.

MRS. WHITE. (*Offering a chair.*) Won't you please be seated?

(*Sampson stands quite still.*)

SAMPSON. Ah—thank you—no, I think not—I think not. (*Pause.*)

MR. WHITE. (*Awkwardly, trying to help him.*) Fine weather for the time o' year.

SAMPSON. Ah—yes—yes— (*Pause; he makes a renewed effort.*) My name is Sampson—I've come—

MRS. WHITE. Perhaps you was wishful to see Herbert; he'll be home in a minute. (*Pointing.*) Here's his breakfast waiting—

SAMPSON. (*Interrupting her hastily.*) No, no! (*Pause.*) I've come from the electrical works—

MRS. WHITE. Why, you might have come *with* him.

(*Mr. White sees something is wrong, tenderly puts his hand on her arm.*)

SAMPSON. No—no—I've come—*alone.*

MRS. WHITE. (*With a little anxiety.*) Is anything the matter?

SAMPSON. I was asked to call—

MRS. WHITE. (*Abruptly.*) Herbert! Has anything happened? Is he hurt? Is he hurt?

MR. WHITE. (*Soothing her.*) There, there, Mother. Don't you jump to conclusions. Let the gentleman speak. You've not brought bad news, I'm sure, sir.

SAMPSON. I'm—sorry—

MRS. WHITE. Is he hurt?

(*Sampson bows.*)

MRS. WHITE. Badly?

SAMPSON. Very badly. (*Turns away.*)

MRS. WHITE. (*With a cry.*) John—! (*She instinctively moves towards White.*)

MR. WHITE. Is he in pain?

SAMPSON. He is not in pain.

MRS. WHITE. Oh, thank God! Thank God for that! Thank— (*She looks in a startled fashion at Mr. White—realizes what Sampson means, catches his arm and tries to turn him towards her.*) Do you mean—?

(*Sampson avoids her look; she gropes for her husband; he takes her two hands in his, and gently lets her sink into the armchair above the fireplace, then he stands on her right, between her and Sampson.*)

MR. WHITE. (*Hoarsely.*) Go on, sir.

SAMPSON. He was telling his mates a story. Something that had happened here last night. He was laughing, and wasn't noticing and—and— (*hushed*) the machinery caught him—

(*A little cry from Mrs. White, her face shows her horror and agony.*)

MR. WHITE. (*Vague, holding Mrs. White's hand.*) The machinery caught him—yes—and him the only child—it's hard, sir—very hard—

SAMPSON. (*Subdued.*) The Company wished me to convey their sincere sympathy with you in your great loss—

MR. WHITE. (*Staring blankly.*) Our—great—loss—!

SAMPSON. I was to say further— (*as if apologizing*) I am only their servant— I am only obeying orders—

MR. WHITE. Our—great—loss—

SAMPSON. (*Laying an envelope on the table and edging towards the door.*) I was to say, the Company disclaims all responsibility, but, in consideration of your son's services, they wish to present you with a certain sum as compensation. (*Gets to door.*)

MR. WHITE. Our—great—loss— (*Suddenly, with horror.*) How—how much?

SAMPSON. (*In the doorway.*) Two hundred pounds.

(*Exit.*)

(Mrs. White gives a cry. The old man takes no heed of her, smiles faintly, puts out his hands like a sightless man, and drops, a senseless heap, to the floor. Mrs. White stares at him blankly and her hands go out helplessly towards him.)

CURTAIN

SCENE III:

(Night. On the table a candle is flickering its last gasp. The room looks neglected. Mr. White is dozing fitfully in the armchair. Mrs. White is in the window peering through the blind.)

(Mr. White starts, wakes, looks around him.)

MR. WHITE.   *(Fretfully.)* Jenny—Jenny.

MRS. WHITE.   *(In the window.)* Yes.

MR. WHITE.   Where are you?

MRS. WHITE.   At the window.

MR. WHITE.   What are you doing?

MRS. WHITE.   Looking up the road.

MR. WHITE.   *(Falling back.)* What's the use, Jenny? What's the use?

MRS. WHITE.   That's where the cemetery is; that's where we've laid him.

MR. WHITE.   Ay—ay—a week today—what o'clock is it?

MRS. WHITE.   I don't know.

MR. WHITE.   We don't take much account of time now, Jenny, do we?

MRS. WHITE.   Why should we? He don't come home. He'll never come home again. There's nothing to think about—

MR. WHITE.   Or to talk about. *(Pause.)* Come away from the window; you'll get cold.

MRS. WHITE.   It's colder where *he* is.

MR. WHITE.   Ay—gone forever—

MRS. WHITE.   And taken all our hopes with him—

MR. WHITE.   And all our *wishes*—

MRS. WHITE.   Ay, and all our— *(With a sudden cry.)* John!

(She comes quickly to him; he rises.)

MR. WHITE.   Jenny! What's the matter?

MRS. WHITE.   *(With dreadful eagerness.)* The paw! The monkey's paw!

MR. WHITE.   *(Bewildered.)* Where? Where is it? What's wrong with it?

MRS. WHITE.   I want it! You haven't done away with it?

MR. WHITE.   I haven't seen it—since—why?

MRS. WHITE.   I want it! Find it! Find it!

MR. WHITE.   (*Groping on the mantelpiece.*) Here! Here it is! What do you want of it? (*He leaves it there.*)

MRS. WHITE.   Why didn't I think of it? Why didn't *you* think of it?

MR. WHITE.   Think of what?

MRS. WHITE.   The *other two* wishes!

MR. WHITE.   (*With horror.*) What?

MRS. WHITE.   We've only had one.

MR. WHITE.   (*Tragically.*) Wasn't that enough?

MRS. WHITE.   No! We'll have one more. (*White crosses to Right Center. Mrs. White takes the paw and follows him.*) Take it. Take it quickly. And wish—

MR. WHITE.   (*Avoiding the paw.*) Wish what?

MRS. WHITE.   Oh, John! John! Wish our boy alive again!

MR. WHITE.   Jenny! Are you mad?

MRS. WHITE.   Take it. Take it and wish. (*With an outburst of grief.*) Oh; my boy! My boy!

MR. WHITE.   Get to bed. Get to sleep. You don't know what you're saying.

MRS. WHITE.   We had the first wish granted—why not the second?

MR. WHITE.   (*Hushed.*) He's been dead ten days, and—Jenny! Jenny! I only knew him by his clothing—if you wasn't allowed to see him then—how could you bear to see him *now*?

MRS. WHITE.   I don't care. Bring him back.

MR. WHITE.   (*Shrinking from the paw.*) I daren't touch it!

MRS. WHITE.   (*Thrusting it in his hand.*) Here! Here! Here!

MR. WHITE.   (*Trembling.*) Jenny!

MRS. WHITE.   (*Fiercely.*) Wish. (*She goes on frantically whispering "Wish."*)

MR. WHITE.   (*Shuddering, but overcome by her insistence.*) I—I—wish—my son—alive again.

(*He drops it with a cry. The candle goes out. Utter darkness. He sinks into a chair. Mrs. White hurries to the window and draws the blind back. She stands in the moonlight. Pause.*)

MRS. WHITE.   (*Drearily.*) Nothing.

MR. WHITE.   Thank goodness!

MRS. WHITE.   Nothing at all. Along the whole length of the road not a living thing. (*Closes blind.*) And nothing, nothing, nothing left in our lives, John.

MR. WHITE.   Except each other, Jenny—and memories.

MRS. WHITE.   (*Coming back slowly to the fireplace.*) We're too old. We were only alive in him. We can't begin again. We can't feel anything now, John, but emptiness and darkness. (*She sinks into armchair.*)

MR. WHITE.   'Tisn't for long, Jenny. There's that to look forward to.

MRS. WHITE.   Every minute's long, now.

MR. WHITE.   (*Rising.*) I can't bear the darkness!

MRS. WHITE.   It's dreary—dreary.

MR. WHITE.   (*Crosses to dresser.*) Where's the candle? (*Finds it and brings it to table.*) And the matches? Where are the matches? We mustn't sit in the dark. 'Tisn't wholesome. (*Lights match; the other candlestick is close to him.*) There. (*Turning with the lighted match towards Mrs. White, who is rocking and moaning.*) Don't take on so, Mother.

MRS. WHITE.   I'm a mother no longer.

MR. WHITE.   (*Lights candle.*) There now; there now. Go on up to bed. Go on, now—I'm coming.

MRS. WHITE.   Whether I'm here or in bed, or wherever I am, I'm with my boy, I'm with —

(*A low single knock at the street door.*)

MRS. WHITE.   (*Starting.*) What's that!

MR. WHITE.   (*Mastering his horror.*) A rat. The house is full of 'em.

(*A louder single knock; she starts up. He catches her by the arm.*)

Stop! What are you going to do?

MRS. WHITE.   (*Wildly.*) It's my boy! It's Herbert! I forgot it was a mile away! What are you holding me for? I must open the door!

(*The knocking continues in single knocks at irregular intervals, constantly growing louder and more insistent.*)

MR. WHITE.   (*Still holding her.*) Jenny, for the love of —!

MRS. WHITE.   (*Struggling.*) Let me go!

MR. WHITE.   Don't open the door!

(*He drags her Up Right.*)

MRS. WHITE.   Let me go!

MR. WHITE.   Think what you might see!

MRS. WHITE.   (*Struggling fiercely.*) Do you think I fear the child I bore! Let me go! (*She wrenches herself loose and rushes to the door which she tears open.*) I'm coming, Herbert! I'm coming!

MR. WHITE.   (*Cowering in the extreme corner Up Left.*) Don't do it! Don't do it!

(*Mrs. White is at work on the outer door, where the knocking still continues. She slips the chain, slips the lower bolt, unlocks the door.*)

MR. WHITE.   (*Suddenly.*) The paw! Where's the monkey's paw?

(*He gets on his knees and feels along the floor for it.*)

MRS. WHITE.   (*Tugging at the top bolt.*) John! The top bolt's stuck. I can't move it. Come and help. Quick!

MR. WHITE.   (*Wildly groping.*) The paw! There's a wish left.

(*The knocking is now loud, and in groups of increasing length between the speeches.*)

MRS. WHITE.   Do you hear him? John! Your child's knocking!

MR. WHITE.   Where is it! Where did it fall?

MRS. WHITE.   (*Tugging desperately at the bolt.*) Help! Help! Will you keep your child from his home?

MR. WHITE.   Where did it fall? I can't find it—I can't find—

(*The knocking is now thunderous, and there are blows upon the door as of a body beating against it.*)

MRS. WHITE.   Herbert! Herbert! My boy! Wait! Your mother's opening to you! Ah! It's moving! It's moving!

MR. WHITE.   Heaven forbid! (*Finds the paw.*) Ah!

MRS. WHITE.   (*Slipping the bolt.*) Herbert!

MR. WHITE.   (*Has raised himself to his knees; he holds the paw high.*) I wish him dead. (*The knocking stops abruptly.*) I wish him dead and at peace!

MRS. WHITE.   (*Flinging the door open simultaneously.*) Herb—

(*A flood of moonlight. Emptiness. The old man sways in prayer on his knees. The old woman lies half swooning, wailing against the doorpost.*)

CURTAIN

Looking into the Plot

1. Arrange these incidents in the order in which they occur in the story.
   (a) Mr. White takes the monkey's paw and makes his first wish.
   (b) Mr. Sampson tells the Whites of Herbert's accidental death.
   (c) The Sergeant shows the monkey's paw to the Whites.
   (d) Herbert knocks at the door of his parents' home.
   (e) The Sergeant-Major knocks at the Whites' door.
   (f) Mr. White uses his last wish to return Herbert to his grave.

2. How many people could use the paw's magic power? How many wishes could each be granted?

3. What was the final wish of the first person ever to use the paw?

4. What does the Sergeant say when Mrs. White asks him whether he would take three more wishes if he had the chance?

5. How does the 200 pounds come to the Whites? Who brings it? Why?

Thinking It Through

1. Early in the play certain events occur which are strangely paralleled later on. What do the following incidents foreshadow?
   (a) Sergeant-Major Morris enters the Whites' house after repeated, loud knocking at the door.
   (b) The first owner of the paw wished for death on his third wish.

2. You will recall that *dramatic irony* is a tool the playwright uses to heighten the tension in the play by having a character say something that is much more important than she or he realizes at the time.

   Name the speaker of each of the following lines, and tell why the statement is ironic:
   (a) "I've got to keep a cool head, a steady eye, and a still hand. The fly wheel might gobble me up." (*Scene I*)
   (b) "I don't see the money and I bet I never shall." (*Scene I*)
   (c) "Takes him half an hour to change and wash. He's just by the cemetery now." (*Scene II*)

3. Herbert is not disturbed by the Sergeant's hints of doom. He says, "You've only got to wish for things that *can't* have any bad luck." The Sergeant shakes his head and says, "Ah!" What is the Sergeant thinking?

4. The Sergeant-Major says he received the paw from a holy man who "wanted to show that fate ruled people." Do you think what happened to

the Whites proved that the holy man was correct? What do you think was responsible for Herbert's death?

5. What is Mr. White's final wish? Why?

Building Vocabulary

The following sentences are based on the play. Decide which of the words following the sentences best fits each blank. Write your answers on a separate sheet of paper.

1. The Sergeant says of the paw, "Let the _____ thing burn."

2. The Sergeant, remembering how he first got the monkey's paw, speaks _____ of his experiences.

3. Mr. White sees something horrible in the fire and gives an _____ cry.

4. Mr. White tries to _____ Herbert's attention from the chess game.

5. An air of comfort _____ the room, with its old-fashioned armchairs and cheerful fireplace.

> pervades   pensively   infernal
> distract   involuntary   spell

Writing Projects

1. Pretend that you are Sergeant-Major Morris. Write a letter to an old army buddy telling him what happened to the White family. Use the list of events as you arranged them in "Looking into the Plot" (page 137). Be sure to include the Sergeant-Major's feelings and opinions in your **narrative**. (*For help with this assignment see Writing Manual, p. 202.*)

2. When W. W. Jacobs wrote the short story "The Monkey's Paw" (on which this play is based), he gave his own twist to an old tale of three wishes. In the classic version, a poor old couple is granted three wishes. The wife wastes the first wish on a new cooking pot. Her angry husband then wishes that the pot were stuck on her head, and, finally, the third wish must be used to free her.

Tell, in the form of a **short story** or **diary**, the tale of the first owner of the monkey's paw. (You will recall the Sergeant tells the Whites that this man asked for death as his final wish.) Give the man a name, and try to imagine what experiences might have led to such a desperate wish. (*For help with this assignment see Writing Manual, p. 202.*)

Dracula

Hamilton Deane and John L. Balderston
Adapted from Bram Stoker's novel, *Dracula*

WEREWOLVES, VAMPIRES, BATS, the "undead" that walk in the night—these are the elements of the folk tales that have grown up around the legend of Count Dracula. The model for Dracula was a real person, a fifteenth century Romanian nobleman, much feared and hated. Although he never drank the blood of the living, he earned the name Vlad the Impaler because one of his favorite cruelties was to kill his enemies by impaling them on a wooden pole.

Using the material of the legends, Bram Stoker, in 1897, published his novel *Dracula*, destined to become a classic and probably the most famous horror story of all time. In *Dracula*, Stoker created a vampire who could, at will, assume the shape of a werewolf, a bat, or his centuries-old earthly form as a man. But Dracula is also a living, compelling dramatic presence in the story, an aristocratic, elegant nobleman whose power is difficult to resist.

In 1927, Hamilton Deane's dramatization of the story was presented in London, and since then has appeared numerous times and in various adaptations. The version here is the result of a collaboration between Deane and John L. Balderston. As a play, the story has had many revivals on the American stage; as a movie, it made Bela Lugosi famous in the 1930s. More recently, Frank Langella won fame on stage and screen as the suave, intense, hypnotic count.

The extraordinary popularity of the novel and play has led to numerous spin-offs of television and movie vampires. None has achieved the sustained horror of the play you are about to read.

Vocabulary Preview

SANITARIUM (san-uh-TAIR-ee-um) an institution for the treatment of long-term diseases or mental illness

After six months of rest and treatment, she left the *sanitarium* completely cured.

MEDIEVAL (meed-ee-EE-vul) in the style of the Middle Ages (about 600 to 1450)

We visited a twelfth-century cathedral in the *medieval* Italian town.

TAPESTRY (TAP-ih-stree) a heavy, woven cloth with decorative designs and pictures, used as a wall hanging

A hand-woven *tapestry* on the wall of the palace showed a medieval hunting scene.

ASTUTE (uh-STOOT) having a shrewd mind

The townspeople selected their most *astute* citizen to represent them at the meeting.

INCISIVE (in-SY-siv) keen, sharp

Her *incisive* criticism of the movie made us see its weaknesses.

POSTERITY (po-STAIR-uh-tee) future generations

Although his work was not appreciated during his lifetime, he was sure that *posterity* would recognize him.

LOATHING (LOH-thing) strong dislike; disgust

He felt nothing but *loathing* when he remembered his captors and their ugly behavior.

LAIR (LAIR) the den or resting place of a wild beast

The lioness kept her cubs safe in the *lair*.

CUNNING (KUN-ing) craftiness; skill, especially at deceiving

He overcame his enemies with *cunning*, not physical strength.

DEFIANT (duh-FY-unt) openly disobedient

The *defiant* child was sent to her room.

ENTICE (en-TYS) tempt; lure

This saucer of milk will *entice* the kitten to come out of the tree.

Other Words You Will Need to Know

ANEMIA (uh-NEE-mee-uh) a blood disease which leaves its victims pale and
weak

WOLFSBANE (WOOLFS-bayn) a poisonous yellow plant, found in Asia

CONVULSED (kun-VULST) upset to the point of shaking

OPPRESSIVE (uh-PRES-iv) harsh; hard to bear

LANGUID (LANG-gwid) without energy

REPULSION (ruh-PUL-shun) feeling of disgust

OCCULT (oh-KULT) relating to mystical or magical acts or beliefs

TRANSMUTE (tranz-MYOOT) change the form of

DEMATERIALIZATION (dee-muh-tir-ee-uh-lyz-AY-shun) disintegration; breaking
apart

ABHORS (ab-HORZ) hates

STAKE (STAYK) a wooden stick with a sharp point at one end

PREPOSTEROUS (prih-POS-tur-us) senseless

MANIACAL (muh-NY-uh-kul) insane

AFFRONT (uh-FRUNT) insult

BENEFACTORS (BEN-uh-fak-turz) people who help

DISPENSATION (dis-pen-SAY-shun) special permission

HOST (HOHST) a wafer used in the Catholic church as a holy symbol

Characters

Miss Wells, maid
John Harker, betrothed to Lucy Seward
Dr. Seward, Director of a sanitarium
Abraham Van Helsing, doctor; friend of Dr. Seward
R. M. Renfield, patient at the sanitarium
Butterworth, attendant at sanitarium
Lucy Seward, Dr. Seward's daughter
Count Dracula

Setting

Act One
The library in Dr. Seward's Sanitarium, Purley, England

Act Two
    Lucy's bedroom; following day

Act Three
    SCENE 1
    The library, 32 hours later
    SCENE 2
    A vault, just after sunrise

Dracula   ACT ONE

The library on the ground floor of Dr. Seward's Sanitarium at Purley.
Room is medieval, the walls are stone with vaulted ceiling supported by
two stone pillars, but is comfortably furnished in modern style. Wooden
paneling around walls. Tapestries hang on the wall. Medieval fireplace in
wall Right. Fire burning. There is a couch Right Center, a large armchair
Right. At Left, a desk with armchair back of it, a small chair to Right of
desk. Double doors in the rear wall. Large double window across angle
of room, Left rear, leading out into garden. The curtains are drawn.
Door Downstage Left. Invisible sliding panel in bookcase rear wall Right.

Maid, an attractive young girl, enters, showing in John Harker. Harker is
a young man of about twenty-five, handsome in appearance; a typical
Englishman, but in manner direct, explosive, incisive and excitable.

HARKER.   (*Agitated.*) You're sure Miss Lucy is no worse?

MAID.   (*Soothingly.*) Just the same, sir.

(*Dr. Seward comes in, Downstage Left. He is a psychiatrist of about fifty-*
five, intelligent, but a typical specialist who lives in a world of textbooks
and patients, not a man of action or force of character. The Maid exits,
closing doors.)

SEWARD.   Oh! John.

HARKER.   (*As Seward extends hand.*) Doctor Seward. What is it? Why have
you sent for me?

SEWARD.   My dear John. I told you in my wire there was nothing new.

HARKER.   You said "no change, don't worry," but to "come at once."

SEWARD.   (*Approvingly.*) And you lost no time.

HARKER.   I jumped in the car and burned up the road from London. Oh,
Doctor, surely there must be something *more* we can do for Lucy. I'd
give my life gladly if it would save her.

SEWARD.   I'm sure you would, my boy. You love her with the warm blood of
youth, but don't forget I love my daughter, too. She's all I have. You
must see that nothing medical science can suggest has been left undone.

HARKER.   (*Bitterly.*) Medical science couldn't do much for Mina. Poor Mina.

SEWARD.   Yes, poor Mina. She died after these same incredible symptoms
that my Lucy has developed.

HARKER.   *My* Lucy too.

SEWARD. *Our* Lucy, then.

(*Wild, maniacial laugh is heard offstage left.*)

HARKER. Good God, what was that?

SEWARD. (*Sits at desk.*) Only Renfield. A patient of mine.

HARKER. But you never keep violent patients here in your sanitarium. Lucy mustn't be compelled to listen to raving madmen.

SEWARD. I quite agree, and I'm going to have him sent away. Until just lately he was always quiet. I'll be sorry to lose him.

HARKER. What!

SEWARD. An unusual case. Zoophagous.

HARKER. What's that?

SEWARD. A life-eating maniac.

HARKER. What?

SEWARD. Yes, he thinks that by absorbing lives he can prolong his own life.

HARKER. Good Lord!

SEWARD. Catches flies and eats them. And by way of change, he feeds flies to spiders. Fattens them up. Then he eats the spiders.

HARKER. Good God, how disgusting. (*Sits.*) But tell me about Lucy. Why did you send for me?

SEWARD. Yesterday I wired to Holland for my old friend Van Helsing. He'll be here soon. The car has gone down to the station for him now. I'm going to turn Lucy's case over to him.

HARKER. Another specialist on anemia?

SEWARD. No, my boy, whatever this may be, it's not anemia, and this man, who speaks a dozen languages as well as his own, knows more about mysterious diseases than anyone alive.

HARKER. Heaven knows it's mysterious enough, but surely the symptoms are clear.

SEWARD. So were poor Mina's. Perfectly clear. (*A dog howls at a distance. Other dogs take up the chorus far and near.*) There they are, at it again, every dog for a mile around.

HARKER. (*Crosses to window.*) They seem howls of terror.

SEWARD. We've heard that chorus every night since Mina fell ill.

HARKER. When I was traveling in Russia, and the dogs in the village barked like that, the natives always said wolves were prowling about.

SEWARD. I hardly think you'll find wolves prowling around Purley, twenty miles from London.

HARKER. Yet your old house might be in a wilderness. (*Looks out of win-*

dow.) Nothing in sight except that place Carfax that Count Dracula has taken.

SEWARD.   Your friend, the Count, came in again last evening.

HARKER.   He's no friend of mine.

SEWARD.   Don't say that. He knows that you and I gave our blood for Lucy as well as for Mina, and he's offered to undergo transfusion himself if we need another volunteer. (*Sits on couch.*)

HARKER.   By Jove, that's sporting of him. I see I've misjudged him.

SEWARD.   He seems genuinely interested in Lucy. If he were a young man I'd think . . .

HARKER.   What!

SEWARD.   But his whole attitude shows that it isn't that. We need sympathy in this house, John, and I'm grateful for it.

HARKER.   So am I. Anyone who offers to help Lucy can have anything I've got.

SEWARD.   Well, I think he does help Lucy. She always seems cheered up when he comes.

HARKER.   That's fine. May I go to Lucy now?

SEWARD.   (*Rises.*) We'll go together. (*Bell rings off.*) That must be Van Helsing. You go ahead and I'll come presently.

(*Harker exits. Maid shows in Abraham Van Helsing, who enters briskly. Man of medium height, in his early fifties, with clean-shaven, astute face, shaggy gray eyebrows and a mass of gray hair which is brushed backward showing a high forehead. Dark, piercing eyes set far apart; nervous, alert manner; an air of resolution, clearly a man of resourceful action. Incisive speech, always to the point; raps his words out sharply and quickly. Van Helsing carries small black bag.*)

MAID.   Professor Van Helsing.

SEWARD.   (*He and Van Helsing shake hands warmly as Maid goes out.*) My dear Van Helsing, I can never repay you for this.

VAN HELSING.   Were it only a patient of yours instead of your daughter, I would have come. You once rendered me a service.

SEWARD.   Don't speak of that. You'd have done it for me. (*Starts to ring.*) Let me give you something to eat. (*Stopped by Van Helsing's gesture.*)

VAN HELSING.   (*Places bag on table back of couch.*) I dined on the boat train. I do not waste time when there is work to do.

SEWARD.   Ah, Van Helsing, you cast the old spell on me. I lean on you before you have been two minutes in my house.

VAN HELSING.   You wrote of your daughter's symptoms. Tell me more of the other young lady, the one who died.

SEWARD.   (*Shows Van Helsing to chair. Seward sits at desk.*) Poor Mina Weston. She was a girl just Lucy's age. They were inseparable. She was on a visit here when she fell ill. As I wrote you, she just grew weaker; day by day she wasted away. But there were no anemic symptoms; her blood was normal when analyzed.

VAN HELSING.   You said you performed transfusion.

SEWARD.   Yes, Sir William Briggs ordered that. (*Baring forearm.*) You see this mark? Well, Lucy herself, and her fiancee, John Harker, gave their blood as well.

VAN HELSING.   So . . . Three transfusions . . . And the effect?

SEWARD.   She rallied after each. The color returned to her cheeks, but the next morning she would be pale and weak again. She complained of *bad dreams*. Ten days ago we found her in a stupor from which nothing could rouse her. She . . . died.

VAN HELSING.   And . . . the other symptoms?

SEWARD.   None, except those two little marks on the throat that I wrote you about.

VAN HELSING.   And which perhaps brought me here so quickly. What were they like?

SEWARD.   Just two little white dots with red centers. (*Van Helsing nods grimly.*) We decided she must have run a safety pin through the skin of her throat, trying in her delirium to fasten a scarf or shawl.

VAN HELSING.   Perhaps. And your daughter's symptoms are the same?

SEWARD.   Precisely. She too speaks of *bad dreams*. Van Helsing, you've lived in the tropics. May this not be something alien to our medical experience in England?

VAN HELSING.   (*Grimly.*) It may indeed, my friend.

(*Laugh is heard from behind curtain at window. Van Helsing rises, followed by Seward, who crosses to window and draws curtains. Renfield is standing there. Repulsive youth, face distorted, shifty eyes, tousled hair.*)

SEWARD.   (*Astounded, drawing Renfield into room.*) Renfield. How did you . . . ?

VAN HELSING.   Who is this man?

SEWARD.   (*Crosses to bell; rings.*) One of my patients. This is gross carelessness.

VAN HELSING.   Did you hear us talking?

RENFIELD.   Words . . . words . . . words . . .

SEWARD.   Come, come, Renfield, you know you mustn't wander about this way. How did you get out of your room?

RENFIELD.   (*Laughs.*) Wouldn't you like to know?

SEWARD.   How are the flies? (*To Van Helsing.*) Mr. Renfield makes a hobby of eating flies. I'm afraid you eat spiders, too, sometimes. Don't you, Renfield?

RENFIELD.   Will you walk into my parlor, said the spider to the fly. Excuse me, Doctor, you have not introduced me to your friend.

SEWARD.   (*Reprovingly.*) Come, come, Renfield.

VAN HELSING.   Humor him.

(*Enter Maid.*)

SEWARD.   Tell the Attendant to come here at once.

MAID.   Yes, sir. (*Exits.*)

SEWARD.   Oh, very well. Professor Van Helsing, Mr. Renfield, a patient of mine.

(*Van Helsing steps toward him. They shake hands. Van Helsing rubs Renfield's fingers with his thumb and Renfield jerks hand away.*)

RENFIELD.   Ah, who does not know of Van Helsing! Your work, sir, in investigating certain obscure diseases, not altogether unconnected with forces and powers that the ignorant herd do not believe exist, has won you a position that posterity will recognize.

(*Enter Attendant dressed in uniform. He starts at seeing Renfield, then looks at Seward sheepishly.*)

SEWARD.   (*As severely as his mild nature permits.*) Butterworth, you have let your patient leave his room again.

ATTENDANT.   No, really, sir, I locked the door on him, and I've got the key in my pocket now.

SEWARD.   But this is the second time. Only last night you let him escape and he tried to break into Count Dracula's house across the grounds.

ATTENDANT.   He didn't get out the door this time, sir, and it's a drop of thirty feet out of the windows. (*Crosses to Renfield.*) He's just an eel. Now you come with me. (*As they start toward door; holds Renfield by coat collar and right arm.*)

SEWARD.   Renfield, if this happens again you will get no more sugar to spread out for your flies.

RENFIELD.   (*Drawing himself up.*) What do I care for flies . . . now? (*Attendant gives Van Helsing a look.*) Flies. Flies are but poor things. (*As he speaks he follows with his eyes a fly. Attendant sees fly too; releases Renfield indulgently. With a sweep of his hand he catches fly, holds closed hand to ear as if listening to buzz of fly as he crosses a few steps, then carries it to his mouth. Then seeing them watching him, releases it quickly.*) A low form of life. Beneath my notice, I don't care a pin about flies.

ATTENDANT.   Oh, don't you? Any more of your tricks and I'll take your new spider away.

RENFIELD.   (*Babbles; on knees.*) Oh, no, no! Please, dear Mr. Butterworth, please leave me my spider. He's getting so nice and fat. When he's had another dozen flies he'll be just right, just right. (*Gives little laugh. Rubs hands together, then catches fly and makes gesture of eating.*)

VAN HELSING.   Come, Mr. Renfield, what makes you want to eat flies?

RENFIELD.   (*Rises.*) The wings of a fly, my dear sir, typify the aerial powers of the psychic faculties.

SEWARD.   (*To attendant, wearily.*) Butterworth, take him away.

VAN HELSING.   One moment, my friend. (*To Renfield.*) And the spiders?

RENFIELD.   (*Impressively.*) Professor Van Helsing, can you tell me why that one great spider lived for centuries in the tower of the old Spanish church —and grew and grew? He never ate, but he drank, and he *drank*. He would come down and drink the oil of all the church lamps.

SEWARD.   (*To attendant.*) Butterworth.

RENFIELD.   One moment, Doctor Seward . . . (*Van Helsing gets wolfsbane from bag on table.*) I want you to send me away, now, *tonight*, in a straitjacket. Chain me so I can't escape. This is a sanitarium, not a lunatic asylum. This is no place for me. My cries will disturb Miss Lucy, who is ill. They will give your daughter *bad dreams*, Doctor Seward, *bad dreams*.

SEWARD.   (*Soothingly.*) We'll see about all this in the morning. (*Nods to Attendant, who moves toward Renfield.*)

VAN HELSING.   Why are you so anxious to go?

RENFIELD.   (*Crosses to Van Helsing; hesitates, then with gesture of decision.*) I'll tell *you*. Not that fool Seward. He wouldn't understand. But you . . . (*A large bat dashes against window. Renfield turns to the window, holds out his hands and gibbers.*) No, no, no, I wasn't going to say anything . . .

(*Attendant crosses up; watches Renfield.*)

SEWARD.   What was that?

RENFIELD.   (*Looks out window, then turns.*) It was a bat, gentlemen. Only a bat! Do you know that in some islands of the Eastern seas there are bats which hang on trees all night? And when the heat is stifling and sailors sleep on the deck in those harbors, in the morning *they* are found dead men . . . white, even as Miss Mina was.

SEWARD.   What do you know of Miss Mina? (*Pause.*) Take him to his room!

VAN HELSING.   (*To Seward.*) Please! (*To Renfield.*) Why are you so anxious to be moved from here?

RENFIELD.   To save my soul.

VAN HELSING.   Yes?

RENFIELD.   Oh, you'll get nothing more out of me than that. And I'm not sure I hadn't rather stay. After all, what is my soul good for? Is not . . . (*Turns to window.*) . . . *what I am to receive worth* the loss of my soul?

SEWARD.   (*Lightly.*) What's got him thinking about souls? Have you the souls of those flies and spiders on your conscience?

RENFIELD.   (*Puts fingers in his ears, shuts eyes, distorts face.*) I forbid you to plague me about souls! I don't want their *souls*. All I want is their life. The blood is the life.

VAN HELSING.   So?

RENFIELD.   That's in the Bible. What use are souls to me? (*To Van Helsing.*) I couldn't eat them or dr . . . (*Breaks off suddenly.*)

VAN HELSING.   Or drink . . . (*Holding wolfsbane under his nose, Renfield's face becomes convulsed with rage and loathing. He leaps back.*)

RENFIELD.   You know too much to live, Van Helsing! (*He suddenly lunges at Van Helsing. Seward and Attendant'shout at the attack and as they drag Renfield to door he stops struggling and says clearly:*)

RENFIELD.   I'll go quietly. (*Seward lets go of him.*) I warned you to send me away, Doctor Seward. If you don't, you must answer for my soul before the judgment seat of God!

(*Renfield and Attendant exit. Wild laughter can be heard off. Van Helsing puts wolfsbane in bag as Seward closes door.*)

SEWARD.   My friend, you're not hurt?

VAN HELSING.   No.

SEWARD.   My deepest apologies. You'll think my place shockingly managed.

(*Van Helsing waves apology aside with impatient gesture.*)

What was your herb that excited him so?

VAN HELSING.   Wolfsbane. (*A little look out of window as he crosses.*)

SEWARD.   Wolfsbane? What's that? I thought I knew all the drugs.

VAN HELSING.   It grows only in the wilds of Central Russia.

SEWARD.   But why did you bring it with you?

VAN HELSING.   It is a form of preventive medicine.

SEWARD.   Well, we live and learn. I never heard of it.

VAN HELSING.   Seward, I want you to have that lunatic securely watched.

SEWARD.   Anything you say, Professor Van Helsing, but it's my Lucy I want you to look after first.

VAN HELSING.   I want to keep this man under observation.

SEWARD.   (*Annoyed and hurt.*) An interesting maniac, no doubt, but surely you'll see my daughter.

VAN HELSING.   I must see the records of his case.

SEWARD.   But Doctor . . .

VAN HELSING.   Do you think I have forgotten why I am here?

SEWARD.   (*As they start to go out left.*) Forgive me. Of course I'll show you the records, but I don't understand why you're so curious about Renfield, because in your vast experience . . .

(*They exit. The room is empty for a few seconds; then Lucy enters, supported by Harker. She is a beautiful girl of twenty, clad in filmy white dressing gown, her face unnaturally pale. She walks with difficulty. Round her throat is wound a scarf. She crosses to desk and leans on it as Harker closes door.*)

HARKER.   Why, I thought they were here, Lucy.

LUCY.   John, do you think this new man will be any better than the others?

HARKER.   (*Moving her to the couch.*) I'm sure he will. Anyway, Lucy, now that I'm back I'm going to stay with you till you get over this thing.

LUCY.   (*Delighted.*) Oh, John. But can you? Your work in town?

HARKER.   (*Seating her, then sitting next to her.*) You come first.

LUCY.   (*A change comes over her.*) I . . . don't think you'd better stay, John. (*A look about room.*) Sometimes . . . I feel that I want to be alone.

HARKER.   My dear. How can you say that you don't want me with you when you're so ill? You love me, don't you? (*Taking her hand.*)

LUCY.   (*Affectionately.*) Yes, John, with all my soul.

HARKER.   Just as soon as you're well enough I'm going to take you away. We'll be married next month. We won't wait till June. We'll stretch that honeymoon month to three months and the house will be ready in July.

LUCY.   (*Overjoyed.*) John, you think we could?

HARKER.   Of course, why not? My mother wanted us to wait, but she'll understand, and I want to get you *away*. (*Starts to kiss her. She shudders as
he does so.*) Why do you shrink when I kiss you? You're so cold, Lucy,
always so cold . . . now . . .

LUCY.   (*With tenderness but no hint of passion.*) Forgive me, dear. I am
yours, all yours. (*Clings to him. He embraces her. She sinks back.*) Oh,
John, I'm so tired . . . so tired.

(*Seward and Van Helsing return.*)

SEWARD.   Lucy dear, this is my old friend, Professor Van Helsing.

(*She sits up; extends her hand to him.*)

VAN HELSING.   My dear Miss Seward, (*He kisses Lucy's hand.*) you don't remember poor old Van Helsing. I knew you when you were a little girl. So
high, and now what charm, what beauty. A little pale, yes, but we will
bring the roses back to the cheeks.

LUCY.   You were so kind to come, Professor.

VAN HELSING.   And this, no doubt, is the fortunate young man you are to
marry?

SEWARD.   Yes, John Harker, Professor.

HARKER.   Look here, Professor. I'm not going to get in your way, but if Doctor Seward will have me I'm going to make him give me a bed here until
Lucy gets over this thing. (*Turns to Seward.*) It's absolute hell, being
away in London, and of course I can't do any work.

SEWARD.   You're most welcome to stay, my boy.

VAN HELSING.   Indeed, yes. I should have asked you to stay. I may need
you. (*Takes chair from desk to left of couch; turns to Lucy.*) Now lie
back, so. (*Examines her eyelids carefully and feels her pulse.*) And now
tell me when did this, this weakness first come upon you? (*Sits, after examining eyelids; looks at her gums, examines tips of fingernails, then
takes out watch as he feels her pulse.*)

LUCY.   Two nights after poor Mina was buried I had . . . a bad dream.

VAN HELSING.   (*Releases pulse, after looking at watch.*) A bad dream? Tell me
about it.

LUCY.   I remember hearing dogs barking before I went to sleep. The air
seemed oppressive. I left the reading lamp lit by my bed, but when the
dream came there seemed to come a mist in the room.

VAN HELSING.   Was the window open?

LUCY.   Yes, I always sleep with my window open.

VAN HELSING.   Oh, of course, you're English. (*Laughs.*) We Continentals are not so particular about fresh air. And then . . .

LUCY.   The mist seemed so thick I could just see the lamp by my bed, a tiny spark in the fog, and then . . . (*Hysterically.*) I saw two red eyes staring at me and a livid white face looking down on me out of the mist. It was horrible, horrible!

(*Harker makes move toward her. Van Helsing stops him by a gesture.*)

VAN HELSING.   There, there. (*Soothingly, taking her hands from her face.*) Go on, please.

LUCY.   (*Gives little start when Van Helsing touches her hands. Looks at Harker and starts; and at Seward and starts, then at Van Helsing and relaxes.*) The next morning my maid could scarcely wake me. I felt weak and languid. Some part of my life seemed to have gone from me.

VAN HELSING.   There have been other such dreams?

LUCY.   Nearly every night since then has come the mist . . . the red eyes and that awful face.

(*She puts hands to her face again. Van Helsing soothes her, "There, there, now."*)

SEWARD.   We've tried transfusion twice. Each time she recovered her strength.

LUCY.   But then would come another dream. And now I dread the night. I know it seems absurd, Professor, but please don't laugh at me.

VAN HELSING.   I'm not likely to laugh.

(*Gently, without answering, he unwinds scarf from her throat. She puts hand up to stop him and cries, "No, no." A look at Harker when her neck is bare. As Van Helsing does so he starts, then quickly opens small black bag on table and returns with magnifying glass; examines two small marks on throat. Lucy with eyes closed. Controlling himself with difficulty, Van Helsing puts magnifying glass back in bag, closes it, puts back chair by desk.*)

And how long have you had these little marks on your throat?

(*Seward and Harker start violently and come to couch. They look at each other in horror.*)

LUCY.   Since . . . that first morning.

HARKER.   Lucy, why didn't you tell us?

SEWARD.   Lucy, you've worn that scarf around your throat to hide them!

(*Lucy makes convulsive clutch at throat.*)

VAN HELSING. Do not press her. Do not excite her. (*To Lucy.*) Well?

LUCY. (*Constrained; to Seward and Harker.*) I was afraid they'd worry you, for I knew that . . . Mina had them.

VAN HELSING. (*With assumed cheerfulness.*) Quite right, Miss Lucy, quite right. They're nothing, and old Van Helsing will see that these dreams trouble you no more.

MAID. (*Appears at door.*) Count Dracula.

(*Dracula enters. He is a tall, mysterious man of about fifty. Polished and distinguished. Continental in appearance and manner. Lucy registers attraction to Dracula.*)

SEWARD. Ah, good evening, Count.

DRACULA. Gentlemen. (*He bows to men; then goes to the couch and bows in courtly fashion.*) Miss Seward, how are you? You are looking more yourself this evening.

(*Lucy registers thrill. Alternate moods of attraction and repulsion, unaccountable to herself, affect Lucy in Dracula's presence. But this should be suggested subtly.*)

LUCY. (*Quite natural.*) I feel better already, Count, now that father's old friend has come to help me.

(*Dracula turns to Van Helsing. Lucy looks up at Dracula, recoils, and turns to Harker.*)

SEWARD. Count Dracula, Professor Van Helsing.

(*The two men bow.*)

DRACULA. A most distinguished scientist, whose name we know even in the wilds of Transylvania. (*To Seward.*) But I interrupt a consultation.

SEWARD. Not at all, Count. It's good of you to come, and we appreciate your motives.

HARKER. Doctor Seward has just told me of your offer, and I can't thank you enough.

DRACULA. It is nothing. I should be grateful to be permitted to help Miss Lucy in any way.

LUCY. But you do, Count. I look forward to your visits. They seem to make me better.

VAN HELSING. And so I arrive to find a rival in the field.

DRACULA. (*Crosses to Lucy.*) You encourage me, Miss Seward, to make them more frequent, as I should like to.

LUCY. (*Looking at him fixedly.*) I am always glad to see you.

DRACULA. Ah, but you have been lonely here. And my efforts to amuse you with our old tales will no longer have the same success, now that you have Professor Van Helsing with you, and especially now that Mr. Harker is to remain here.

HARKER. How did you know I was going to stay, Count?

DRACULA. (*Little start.*) Can the gallant lover ask such a question? I inferred it, my friend.

HARKER. You're right. Nothing is going to shift me now until Lucy's as fit as a fiddle again.

DRACULA. Nothing?

LUCY. Please come as before, Count, won't you?

(*Dracula bows to her; kisses her hand. Van Helsing meanwhile has been talking to Maid.*)

VAN HELSING. You understand, you will not answer bells. She must not be alone for a single moment under any circumstances, you understand.

(*As Dracula crosses to below desk, Lucy leans toward him, extends her hand, then recovers herself. Van Helsing registers that he sees her look at Dracula.*)

MAID. Yes, sir.

VAN HELSING. (*To Lucy.*) Good. Your maid will take you to your room. Try to rest for a little, while I talk to your father.

(*Maid comes to couch to get Lucy. Pause, as Lucy looks at Dracula.*)

SEWARD. Wells, remember, don't leave her alone for a moment.

MAID. Oh, no, sir.

(*Lucy exchanges a long look with Dracula as Maid takes her out.*)

DRACULA. Professor Van Helsing, so you have come from the land of the tulip, to cure the nervous prostration of this charming girl. I wish you all the success.

VAN HELSING. Thank you, Count.

DRACULA. Do I appear officious, Doctor Seward? I am a lonely man. You are my only neighbors when I am here at Carfax, and your trouble has touched me greatly.

SEWARD. Count, I am more grateful for your sympathy than I can say.

VAN HELSING. You, like myself, are a stranger in England, Count?

DRACULA. Yes, but I love England and the great London, so different from my own Transylvania, where there are so few people and so little opportunity.

VAN HELSING.   Opportunity, Count?

DRACULA.   For my investigations, Professor.

SEWARD.   I hope you haven't regretted buying that old ruin across there?

DRACULA.   Oh, Carfax is not a ruin. The dust was somewhat deep, but we are used to dust in Transylvania.

HARKER.   You plan to remain in England, Count?

DRACULA.   I think so, my friend. The walls of my castle are broken, and the shadows are many, and I am the last of my race.

HARKER.   It's a lonely spot you've chosen, Carfax.

DRACULA.   It is, and when I hear the dogs howling far and near I think myself back in my Castle Dracula with its broken battlements.

HARKER.   Ah, the dogs howl there when there are wolves around, don't they?

DRACULA.   They do, my friend. And they howl here as well, although there are no wolves. But you wish to consult the anxious father and the great specialist. May I read a book in the study? I am so anxious to hear what the Professor says and to learn if I can be of any help.

SEWARD.   By all means, Count. (*Dracula bows; exits. Seward watches him leave. Dogs howl offstage.*) Very kind of Dracula, with his untimely friendliness, but now what about my daughter?

HARKER.   Yes, Professor, what do you think is the matter with Lucy?

VAN HELSING.   (*Crosses to window, looks out. Long pause before he speaks.*) Your patient, that interesting Renfield, does not like the smell of wolfsbane.

SEWARD.   Good Heavens. What has that got to do with Lucy?

VAN HELSING.   Perhaps nothing.

HARKER.   In God's name, Professor, is there anything unnatural or occult about this business?

SEWARD.   Occult? Van Helsing! Oh . . .

VAN HELSING.   Ah, Seward, let me remind you that the superstitions of today are the scientific facts of tomorrow. Science can now transmute the electron, the basis of all matter, into energy, and what is that but the dematerialization of matter? Yet dematerialization has been known and practiced in India for centuries. In Java I myself have seen things.

SEWARD.   My dear old friend, you can't have filled up your fine old brain with Eastern moonshine.

VAN HELSING.   Moonshine?

SEWARD.   But anyway, come now, what about my daughter?

VAN HELSING. Ah! Seward, if you won't listen to what will be harder to believe than any Eastern moonshine, if you won't forget your textbooks . . . keep an open mind, then, Seward, your daughter's life may pay for your pig-headedness.

HARKER. Go on, go on, Professor!

SEWARD. I am listening.

VAN HELSING. Then I must ask you to listen calmly to what I am going to say. Sit down. (*Van Helsing crosses to window; closes curtains. Seward and Harker exchange glances, then both look at Van Helsing as they sit.*) You have both heard the legends of Central Europe, about the Werewolf, the Vampires?

SEWARD. You mean ghosts, who suck the blood of the living?

VAN HELSING. If you wish to call them ghosts. I call them the undead.

HARKER. (*Quickly.*) For God's sake, man, are you suggesting that Mina, and now Lucy . . .

SEWARD. (*Interrupting.*) Of course, I have read these horrible folk tales of the Middle Ages, Van Helsing, but I know you better than to suppose . . .

VAN HELSING. (*Interrupting.*) That I believe them? I *do* believe them.

SEWARD. (*Incredulously.*) You mean to tell us that vampires actually exist and . . . and that Mina and Lucy have been attacked by one?

VAN HELSING. Your English doctors would all laugh at such a theory. Your police, your public would laugh. (*Impressively.*) *The strength of the vampire is that people will not believe in him.*

SEWARD. (*Shaking head.*) Is this the help you bring us?

VAN HELSING. (*Much moved.*) Do not despise it.

HARKER. (*To Seward.*) Doctor, this case has stumped all your specialists. (*To Van Helsing.*) Go on, Professor.

VAN HELSING. Vampires are rare. Nature abhors them, the forces of good combine to destroy them, but a few of these creatures have lived on for centuries.

HARKER. (*Excited.*) What *is* a vampire?

VAN HELSING. A vampire, my friend, is a man or a woman who is dead and yet not dead. A thing that lives after its death by drinking the blood of the living. It must have blood or it dies. Its power lasts only from sunset to sunrise. During the hours of the day it must rest in the earth in which it was buried. But, during the night, it has the power to prey upon the living. (*Incredulous move from Seward.*) My friend, you are thinking you will have to put me amongst your patients?

SEWARD. Van Helsing, I don't know what to think but I confess I simply can't follow you.

HARKER. What makes you think that Lucy has been attacked by such a creature?

VAN HELSING. (*From now on dominating them.*) Doctor Seward's written account of these ladies' symptoms at once aroused my suspicion. Anemia? The blood of three people was forced into the veins of Miss Mina. Yet she died from loss of blood. Where did it go? Had your specialist any answer? The vampire attacks the throat. He leaves two little wounds, white with red centers. (*Harker rises slowly.*) Seward, you wrote me of those two marks on Miss Mina's throat. An accident with a safety pin, you said. So I thought, I suspected, I did not know, but I came on the instant, and what do I find? These same wounds on Miss Lucy's throat. Another safety pin, Doctor Seward?

SEWARD. Do you mean to say that you've built up all this nightmare out of a safety pin? It's true I can't make out why she hid those marks from us.

VAN HELSING. I could tell you that.

SEWARD. (*Pause.*) What! I don't believe it. Of course Lucy's trouble can't be *that.*

HARKER. I do believe it. This theory accounts for all the facts that nobody has been able to explain. We'll take her away where this thing can't get at her.

VAN HELSING. She will not want to go.

SEWARD. What!

VAN HELSING. If you force her, the shock may be fatal.

HARKER. But why won't she go if we tell her·that her life depends on it?

VAN HELSING. Because the victim of the vampire becomes his creature, linked to him in life and after death.

SEWARD. (*Incredulous, shocked; rises.*) Professor, this is too much!

HARKER. Will Lucy become an unclean thing, a demon?

VAN HELSING. Yes, Harker. *Now* will you help me?

HARKER. Yes, anything. Tell me what to do.

VAN HELSING. It is dangerous work. Our lives are at stake, but so is Miss Lucy's life, so is her soul. We must stamp out this monster.

HARKER. How can we stamp it out now?

VAN HELSING. This undead thing lies helpless by day in the earth or tomb in which it was buried.

SEWARD. A corpse, in a coffin?

VAN HELSING.   A corpse, if you like, but a living corpse, sustained by the blood of the living. If we can find its earth home, a stake driven through the heart destroys the vampire. But this is our task. In such a case the police, all the powers of society, are as helpless as the doctors. What bars or chains can hold a creature who can turn into a wolf or a bat?

HARKER.   A wolf! Doctor Seward, those dogs howling! I told you they howl that way in Russia when wolves are about. And a bat, Renfield said there was a bat.

SEWARD.   Well. What of it?

VAN HELSING.   (*Reflectively.*) Your friend Renfield does not like the smell of wolfsbane.

SEWARD.   But what in the world has your wolfsbane to do with all this?

VAN HELSING.   A vampire cannot stand the smell of wolfsbane.

HARKER.   You suspect that lunatic?

VAN HELSING.   I suspect no one and everyone. Tell me, who is this Count Dracula?

SEWARD.   Dracula? We really know very little about him.

HARKER.   When I was in Transylvania I heard of Castle Dracula. A famous Voivode Dracula who fought the Turks lived there centuries ago.

VAN HELSING.   I will make inquiries by telegraph. No, but after all this Thing must be English. Or at least have died here. His lair must be near enough to this house for him to get back there before sunrise. (*To Seward.*) Oh, my friend, I have only the old beliefs with which to fight this monster that has the strength of twenty men, perhaps the accumulated wisdom and cunning of centuries.

HARKER.   This all seems a nightmare. But I'm with you, Professor.

VAN HELSING.   And you, Doctor Seward?

SEWARD.   It all seems preposterous to me. But everyone else has failed. The case is in your hands at present.

VAN HELSING.   (*Sternly.*) I need allies, not neutrals.

SEWARD.   Very well, then, do what you will.

VAN HELSING.   Good. Then bring your daughter here.

SEWARD.   What are you going to do?

VAN HELSING.   To set a trap. Miss Lucy is the bait.

HARKER.   We can't let you do that!

VAN HELSING.   There's no other way. I believe this Thing knows that I plan to protect Miss Lucy. This will put it on its guard and the first moment she is alone it will no doubt try to get at her, for a vampire must have blood or its life in death ceases.

HARKER.   No, I forbid this.

SEWARD.   She's my daughter, and I consent. We'll show the Professor he's mistaken.

HARKER.   You allow it only because you don't believe, and I do believe. Doctor, I've heard that lunatic laugh; life-eating, you said he was, and you subject Lucy to that risk.

VAN HELSING.   (*Interrupting harshly.*) I must be master here or I can do nothing! I must know in what form this Thing comes before I can plan how to stamp it out. Bring your daughter here.

(*Seward turns and sees Harker looking at him; stares at Harker. There is a short pause, then Harker reluctantly exits. Seward follows him. Van Helsing thinks a moment, then looks about, noting the positions of doors, furniture, etc. He then turns out lights. The room is dark except for the firelight. Van Helsing moves into firelight, looks at couch, then walks back to door and turns, looking at couch, satisfying himself that the light from the fire is sufficient to see anything that happens. Opens curtains. Suddenly, the double doors open sharply and Van Helsing starts violently; the Attendant enters.*)

ATTENDANT.   Beg pardon, sir. Is Doctor Seward here?

VAN HELSING.   What do you want with him?

ATTENDANT.   Old Flycatcher's escaped again, sir.

VAN HELSING.   Escaped, how?

ATTENDANT.   Out of the window. The door's still locked and I was in the corridor all the while. It's a drop of thirty feet to the stone flagging. That loonie's a flyin' squirrel he is.

VAN HELSING.   (*Commandingly.*) Say nothing to Doctor Seward at present. Nothing, do you hear? Now go.

(*Attendant exits. Van Helsing switches on lights again. Enter Lucy, supported by Harker and Seward.*)

LUCY.   Oh! Oh!

SEWARD.   Lucy, you have nothing to fear.

(*They take her to the couch.*)

VAN HELSING.   I want you to lie down here, my dear.

LUCY.   But, Doctor . . .

VAN HELSING.   You trust me, do you not? (*She smiles weakly at him; nods. They place her on the couch.*) I want you to lie here for just a little.

LUCY.   But I am so frightened.

VAN HELSING.   Make your mind passive. Try not to think. Sleep if you can.

LUCY.   I dare not sleep. It is when I sleep . . .

    (*Harker takes her hand.*)

VAN HELSING.   (*Arranging her on the couch, head on pillows, soothingly.*) I know, my dear. I know. I am going to cure you, with God's help.

LUCY.   Oh, but Father. . . .

SEWARD.   You must do as the Professor says. Come, Harker.

VAN HELSING.   Come, Harker.

    (*Van Helsing leads Seward to the door. Seward exits. Harker lingers and Van Helsing calls him. Van Helsing switches off lights as he and Harker go out. No movement. Lucy closes her eyes. Low howl is heard outside, howl of a wolf. It is followed by a distant barking of dogs. Firelight grows dimmer. Dracula's hand appears from back of couch, then his face. Lucy screams; swoons. Harker and Seward are heard offstage.*)

HARKER.   Lucy! Lucy!

SEWARD.   Professor, what is it?

    (*Van Helsing enters, followed by Seward and Harker. Van Helsing switches on lights. They are just in front of door as a bat flies in the room from window to center, then out of the window.*)

VAN HELSING.   You saw?

SEWARD.   What was that?

HARKER.   Lucy, Lucy, speak to me!

VAN HELSING.   Take her to her room, Harker, quickly.

    (*Harker carries Lucy to door as Dracula enters. He looks about, his glance taking in everyone.*)

DRACULA.   (*Mildly, sympathetically.*) The patient is better, I hope?

    (*Renfield gives a wild laugh offstage right. Van Helsing, Seward and Harker turn. Renfield gives a second wild laugh.*)

CURTAIN

ACT TWO

Lucy's bedroom. Window Right rear, closed but curtains open. Chairs, small table with toilet articles on it by window. Couch against wall up Left

Center. Mirror on wall. Small stand, with flowers in vase, near couch. Doors, Right, leading into bedroom, Left, leading into hall. Arch Left Center.

The next evening.

Dogs howling. As curtain rises, Maid enters from bedroom, glances up at window over her left shoulder, takes a few steps, looks back over right shoulder, then to couch and takes newspaper. Sits on couch; reads newspaper. As she turns a page, Attendant knocks on hall door.

MAID. (*Starts.*) Who is that?

ATTENDANT. (*Enters; smiles at her.*) Excuse me, Miss. Did you happen to have seen anything of the Guv'ner's pet looney? He's out again, he is.

MAID. (*Holding paper.*) And what would he be doing here? You'll not hold your job, you won't, if you can't keep that man safe and sound. Why, he gets out every night. (*She crosses toward bedroom door.*)

ATTENDANT. Don't go, miss.

MAID. Miss Lucy's asked for the evening paper.

(*Maid smiles as she goes off; indicates speedy return. Attendant looks out of window and then looks under couch. Maid returns. Her line comes just as Attendant bends over, causing him to jump back, frightened.*)

MAID. Well, have you found him?

ATTENDANT. No, I haven't. (*Confidentially.*) And I'll tell you, Miss, this job is gettin' on my nerves.

MAID. Your nerves? And what about *my* nerves? Isn't it enough to have dogs howling every night and foreign counts bobbing up out of the floor, and Miss Lucy taking on the way she does, with everybody having their veins drained of blood for her, and this Dutch Sherlock Holmes with the X-ray eyes about, without you letting that Renfield loose?

ATTENDANT. (*Grieved.*) I haven't let him loose. Just now I hears a noise like a wolf howling. I opens his door with me key, and what do I see but his legs goin' through the window as though he was goin' to climb down that smooth wall. He ain't human, he ain't.

MAID. Climb down the wall?

ATTENDANT. (*Gloomily.*) I don't expect no one to believe it, but I seen it, and what's more, I grabbed hold of his feet, I did.

MAID. (*Laughs unbelievingly.*) Climbing down, head first, like a bat?

ATTENDANT. Queer your mention of bats, for just as I got hold of him, a big bat flies in the window and hits me in the face.

MAID. (*Mysteriously.*) I know where that bat came from.

ATTENDANT. (*Startled.*) You do? Where?

MAID. Out of your belfry. (*Crosses to head of couch and arranges pillows, then to dresser.*)

ATTENDANT. No, miss, it's the truth I'm tellin' you. (*Look from her.*) Out that bat flies, and the looney is gone, but I heard 'im laugh. And what a laugh! I'll catch it from the Guv'ner for this.

MAID. (*At dressing table.*) If you tell the Governor any such tales he'll shut you up with the looney.

ATTENDANT. Gosh, miss, but you're a smart one. That's just what I've been thinkin', and I daren't tell him what I see or what I heard. But he's harmless, this guy.

MAID. (*Ironically.*) Wouldn't hurt a fly, would he?

ATTENDANT. Hurt a fly? Oh, no, not him. He only *eats* 'em. Why, he'd rather eat a few blue-bottles than a pound of the best steak, and what he does to spiders is a crime.

MAID. It seems to me somebody will be coming after *you* in a minute, you and your spiders.

ATTENDANT. I say, miss. This is a queer neighborhood. (*Looking out of window.*) What a drop that is to the ground. (*Turns to her.*) You don't have to be afraid of burglars, do you? No way of getting up here unless they fly. Don't you never feel a bit lonesome like, out there (*Points to window.*) on your nights off?

MAID. Just lately I have a bit. (*Looks toward window.*) I never noticed trees had such shadows before.

ATTENDANT. Well, if you feel you'd like an escort, miss.

MAID. I'll not walk with you in your uniform. People might be taking me for one of your loonies.

ATTENDANT. (*Puts arm around her.*) In mufti, then, tomorrow night.

MAID. I say, you haven't wasted much time, have you?

ATTENDANT. I've had my eye on you.

MAID. Better keep that eye on your looney, or you'll be looking for a new job. (*Attendant tries to kiss her. She pushes him off and slaps him.*) Here, you. Be off. Your Governor will be in any minute. (*Gestures to door.*) Go find your looney.

ATTENDANT. Oh, all right, but I've got somethin' here that'll tempt him back to his room.

MAID. Why, what's that?

(*He fumbles in pocket. She comes up to him.*)

ATTENDANT. (*Takes white mouse by tail out of pocket; holds it in her face.*) This here.

MAID. (*Screams; climbs on chair; holds skirt.*) Take it away! Take it away!

ATTENDANT. (*Mouse climbs up his arm to shoulder. To mouse.*) Come on, Cuthbert. We ain't too popular. (*Offended, walks off left with dignity, remarking from door:*) Some people have no sense of humor.

SEWARD. (*Enters hastily from bedroom.*) What was that?

MAID. (*Puts down her skirt.*) Pardon, sir. He frightened me with that . . . that animal.

SEWARD. (*Agitated.*) Animal, what animal?

MAID. A white mouse, sir.

SEWARD. (*Relieved.*) You mustn't scream, not in this house, *now*.

MAID. I'm sorry, sir, but that nasty little beast . . .

SEWARD. You alarmed Miss Lucy so. She's dreadfully upset as it is by something in the paper.

MAID. Oh, do you mean about that Hampstead Horror, sir? The lady in white who gives chocolates to little children.

SEWARD. (*Interrupts impatiently.*) Never mind that, but I will not have Miss Lucy disturbed.

(*Seward returns to bedroom. Dogs howl. Lights go out. Maid screams. Green spot comes up on Dracula who stands in center of room. Maid screams again as she sees him.*)

DRACULA. (*Soothingly.*) Forgive me. My footfall is not heavy, and your rugs are soft.

MAID. It's all right, sir, but how did you come in?

DRACULA. (*Smiling.*) The door of this room was ajar, so I did not knock. How is Miss Lucy and her nervous prostration?

MAID. I think she's better, sir.

DRACULA. Ah, good. But the strain of Miss Lucy's illness has made you also ill.

MAID. How did you know, sir? But it's only a pain in my head that runs down into the neck.

DRACULA. (*Winningly.*) I can remove this pain.

MAID. I don't understand, sir.

DRACULA. Such pains yield readily to suggestion.

MAID. (*Raises arm slightly to shield herself.*) Excuse me, sir, but if it's hypnotism you mean, I'd rather have the pain.

DRACULA. Ah, you think of hypnotism as an ugly waving of arms and many passes. That is not my method. (*As he speaks he gestures quietly with his left hand and she stares at him, fascinated. Placing his left thumb against her forehead, he stares straight into her eyes. She makes a feeble effort to remove his hand, then remains still. He now speaks coldly; turns her face front before speaking.*) What is given can be taken away. From now on you have no pain. And you have no will of your own. Do you hear me?

MAID. (*Murmurs.*) I hear you.

DRACULA. When you awake you will not remember what I say. Doctor Seward ordered you today to sleep with your mistress every night in the same bed because of her bad dreams. Is it not so?

MAID. (*Murmurs.*) Yes, Master.

DRACULA. Your mistress is threatened by horror and by death, but I will save her. A man whose will is at cross purposes with mine has come to this house. I will crush him. Receive your orders. You hear me?

MAID. Yes, Master.

DRACULA. Hear and obey. From now on you will carry out any suggestion that reaches you from my brain instantly without question. When I will you to do a thing it shall be done. My call will reach you soon.

(*Green spot dims out slowly. Dracula exits through window. Lights come on. Dogs howl outside. Maid looks up at window as Van Helsing enters left. She starts when door shuts.*)

VAN HELSING. (*His face is paler. He looks drawn and weak. He carries box tied with string.*) You've not left your mistress alone?

MAID. Doctor Seward is with her, sir. (*Sways a little.*)

VAN HELSING. (*Looking at her keenly.*) What's wrong with you, my girl?

MAID. Nothing, sir.

VAN HELSING. You've just had a severe shock.

MAID. It's nothing, sir. I . . . I suddenly felt queer. (*Looks toward window.*) That's all. I can't remember anything.

VAN HELSING. Mr. Harker has just arrived. Ask Doctor Seward to come here. Remain with Miss Lucy yourself.

MAID.   Yes, sir. She's dreadfully upset, sir.

VAN HELSING.   Upset over what?

MAID.   It's in the evening paper, sir. About the Hampstead Horror. (*Van Helsing motions Maid to silence.*) Yes, sir.

VAN HELSING.   (*Shaken.*) Oh, God, she has seen it!

(*Maid goes into bedroom. Harker enters left.*)

HARKER.   (*Worried.*) Everything just the same? (*Van Helsing nods. Harker closes door.*) When I leave this house even for a few hours I dread what I . . . I dread what I may find when I come back.

VAN HELSING.   And well you may, my friend. (*He places box on table under mirror.*)

HARKER.   God must have sent you here to help us. Without you there'd be no hope. And this morning, Professor, when you opened your veins to revive Lucy again . . .

VAN HELSING.   It was the least I could do, for my lack of foresight was responsible for this attack.

HARKER.   Don't say that.

VAN HELSING.   Her maid slept with her and yet we found the wolfsbane thrown off the bed to the floor.

HARKER.   She was so weak, so pale, the two little wounds opened fresh again.

VAN HELSING.   (*With gesture to box.*) I have prepared a stronger defense. But our main task is not defense, but attack. What have you found in London?

HARKER.   A lot, but heaven knows what it means or whether it's any use.

VAN HELSING.   I, too, have had news of which I can make nothing.

SEWARD.   (*Enters.*) Ah, John, back from town.

HARKER.   Yes. (*Sits.*)

VAN HELSING.   We must try to piece together what we have learned today. (*Producing telegram of several sheets.*) My colleague in Bucharest wires that the Dracula family has been extinct for five hundred years.

SEWARD.   Can the Count be an impostor?

VAN HELSING.   (*Referring to telegram.*) The castle he calls his own is a desolate ruin near the border. It was built, as you said, Harker, by the terrible Voivode Dracula, who was said to have had dealings with evil spirits. He was the last of his race. But for many generations the peasants have believed the Castle Dracula inhabited by a vampire.

HARKER.   Then it must be he.

VAN HELSING. (*Shakes head; puts telegram back in pocket.*) My friends, I am bewildered.

SEWARD. But surely this confirms your suspicions. I was incredulous till I saw that creature hovering over Lucy.

VAN HELSING. A vampire from Transylvania cannot be in England.

SEWARD. But why?

VAN HELSING. Because, as I have told you, the vampire must rest by day in the earth in which the corpse it inhabits was buried.

HARKER. (*Rises.*) In the earth.

VAN HELSING. The vampire must return to its burial place by sunrise.

HARKER. (*Excited.*) I found today that Dracula arrived at the Croydon airdrome in a three-engined German plane, on March sixth.

SEWARD. March the sixth? Three days before Mina first was taken ill.

HARKER. This plane had made a nonstop flight from Sekely in Transylvania. It left just after sunset. It arrived two hours before dawn. It carried only the Count and six packing cases.

VAN HELSING. Did you learn what was in those cases?

HARKER. He told the customs people he wanted to see whether Transylvania plants would grow in a foreign climate in their native soil.

VAN HELSING. Soil? What was in those boxes?

HARKER. Just plain dirt. He left in a truck, with the six coffinlike boxes, before sunrise.

VAN HELSING. Before sunrise! The King of Vampires, my friends. (*Crosses between Seward and Harker.*) This creature is the terrible Voivode Dracula himself! In his satanic pride and contempt, he even uses his own name. For who could suspect? For five hundred years he has been fettered to his castle because he must sleep by day in his graveyard. Five centuries pass. The airplane is invented. His chance has come, for now he can cross Europe in a single night. He prepared six coffins filled with the earth in which he must rest by day. He leaves his castle after sunset. By dawn he is in London and safe in one of his cases—a great risk, but he has triumphed. He has reached London with its teeming millions, with its "opportunity," as he said.

SEWARD. God protect my Lucy!

HARKER. (*To Van Helsing, new tone.*) I saw the estate agent from whom he bought Carfax here and got the address of four old houses he has leased in different parts of London.

VAN HELSING. One of his coffin retreats is in each of those houses.

SEWARD.   Two heavy boxes were delivered at Carfax the day after he took possession.

VAN HELSING.   He has scattered them, for safety. If we can find all six, we can destroy him.

SEWARD.   But how?

VAN HELSING.   His native earth will no longer receive his unclean form if each box is sanctified with holy water.

HARKER.   Then we must get at those boxes, tear them open one by one. If we find him, Professor, I demand that my hand shall drive the stake into this devil's heart and send his soul to hell!

(*Seward motions no noise because of Lucy.*)

VAN HELSING.   Your plan is too dangerous.

SEWARD.   But why? These attacks on Lucy continue. Are we to delay while my child is dying?

HARKER.   No, not for a moment.

VAN HELSING.   Patience, my friends. This creature is more than mortal. His cunning is the growth of the ages. What if we find five of his boxes and close them against him, and cannot find the sixth?

SEWARD.   Well?

VAN HELSING.   Then he will bury himself in his last refuge, where we can never find him and sleep until we are all dead.

HARKER.   Then Lucy will be safe.

VAN HELSING.   For her life, yes, but his unclean kiss has claimed her for his own. When she dies she will become as he is, a foul thing of the night. The vampire can wait. No, my friends, there is only one way to save her from him, to destroy him.

SEWARD.   You're right, as always.

VAN HELSING.   We have one great advantage. By day he is a coffined corpse. Of our search by day he can know nothing, if we leave no traces.

HARKER.   God, this delay!

VAN HELSING.   We must make the round of his houses and find all six boxes, without his knowledge, and *then* we act.

SEWARD.   But what about the caretakers or servants?

VAN HELSING.   All the houses will be empty. The vampire plays a lone hand.

(*Maniacal laugh heard behind curtains of window. Seward crosses quickly to window.*)

SEWARD.   Renfield!

(*He grabs Renfield by arm and throws him into room. Renfield laughs cunningly.*)

VAN HELSING.   He's been here all the time we've been talking.

SEWARD.   Did you hear what we were saying, man?

RENFIELD.   Yes, I heard . . . something . . . enough . . . (*With gestures to Seward and Harker.*) Be guided by what he says. (*Points to Van Helsing.*) It is your only hope. It is her only hope. (*Crosses to Van Helsing.*) It is *my* only hope. (*Falls on knees before Van Helsing.*) Save my soul! Save my soul! I am weak. You are strong. I am crazy. You are sane. You are good and he is evil.

VAN HELSING.   (*Impressively.*) I will save you, Renfield, but you must tell me what you know. Everything.

RENFIELD.   (*Rises.*) Know? What should I know? I don't know anything. (*Taps head.*) You say I'm mad and Doctor Seward will tell you about that. You musn't pay any attention to anything I say.

SEWARD.   We can't waste time with this fellow. I'll have him taken away. (*Crosses to bell.*)

RENFIELD.   (*To Seward.*) Fool, fool, and I thought you were wise! The whole world is mad just now, and if you want help you must come to a madman to get it. (*Little laugh, cunningly.*) But I'll not give it to you, I'm afraid. (*Turns to window.*) A wise madman will obey him who is strong and not the weak.

VAN HELSING.   (*Moves to him fiercely.*) Him? Whom do you mean?

RENFIELD.   Need we mention names among friends? Come, Professor, be reasonable. What have I got to gain by being on your side? The Doctor keeps me shut up all day, and if I'm good he gives me a little sugar to spread out for my flies, but on the other hand, if I serve *him.* . . . (*Points to window.*)

VAN HELSING.   (*Sharply, taking him by coat.*) The blood is the life, eh, Renfield? (*Dragging him again.*) What have you to do with Count Dracula?

RENFIELD.   (*Convulsed with terror.*) Dracula! (*Drawing himself up defiantly.*) I never even heard the name before!

VAN HELSING.   You are lying!

RENFIELD.   Madmen, Professor, lack the power to discriminate between truth and falsehood, (*Breaks away.*) so I take no offense at what most men would consider an affront. (*Crosses to Seward.*) Send me away! I asked you to before and you wouldn't. If you only knew what has happened since then. I dare not tell you more. I dare not! I should die in torment if I betrayed . . .

VAN HELSING.   Doctor Seward will send you away if you speak.

SEWARD.   Yes, Renfield. (*Renfield moans.*) I offer you your soul in exchange for what you know.

RENFIELD.   God will not damn a poor lunatic's soul. God knows the devil is too strong for us who have weak minds. But send me away. I want you to promise, Doctor Seward!

SEWARD.   If you will speak.

VAN HELSING.   Come, Renfield.

RENFIELD.   (*Pause. Looks at Seward, Van Helsing, Harker, and Seward again, then speaks as a sane man.*) Then I will tell you. Count Dracula is . . . (*Bat comes in window; flies out again. Renfield rushes to window with arms outstretched, screaming.*) Master! Master, I didn't say anything! I told them nothing. I'm loyal to you. I am your slave.

(*Seward and Harker rush to window.*)

SEWARD.   (*Looking out window.*) There's a big bat flying in a circle. It's gone.

HARKER.   What's that, just passing that small shrub? It looks like a big gray dog.

VAN HELSING.   Are you sure it was a dog?

HARKER.   Well, it might easily be a wolf. Oh, but that's nonsense. Our nerves are making us see things.

VAN HELSING.   Come, Renfield. What were you about to say?

RENFIELD.   Nothing, nothing.

(*Lucy comes in from bedroom with newspaper.*)

LUCY.   Professor, have you seen what's in this . . .

VAN HELSING.   Miss Lucy, give it to . . .

RENFIELD.   (*Crosses to her.*) Are you Miss Seward?

LUCY.   I am.

(*Seward moves closer to her; indicates Harker to ring bell.*)

RENFIELD.   Then, I beg you, leave this place at once!

(*She turns to him. Van Helsing motions silence to others.*)

LUCY.   But this is my home. Nothing would induce me to leave.

RENFIELD.   (*Sane.*) Oh, that's true. You wouldn't go if they tried to drag you away, would you? It's too late. What a fool I am. I shall be punished for this and it can't do any good. It's too late. (*In tone of pity.*) You are so young, so beautiful, so pure. Even I have decent feelings sometimes, and I must tell you, and if you don't go your soul will pay for it. You're in the power of . . . (*Bat flies in window and out. Renfield rushes to win-*

dow and screams. *Seward moves toward couch. Harker crosses to Lucy to protect her.*) The Master is at hand!

(*Renfield crosses back on knees. Attendant appears at door.*)

SEWARD. Butterworth!

(*Seward helps Renfield up, then Attendant grasps him and takes him to door.*)

RENFIELD. (*At door.*) Goodbye, Miss Seward. Since you will not heed my warning, I pray that I may never see your face again.

(*He exits with Attendant.*)

LUCY. What did he mean, Professor? What did he mean? Why did he say that?

(*She goes off into bedroom, in hysterics. Harker follows her.*)

SEWARD. That crazy thing in league with the devil; horrible, and Lucy already upset by something in the paper.

VAN HELSING. Go in and get that paper from her.

SEWARD. Whatever it is, she keeps on reading that article again and again.

VAN HELSING. Take it away from her, man, and come back to me. (*Places hand on forehead as if faint.*)

SEWARD. Don't overdo it, Van Helsing. God knows where we should be if you went under. After a transfusion operation, at your age you really ought to be in bed . . . the loss of so much blood is serious.

VAN HELSING. I never felt more fit in my life.

SEWARD. I only ask you not to overestimate your strength now, when we lean on you. (*As he exits.*) Feeling fit, are you? Just look at yourself in the glass.

(*Van Helsing, alone, registers as tired and exhausted, and walks slowly across room, looking at his drawn face in mirror. Dracula, with stealthy tread, in evening dress and cloak as before, enters from window and walks slowly to directly behind Van Helsing.*)

VAN HELSING. (*Looking at himself, touching face, shakes head.*) The devil.

DRACULA. Come. (*Van Helsing turns suddenly to him and looks back into the mirror.*) Not as bad as that. (*Suave, cold, ironical.*)

VAN HELSING. (*Long look in mirror, then turns to Dracula. Controlling himself with difficulty.*) I did not hear you, Count.

DRACULA. I am often told that I have a light footstep.

VAN HELSING. I was looking in the mirror. Its reflection covers the whole room, but I cannot see . . .

(*Pause. He turns to mirror. Dracula, face convulsed by fury, picks up small vase with flowers from stand, smashes mirror, pieces of mirror and vase tumbling to floor. Van Helsing steps back; looks at Dracula with loathing and terror.*)

DRACULA. (*Recovering composure.*) Forgive me, I dislike mirrors. They are the playthings of man's vanity. And how's the fair patient?

VAN HELSING. (*Meaningly.*) The diagnosis presents difficulties.

DRACULA. I feared it might, my friend.

VAN HELSING. Would you care to see what I have prescribed for my patient?

DRACULA. Anything that you prescribe for Miss Lucy has the greatest interest for me.

(*Van Helsing crosses to table to get box. Dracula crosses, meets Van Helsing coming back with box. Van Helsing deliberately turns away from him, goes to small table right of arch, turns front as he opens pocketknife and, in cutting string of parcel, cuts his finger. He gives slight exclamation of pain; holds up finger covered with blood. Dracula starts for Van Helsing with right hand raised, then keeping control with difficulty, turns away so as not to see blood. Van Helsing stares at him a moment, then walks up and sticks bleeding finger in front of him.*)

VAN HELSING. The prescription is a most unusual one.

(*Dracula, baring teeth, makes sudden snap at finger. Van Helsing turns away quickly; ties handkerchief around it. Dracula again regains poise with an effort.*)

DRACULA. The cut is not deep. I . . . looked.

VAN HELSING. (*Opening parcel.*) No, but it will serve. Here is my medicine for Miss Lucy. (*Dracula comes up to Van Helsing, who quickly holds handful of wolfsbane up to his face. Dracula leaps back, face distorted with rage and distress, shielding himself with cloak. Putting wolfsbane back in box.*) You do not care for the smell?

DRACULA. You are a wise man, Professor, for one who has not lived even a single lifetime.

VAN HELSING. You flatter me, Count.

DRACULA. But not wise enough to return to Holland at once, now that you have learned what you have learned.

VAN HELSING. (*Shortly.*) I preferred to remain. (*Meaningly.*) Even though a certain lunatic here attempted to kill me.

DRACULA. (*Smiling.*) Lunatics are difficult. They do not do what they are told. They even try to betray their benefactors. But when servants fail to obey orders, the Master must carry them out for himself.

VAN HELSING. (*Grimly.*) I anticipated as much.

DRACULA. (*Gazing at him intently.*) In the past five hundred years, Professor, those who have crossed my path have all died, and some not pleasantly. (*Continues to gaze at Van Helsing; lifts his arm slowly; says with terrible emphasis and force.*) Come . . . here. (*Van Helsing pales, staggers, then slowly takes three steps toward Dracula. Very slight pause as Van Helsing attempts to regain control of himself, then takes another step toward Dracula; pauses, places hand to brow, then completely regains control of himself and looks away.*) Ah, your will is strong. Then I must come to you. (*Advances to Van Helsing, who takes out of breast pocket small velvet bag. Dracula stops.*) More medicine, Professor?

VAN HELSING. More effective than wolfsbane, Count.

DRACULA. Indeed? (*Starts for Van Helsing's throat. Van Helsing holds bag out toward him. Dracula's face becomes convulsed with terror and he retreats left before Van Helsing, who follows him.*) Sacrilege.

VAN HELSING. (*Continuing to advance.*) I have a dispensation.

(*Van Helsing has cut him off from the door and unpityingly presses him toward window. Dracula, enraged and snarling, backs out of the window. As Dracula is just outside the window he spreads his cape like a bat and gives a long satirical laugh as he makes exit. Van Helsing almost collapses; puts bag back in pocket; crosses himself; mops perspiration from brow with handkerchief. A shot is heard. Van Helsing leaps up; rushes to window. Bat circles almost into his face. He staggers back. Seward hurries in, carrying newspaper.*)

SEWARD. Van Helsing, what was that? (*Dropping newspaper on table.*)

VAN HELSING. A revolver shot. It came as a relief. That at least is something human.

SEWARD. Who broke the mirror?

VAN HELSING. I.

(*Harker enters.*)

HARKER. Sorry if I startled you. I saw that infernal bat around this side of the house. I couldn't resist a shot.

SEWARD. Did you hit it?

HARKER. Why, I . . .

VAN HELSING. The bullet was never made, my friend, that could harm *that* bat. *My* weapons are stronger.

HARKER. What do you mean?

VAN HELSING. Dracula has been here.

SEWARD. Good God!

HARKER. How did he get in?

VAN HELSING. You ask how the Vampire King, during the hours of night, the hours that are his, comes and goes? As the wind, my friend, as he pleases. He came to kill me. But I carry a power stronger than his.

HARKER. What power?

VAN HELSING. I expected an attack. I secured a dispensation from the Cardinal. I have with me . . . (*Crosses himself.*) . . . the Host. (*Harker crosses himself.*) He came. I proved my case if it needed proof. The mirror does not reflect this *man that was*, who casts no shadow. See, I cut my finger, *it* leapt at the blood, but before the sacred wafer *it* fled.

SEWARD. Lucy must not know.

VAN HELSING. (*Gently, worried.*) Miss Lucy knows more than you think.

HARKER. How can she? If she knew, she'd tell me.

VAN HELSING. As these attacks continue she comes more and more under his power. There is a mystic link between them. (*Seward sighs.*) Oh, it is hard to bear, but you must face it. It may be that he can already learn what passes in her mind. And so Miss Lucy must not be told that we know about earth boxes, for he may learn whatever she knows.

(*Lucy enters.*)

SEWARD. But Professor, that would mean that Lucy is in with this creature. That's impossible.

(*Lucy crosses to table; takes newspaper.*)

VAN HELSING. No, no, Miss Lucy, you must not.

HARKER. Lucy, what's in this paper that's upset you?

LUCY. (*Hands newspaper to Harker.*) Read it, John.

(*Harker takes newspaper; reads. Van Helsing moves as if to stop him, then checks himself.*)

VAN HELSING. No, Harker, no.

LUCY. Read it!

(*Lucy sits on couch. They all listen.*)

HARKER. (*Reading.*) "The Hampstead Horror. Further attacks on small children, committed after dark by a mysterious and beautiful woman in Hampstead, are reported today. Narratives of three small girls, all under ten years of age, are alike in essential details. Each child speaks of a beautiful lady in white who gave her chocolates, enticed her to some secluded corner and there bit her slightly in the throat." (*He looks at Seward and Lucy.*)

LUCY.   Go on.

HARKER.   (*Reading.*) "The wounds are trivial. The children suffered no other harm and do not seem to have been frightened. Indeed, one small girl told her mother she hoped she might see the beautiful lady again."

(*He turns to Lucy. Seward takes paper from Harker.*)

VAN HELSING.   So soon . . . so soon.

(*Harker and Seward look at each other.*)

SEWARD.   You know what has been happening, Lucy? (*Lucy nods.*)

HARKER.   Professor Van Helsing knows, too, Lucy, and he knows how to protect you.

LUCY.   Is it not too late?

VAN HELSING.   No, Miss Lucy, it is not too late.

SEWARD.   These poor innocent children . . .

VAN HELSING.   (*To Seward.*) You think Count Dracula . . .

LUCY.   (*Shudders.*) Not that name.

VAN HELSING.   You think the Werewolf has done this too?

SEWARD.   Of course, in the form of a woman. Who else could it be?

VAN HELSING.   It is worse. Far worse.

HARKER.   Worse? What do you mean?

(*Lucy is motionless, her face frozen in horror.*)

VAN HELSING.   Miss Lucy knows.

LUCY.   The woman in white . . . is Mina.

HARKER.   Mina. But she's dead, Lucy.

LUCY.   She has joined . . . the Master.

SEWARD.   Oh, God, have pity on us all. (*Drops newspaper on chair.*)

VAN HELSING.   My dear Miss Lucy, I will not ask you how you know. After tonight no more little children will meet the woman in white. She will remain at rest in the tomb where you laid her. And her soul, released from this horror, will be with God.

LUCY.   How can you do this?

VAN HELSING. Do not ask me.

LUCY. (*Takes hold of Van Helsing's arm.*) Professor, if you can save Mina's soul after her death, can you save mine?

HARKER. Oh, Lucy! (*Sitting on couch, arm around her.*)

VAN HELSING. (*Takes her hand.*) I will save you. I swear it. In this room tonight.

LUCY. Then promise me one thing. Whatever you plan to do, whatever you know, do not tell me. (*Turns to Harker.*) Not even if I beg you to tell me, swear that you will not, now, while I am still yours, while I am myself, promise it.

HARKER. I promise it. (*Takes her in his arms; tries to kiss her.*)

LUCY. (*Breaks away from him, horrified.*) No, no, John! You musn't kiss me. Promise that you never will, not even if I beg you to.

HARKER. I promise.

VAN HELSING. My dear Miss Lucy, from tonight on one of us will be awake all night, here in this room, next to your bedroom, with your door open.

LUCY. (*Murmurs.*) You are so good.

VAN HELSING. Yes, and I will make the room safe for you. Your maid will be with you. (*Harker talks to Lucy on couch while Van Helsing takes handful of wolfsbane.*) Doctor, rub these over the window in the little room there. See, like this. (*He starts rubbing around edge of window.*) Rub it around the sashes and especially above the lock. (*Seward watches Van Helsing rubbing, then takes wolfsbane from Van Helsing quickly, and goes out through arch. Van Helsing turns, goes to table and takes out wreath of wolfsbane.*) See, I have made this wreath that you must wear around your neck tonight. While you wear this those . . . dreams . . . cannot come to you. (*Hangs wolfsbane around her neck. Takes out of pocket crucifix on cord, which he also hangs around her neck.*) Swear to me that you will not take these off.

LUCY. I promise.

VAN HELSING. Swear it on the cross.

LUCY. (*Kisses cross.*) I swear it!

(*Van Helsing crosses toward door.*)

HARKER. Professor, surely the Host is more powerful than this wolfsbane.

VAN HELSING. Of course.

HARKER. Then leave the Host with her, nothing can harm her then.

VAN HELSING. No, the Host cannot be used where there has been pollution. (*Screams off left.*) What is it?

(*Attendant enters left. Maid comes in from bedroom; Seward enters from arch.*)

ATTENDANT. It's Renfield, sir.

SEWARD. Why haven't you got him locked up?

ATTENDANT. Because he's barred himself in, sir. He got hold of one of the patients. He had her by the throat.

(*He exits. Lucy rises.*)

VAN HELSING. Ah, human blood now! (*Starting.*) Come, Seward! Come, Harker!

SEWARD. I should have had him sent away!

(*Maid crosses to Lucy. Van Helsing and Seward exit. Harker hesitates, then follows them off. Harker ad libs during exit, "It's all right, Lucy. I'll be right back," etc.*)

LUCY. John . . . (*To maid.*) Don't you leave me, too.

MAID. Of course I won't, Miss Lucy. It's nothing but a quarrel among the patients. Mr. Harker will be back soon. (*Maid places her on couch. Lucy swoons. Maid gets smelling salts.*) Here, Miss Lucy. (*Dracula's face appears back of tapestry on rear wall; disappears. Maid steps down right, gets message, then returns. Puts salts back on dresser; crosses to Lucy.*) These evil-smelling flowers have made you faint. (*Takes crucifix and wreath from around Lucy's neck, throws them on floor; crosses two steps down right. Another message comes to her. Puts hand to head, turns slowly, looks at window, steps toward couch.*) It is so close, Madam. A little air. (*Turns to window. Lucy moans again. Maid pulls back latch; opens window. As window opens, clouds of mist roll in. Steps down. Gets message. Switches out lights, then exits into bedroom. The stage is now dark. Dogs without, far and near, howl in terror. A gauze curtain comes down and a green light dims up covering the couch and center of the stage, revealing Dracula standing center with back to audience, hands outstretched to resemble a large bat. As he moves up a few steps, Lucy slowly rises from couch and falls into his arms. A long kiss and then, as she falls back on his right arm, he bares her throat and starts to bite her as:*)

CURTAIN

ACT THREE

SCENE I:

The library. Thirty-two hours later, shortly before sunrise.

A stake and hammer are on desk. Dogs howl. Curtains move as if some-one is entering window. Then chair back of desk, which is turned Upstage, moves around, facing front. After a moment, Ven Helsing enters with Seward. Van Helsing paces up and down; Seward sits at desk. The Center doors are flung open and the Attendant comes in.

VAN HELSING.   What is it?

ATTENDANT.   (*To Van Helsing.*) Anybody who wants my job, sir, can have it.

(*Seward rouses himself.*)

SEWARD.   What's the matter?

ATTENDANT.   I knows what I knows, and what I seen I saw, and I hops it by the first train, and don't ask for no wages instead of notice.

VAN HELSING.   Where's Renfield?

ATTENDANT.   If you asks me, I says he's probably payin' a little visit to hell.

SEWARD.   You've let him escape again?

ATTENDANT.   Look here, sir. Having, so to speak, resigned, I don't have to put up with any more from any of you. (*Look at Van Helsing and Seward.*) What a man can't help, he can't help, and that's that.

(*Seward sinks back on desk, head in hands.*)

VAN HELSING.   Can't you see, man, that Doctor Seward is not well? Will you desert him when he needs all the help he can get?

ATTENDANT.   Puttin' it that way, sir, I ain't the man to run under fire. But I'm sick and tired of being told off for what ain't my fault.

VAN HELSING.   We don't blame you. No bolts or bars could hold Renfield.

ATTENDANT.   (*Seward looks up at him.*) Now, sir, you're talkin' sense. I had him in a straitjacket this time. Nearly all yesterday I worked at clampin' bars across the window. Now I finds them bars pulled apart like they was made o' cheese and him gone.

VAN HELSING.   Then try to find him.

ATTENDANT.   Find him, sir? Find him? I can't chase him up and down the wall. I ain't no bloody mountain goat! (*Exits.*)

VAN HELSING.   The Thing mocks us. A few hours after he finds out what we know, and what we have done, he comes here, and drags that poor creature of his to himself.

SEWARD. (*In dull, hopeless tone.*) What can the vampire want with Renfield?

VAN HELSING. Renfield is serving an apprenticeship to join the Vampire King after his death. We must prevent that.

SEWARD. What does Renfield matter? If we are beaten, then there is no hope.

VAN HELSING. (*Crosses to him.*) We dare not despair, Seward.

SEWARD. To figure out in advance what anyone would do who got on his track!

VAN HELSING. I thought we had him when we broke into Carfax and found two earth boxes there and then found one box in each of his four other houses, and when I pried up the lid of the sixth box I was sure we would find him there, helpless.

SEWARD. (*Bitterly.*) Empty.

VAN HELSING. An empty packing case, left as a blind.

SEWARD. He only brought six in his plane, so there can be only the one left.

VAN HELSING. Only one, but hidden where we can never find it. And now we've put him on his guard.

SEWARD. Yes. (*Chair turns back. Curtains flap out. Seward looks at wrist watch.*) It's not half an hour till sunrise. (*Rises and crossing to fireplace.*) Poor John has been sitting up with Lucy for nine hours. She'll be safe at dawn and he can get some sleep, if anyone can sleep in this house.

VAN HELSING. Whoever else sleeps or does not sleep, Miss Lucy will sleep at dawn.

SEWARD. Another horror?

VAN HELSING. Oh, you've noticed how she keeps awake all night now and sleeps by day.

SEWARD. Is that part of . . . the change?

VAN HELSING. Of course. And sometimes the look that comes into her face.

SEWARD. (*Turns face away in horror.*) Don't, man. I can't bear it!

VAN HELSING. We must face the facts, for her sake.

SEWARD. How could it have got at her with the wolfsbane and the cross around her neck? (*Pause.*) Suggestion, conveyed from the Monster?

VAN HELSING. Yes. He must have impelled the maid to take away the wolfsbane and cross and open the window. I should have foreseen that.

SEWARD. Don't blame yourself. The devil is more cunning than we are. (*Sits on couch.*) Yet Lucy seems better. Until this last attack she's always been exhausted, but at sunset last night, when she woke up after sleeping all day . . .

VAN HELSING.   There was blood in her cheeks again.

SEWARD.   Yes, thank goodness.

VAN HELSING.   (*With terrible emphasis.*) My poor friend, *where does that blood come from?*

SEWARD.   What do you suggest now? What fresh horror . . .

(*Door left opens a crack. Long skinny hand protrudes into room. Seward sees it first and starts in alarm. Rises. Van Helsing turns quickly. Door opens slowly and Renfield slinks in.*)

RENFIELD.   Is not half past five in the morning a strange hour for men who aren't crazy to be up and about? (*Crosses to window.*)

VAN HELSING.   (*Aside to Seward.*) We may get help from this thing that's still half-human. (*To Renfield.*) Renfield.

RENFIELD.   (*Crosses, with growing hysteria.*) He's after me! He's going to kill me!

VAN HELSING.   Help us, Renfield, and we'll save you.

RENFIELD.   You, you poor puny man, you measure your brains against his? You don't know what you're dealing with! You, a thick-headed Dutch-man and a fool of a psychiatrist, and a young cub of a boy. Why, not all the soldiers and police in London could stop the Master from doing as he likes.

VAN HELSING.   But God can stop him!

RENFIELD.   God permits evil. Why does he permit evil if He is good? Tell me that?

SEWARD.   How did you escape through those iron bars?

RENFIELD.   (*Cunningly.*) Madmen have a great strength, Doctor.

VAN HELSING.   Come, Renfield, we know you didn't wrench those bars apart yourself.

RENFIELD.   (*Sane.*) No, I didn't. I wanted them there. I hoped they'd keep him out. He did it, then he called to me and I had to come. (*Back to insanity.*) The Master is angry. He promised me eternal life and live things, live things, big ones, not flies and spiders; and blood to drink, always blood. I must obey him but I don't want to be like him. I am mad, I know, and bad, too, for I've taken lives, but they were only little lives. I'm not like him. I wouldn't like a human life. (*Lucy laughs offstage and says, "Oh, John!" as she enters with Harker. Lucy has changed; there is blood in her cheeks, she is stronger and seems full of vitality. She and Harker*) *stop in surprise at seeing Renfield. To Lucy.*) And why did I seek to betray him? For you. (*She smiles.*) I said I'd serve the devil, but I didn't serve him honestly. I don't like women with no blood in them. (*Lucy laughs.*) And yet I warned you and made him angry, and now . . . (*Working into frenzy.*) . . . perhaps he will kill me. (*Lucy laughs.*) And I won't get any more live things to eat. There'll be no more blood.

(*Renfield starts for Lucy's throat. Harker grasps him by right arm, Van Helsing by left arm, then Seward steps in and takes Harker's place as Renfield struggles violently. Seward and Van Helsing bear him away, struggling and screaming.*)

HARKER.   Lucy, darling, you mustn't mind that poor, crazed creature.

LUCY.   (*With low laugh as before.*) I don't. He amuses me.

(*She crosses to the couch and sits.*)

HARKER.   Oh, Lucy, how can you? The poor devil! Thank goodness, it will soon be dawn now.

LUCY.   Dawn. The ebb tide of life. I hate the dawn. How can people like daylight? At night I am really alive. The night was made to enjoy life, and love. (*Harker turns to her; hesitates.*) Come to me, John, my own John.

(*He comes and sits next to her.*)

HARKER.   Lucy, I'm so happy that you are better and strong again.

LUCY.   I've never been so well, so full of vitality. I was only a poor, washed-out, pale creature. I don't know what made you love me, John. There was no reason why you should. But there is *now*.

HARKER.   I worship you.

LUCY.   Then tell me something, John. (*Harker turns slightly away.*) If you love me, you'll tell me. Now don't turn away from me again.

HARKER.   (*Wearily and sadly.*) You made me promise that I wouldn't tell you . . . anything.

LUCY.   Oh, but I release you from your promise. There, now. What were you and Father and the funny Professor doing all day?

HARKER.   I can't tell you. I promised.

LUCY.   (*Angrily.*) You say you love me, but you don't trust me.

HARKER.   I would trust you with my life, my soul.

LUCY.   Then prove it. What were you doing over there in Carfax? With the hammer and the horrible iron stake. (*He shakes his head. She registers anger. He puts his head in his hands, as though crying.*) You don't think I'm asking you because . . . I'm just trying to find out whether you really love me. (*Harker recoils from her, facing up.*) So you try to hide your schemes and your plots. Afraid I'd give them away, are you? You fools. Whatever *he* wants to know, he finds out for himself. He knows what you do. He knows what you think. He knows everything.

HARKER.   Lucy!

(*He puts his head in her lap and sobs. Lucy makes claw-like movement with both her hands, then as he sobs she changes attitude and gently strokes his head.*)

LUCY.   My dear, I'm sorry. Let me kiss away the tears.

(*She starts to kiss him. He quickly rises; backs away a few steps.*)

HARKER.   No, you mustn't kiss me! You made me promise not to let you kiss me.

LUCY.   You don't know why I said that, John darling. It was because I love you so much. I was afraid of what might happen. You've always thought me cold, but I've blood in my veins, hot blood, my John. And I knew if I were to kiss you . . . but I'm not afraid now. Come, will you make me say it?

HARKER.   Lucy, I don't understand you.

LUCY.   (*Moves toward him.*) I love you. I want you. (*Stretches out her arms to him.*) Come to me, my darling. I want you.

HARKER.   (*Goes to her, his resistance overcome, carried away by her passion.*) Lucy, Lucy!

(*He seizes her in his arms. Slowly she takes his head and bends it back. Slowly, triumphantly she bends her head down; her mouth hovers over his. Dogs howl outside. She bends his head further back quickly. Her mouth seeks his throat. Doors center open. Van Helsing rushes in, holding crucifix.*)

VAN HELSING.   Harker! Harker, save yourself! (*Harker rises, draws away. With outstretched arm, Van Helsing holds crucifix between them. Lucy's face becomes convulsed with loathing and rage. She snarls like an animal, retreats, fainting onto the couch. Van Helsing follows, holds crucifix to her; strokes her forehead with left hand.*) I warned you, my poor friend. (*He kneels beside Lucy; begins to chafe her temples. She revives slowly, looks about her, sees cross and seizes it and kisses it passionately. Van Helsing, fervently:*) Oh, thank goodness!

(*Pause. Harker crosses to couch.*)

LUCY. (*Broken-hearted.*) Don't come to me, John. I am unclean.

HARKER. (*Sits beside her.*) My darling, in my eyes you are purity itself.

VAN HELSING. You love her, and in love there is truth. She is pure, and the evil thing that has entered her shall be rooted out.

LUCY. (*In weak voice as in previous acts; to Van Helsing.*) You said you could save Mina's soul.

VAN HELSING. Mina's soul is in heaven.

LUCY. (*Murmurs.*) Tell me how.

(*Seward enters, comes up to group in alarm, but Van Helsing motions silence.*)

VAN HELSING. It is your right to know now. I entered her tomb. I pried open the coffin. I found her there, sleeping, but not dead, not truly dead. There was blood in her cheeks, a drop of blood like a red ruby on the corner of her mouth. With a stake and hammer I struck to the heart. One scream, a convulsion, and then . . . the look of peace that came to her face when, with God's help, I had made her truly dead.

LUCY. If I die, swear to me that you will do this to my body.

VAN HELSING. It shall be done.

HARKER. I swear it.

SEWARD. And I.

LUCY. My lover, my father, my dear friend, you have sworn to save my soul. And now I am done with life. I cannot live on to become . . . what you know.

VAN HELSING. No, no, Miss Lucy, by all you hold sacred, you must not even think of suicide. That would put you in his power forever.

LUCY. I cannot face this horror that I am becoming.

HARKER. (*Rises.*) We will find this *Thing* that has fouled your life, destroy him and send his soul to burning hell, and it shall be by *my* hand.

LUCY. You must destroy him if you can, but with pity in your hearts, not rage and vengeance. That poor soul who has done so much evil needs our prayers more than any other.

HARKER. No, you cannot ask me to forgive.

LUCY. Perhaps I, too, will need your prayers and your pity.

VAN HELSING. My dear Miss Lucy, now, while you are yourself, help me. (*Takes her hand.*)

LUCY. How can I help you? Don't tell me, no, you mustn't tell me anything.

VAN HELSING. Each time the white face, the red eyes came you were pale, exhausted afterwards. But that last time . . .

LUCY. (*Shudders.*) Last time he came he said I was his bride, he would seal me to him for the centuries to come.

VAN HELSING. And then?

LUCY. And then . . . (*Rises; crosses toward door.*) No, no, I can't tell you. I can't.

VAN HELSING. But you must.

SEWARD. You must, Lucy!

LUCY. He scratched open one of his veins. He pressed my mouth down to it. He called it a mystic sacrament. He made me . . . he made me drink . . . I can't, I can't . . . go on. . . . (*Lucy rushes off hysterically. Seward follows her.*)

VAN HELSING. I warned you, my poor friend. I broke in when I heard the dogs howling.

HARKER. The dogs. Then the Werewolf is about.

VAN HELSING. He is pursuing Renfield.

HARKER. We must do something!

VAN HELSING. And at once. I shall leave Renfield here, as I did Miss Lucy. If the *Thing* appears, we three will bar the two doors and the window.

HARKER. (*Crosses Up toward window. Laughs bitterly.*) Bar? Against *that*?

VAN HELSING. Even against *that*, for we shall each carry the sacred element.

HARKER. And then?

VAN HELSING. Then I do not know. It will be terrible, for we do not know his full powers. But this I know. . . . (*Looks at watch.*) It is eight minutes to sunrise. The power of all evil things ceases with the coming of day. His one last earth box is his only refuge. If we can keep him here till daybreak he must collapse. And the stake and the hammer are ready. (*Dogs howl. Harker crosses to window, goes out.*) He is here. Quickly! (*Van Helsing runs to window. Seizes Renfield.*)

RENFIELD. (*As he is dragged in by Van Helsing.*) No, no!

VAN HELSING. But you must, man, and this may save your soul and your life as well.

RENFIELD. No, no, no, not alone! Don't leave me alone! (*Van Helsing shoves him forward. Renfield falls. Van Helsing hurries out, closing door and putting lights out. Renfield slowly rises; looks about him. Renfield howls in terror; crouches in firelight as far away as possible from doors and window. Dracula appears, door center, in pale blue light, in evening clothes, dress and cloak as before. Red light from fireplace covers Dracula. As Dracula moves, Renfield's back is to audience.*) Master! I didn't do it! I said nothing. I am your slave, your dog! (*Dracula steps toward him.*)

Master, don't kill me! Punish me . . . torture me . . . I deserve it . . . but let me live! I can't face God with all those lives on my conscience, all that blood on my hands.

DRACULA.   (*With deadly calm.*) Did I not promise you that you should come to me at your death, and enjoy centuries of life and power over the bodies and souls of others?

RENFIELD.   Yes, Master, I want lives, I want blood, but I didn't want human life.

DRACULA.   You betrayed me. You sought to warn my destined bride against me.

RENFIELD.   Mercy, mercy, mercy, don't kill me!

(*Dracula raises right arm very slowly toward Renfield, who screams, this time in physical pain. Renfield, like a bird before a snake, drags himself to Dracula, who stands motionless. As Renfield reaches Dracula's feet, Dracula, with swift motion, stoops, seizes him by the throat, lifts him up, his grip stifling Renfield's screams. Doors Center are thrown open. Van Helsing switches on lights. Dracula drops Renfield, who falls into corner below couch and remains there during following scene. Dracula starts toward Van Helsing, who takes case containing Host out of inside breast pocket and holds it out toward Dracula in his clenched right fist. Dracula recoils; turns quickly to window. Harker appears through window and holds crucifix toward Dracula in clenched fist. Dracula recoils. Seward enters window, holding crucifix. The three men stand during the following scene with right arms pointing toward Dracula. He turns, walks to fireplace, turns and faces them.*)

DRACULA.   (*Ironically.*) My friends, I regret I was not present to receive your calls at my house.

VAN HELSING.   (*Looks at watch.*) Four minutes until sunrise.

DRACULA.   (*Looking at wrist watch.*) Your watch is correct, Professor.

VAN HELSING.   Your life in death has reached its end.

SEWARD.   By God's mercy.

DRACULA.   (*Harker steps toward Dracula. Dracula, turning to them, suavely.*) Its end? Not yet, Professor. I have still more than three minutes to add to my five hundred years.

HARKER.   And three minutes from now you'll be in hell, where a thousand years of agony will not bring you one second nearer the end of your punishment.

VAN HELSING.   Silence, Harker. Miss Lucy forbade this. She asked for prayer, and for pity. (*To Dracula.*) Make your peace with God, Man-That-Was. We are not your judges, we know not how this curse may have come upon you.

DRACULA. (*Furiously.*) You fools! You think with your wafers, your wolfsbane, you can destroy me, me, the king of my kind? You shall see. Five of my earth boxes you have polluted. Have you found the sixth?

VAN HELSING. You cannot reach your sixth refuge now. Take your true form as Werewolf if you will. Your fangs may rend us, but we have each sworn to keep you here (*looks at watch*) for two minutes and a half, when you must collapse and we can make an end.

DRACULA. *You* keep *me*. Fools, listen and let my words ring in your ears all your lives, and torture you on your deathbeds! I go, I go to sleep in my box for a hundred years. You have accomplished that much against me, Van Helsing. But in a century I shall wake, and call my bride to my side from her tomb, my Lucy, my Queen. (*Harker and Seward move closer.*) I have other brides of old times who await me in their vaults in Transylvania. But I shall set *her* above them all.

HARKER. Should you escape, we know how to save Lucy's soul, if not her life.

DRACULA. (*Moving left.*) Ah, the stake. Yes, but only if she dies by day. I shall see that she dies by night. She shall come to an earth box of mine at her death and await her Master. To do to her what you did to my Mina, Van Helsing, you must find her body, and that you will not.

HARKER. Then she shall die by day.

DRACULA. You will kill her? You lack the courage, you poor rat of flesh and blood!

SEWARD. Silence, John, he is doomed. This is his revenge. He hopes to trouble us . . . afterwards.

VAN HELSING. (*Looks at watch.*) Thirty seconds.

(*They move in.*)

DRACULA. (*Calmly, suavely again.*) I thank you for reminding me of the time.

VAN HELSING. Harker, open the curtains. (*Harker opens curtains. Red light of approaching dawn outside.*) That is the East. The sun will rise beyond the meadow there.

(*Dracula pulls cape over his head.*)

SEWARD. (*Glancing behind, leaves wolfsbane on desk as he looks up at window.*) The clouds are coloring.

HARKER. Daybreak.

(*Harker leaves crucifix on desk. Van Helsing checks watch. Seward and Harker step in.*)

DRACULA. (*Coolly. Turns Upstage, with back to them.*) A pleasant task you have set yourself, Mr. Harker.

VAN HELSING. Ten seconds. Be ready when he collapses.

(*Seward crosses to hold Dracula's cape on Left of Dracula. Harker holds cape on Right of Dracula.*)

HARKER. *The sun!* The stake, Professor, the stake! Hold him, Doctor.

SEWARD. I've got him.

(*Dracula, with loud burst of mocking laughter, vanishes on the word "sun," leaving the two men holding the empty cape. A flash goes off in front of fireplace. Harker backs Down Left, drops empty cape in front of desk. The three men look around them.*)

HARKER. Up the chimney, as a bat. You heard what he said?

SEWARD. God will not permit it. What's to be done now, Van Helsing?

VAN HELSING. (*Crosses, after looking at the prostrate Renfield; motions Harker and Seward to him. Whispers to them.*) We'll trick Renfield into showing us! (*Then, loudly:*) Dare we leave Renfield on earth to become the slave when he dies?

SEWARD. But he's human. We can't do murder?

HARKER. I'll do it if you won't, Doctor!

VAN HELSING. (*To Seward.*) Go to your office and get some painless drug.

RENFIELD. (*Sensing their drift without hearing their words, has been edging toward panel. Looks around room, then at panel.*) They're going to kill me, Master! Save me! I am coming to you.

(*Panel in bookcase opens, Renfield exits and panel closes.*)

VAN HELSING. He has shown us the way! Where does that passage go?

SEWARD. I never knew there was a passage.

(*Harker hastens to desk; gets stake and hammer. They rush to panel.*)

VAN HELSING. Only that devil has the combination. We'll break through somehow. Harker, quick, the hammer.

BLACKOUT

CURTAIN

SCENE II:

A vault.

Absolute darkness. Coffin Right Center and back of gauze drop. Flash of electric torch seen coming slowly downstairs Center. Coffin contains body of Dracula.

VAN HELSING'S VOICE.   Be careful, Seward.

SEWARD'S VOICE.   These stairs go down forever.

VAN HELSING'S VOICE.   May God protect us.

SEWARD'S VOICE.   Is Harker there?

VAN HELSING'S VOICE.   He's gone for a lantern.

SEWARD'S VOICE.   I've got to the bottom.

VAN HELSING'S VOICE.   Be careful. I'm right behind you.

(*Torch flashes around vault and they walk about slowly.*)

SEWARD'S VOICE.   What can this place be?

VAN HELSING'S VOICE.   It seems an old vault. (*Stifled scream from Seward. Torch out. The torch is seen to jerk back.*) What is it? Oh, where are you, man?

SEWARD'S VOICE.   Sorry. I'm all right. A big rat ran across my foot.

(*Light seen coming downstairs. Harker appears carrying lighted lantern which reaches floor; partially illuminates bare vault. He has stake and hammer in left hand.*)

HARKER.   Where are you? What is this place?

VAN HELSING.   We can't see.

(*Harker moves with lantern.*)

HARKER.   The place smells horribly of bats.

VAN HELSING.   It has an animal smell, like the lair of a wolf.

HARKER.   That's what it is.

SEWARD.   (*Still flashing torch about.*) There's absolutely nothing here.

HARKER.   (*At extreme Left with lantern.*) Here's another passage.

VAN HELSING.   (*Moving Left.*) I thought so. That must lead to Carfax. The sixth earth box is hidden somewhere here.

HARKER.   And the monster is in it.

SEWARD.   You can't be sure. (*As he speaks, light from his torch falls on Renfield, stretched on floor. Renfield screams as light falls on him; scurries off right into darkness.*) Renfield!

(*Harker and Van Helsing hurry across.*)

VAN HELSING. Where is he?

SEWARD. Over there somewhere. Even if Renfield knew about this place, that doesn't prove the vampire's here.

VAN HELSING. (*As Seward is speaking Van Helsing moves Right; seizes Renfield.*) It is the vampire's life or yours! (*Drags Renfield into light of lantern.*) Look at him, man, look at him. He knows.

RENFIELD. I know nothing. Let me go! Let me go, I say! (*Breaks away; goes Right.*)

VAN HELSING. He was stretched out here, but he wouldn't let me drag him back. Ah! Here it is. Quick, that stake.

(*Harker and Van Helsing, with stake, pry up stone slab and open coffin. The three men gaze in horror and triumph at coffin.*)

SEWARD. What a horrible undead thing he is lying there!

HARKER. Let me drive it in deep!

(*Van Helsing takes stake from Harker, lowers it into the coffin. Renfield stands at right end of coffin.*)

VAN HELSING. (*Almost in a whisper.*) That's over the heart, Doctor?

SEWARD. (*Back of coffin.*) Yes. (*Van Helsing hands hammer to Harker. Harker raises hammer high over head; pounds stake with full force. Low groan. Silence. Stake remains fixed in Dracula's body.*)

VAN HELSING. See his face now . . . the look of peace.

SEWARD. He is crumbling away.

RENFIELD. We're free!

LUCY. (*Comes down stairway and halts at bottom.*) Father, Father, John!

HARKER. Lucy!

VAN HELSING. (*Takes handful of dust; scatters it over the body.*) Dust to dust . . . ashes to ashes.

CURTAIN

(*The curtain rises again and the entire cast comes Downstage before a black drop for curtain speech.*)

VAN HELSING. (*To Audience.*) Just a moment, ladies and gentlemen! Just a word before you go. We hope the memories of Dracula and Renfield won't give you bad dreams, so just a word of reassurance. When you get home tonight and the lights have been turned out and you are afraid to look behind the curtains and you dread to see a face appear at the window . . . why, just pull yourself together and remember that after all *there are such things*.

THE CURTAIN FALLS

Looking into the Plot

Overview

1. Two women are chosen as victims by Dracula. Who are they? Which one dies? Who is saved while she is alive? Who is saved after death? How?
2. The playwrights use colors to convey impressions of innocence, evil, salvation and damnation.
   (a) What color does Lucy wear? Why is it appropriate for her?
   (b) When Lucy first sees Dracula, it is as if in a dream, through a mist or fog. She remembers only two red eyes looking at her. What association is one expected to make with the color red?
   (c) What color accompanies Dracula as he appears in Lucy's bedroom? What effect might it produce on the audience?
   (d) In Act III, Lucy's cheeks are no longer pale. She is described as having "blood in her cheeks." What are we being told?
   (e) At the end of the play we see Dracula covered by the red light of the fireplace. What flames might these symbolize?
3. All of these sounds are heard offstage during the play, each a result of Dracula's presence: (a) wild, maniacal laughter, (b) the howl of a wolf, (c) a pistol shot. Explain each sound.
4. How do Van Helsing's knowledge, judgment and strong will make him more effective than any other character fighting Dracula? When is Van Helsing's knowledge especially important? When is his judgment? His strong will?

Act I

1. Before Count Dracula even appears onstage, the playwrights prepare the audience for the presence of a vampire. How do these events serve to alert the viewer?
   (a) Seward tells Harker that Renfield has always been a quiet patient. Recently he has become wild and uncontrollable.

(b) Ever since Mina became ill, the dogs in the village have been howling as if in terror, as though wolves were present.

(c) After each blood transfusion, Mina grew stronger, but in the morning she was pale again and showed two little marks' on the throat.

Can you think of any other clues the writers provide?

2. Lucy appears with a scarf around her throat. What is she hiding? Who else had a similar injury?

3. Renfeld is an inmate of the sanitarium because of a strange illness. What is it? Why does it make him particularly susceptible to Dracula's power?

4. Several times a bat appears, trying to fly into the window. What does its purpose seem to be?

Act II

1. Dracula offers to hypnotize the maid to rid her of the pain in her head. What is his real purpose?

2. Van Helsing says that a vampire from Transylvania cannot be in England. Why not? How does travel by plane make Dracula's presence possible?

3. Van Helsing confirms his suspicions that Dracula is a vampire with three tests. One is accomplished with a mirror; the second with a cut in Van Helsing's finger; the third with a handful of wolfsbane. Explain the significance of each test. How do Dracula's reactions prove that Van Helsing's suspicions are right?

4. Lucy is drawn to a newspaper story which she reads with dread. What is it about? Who is the mysterious and beautiful woman in the news report?

5. Lucy asks Harker to promise that he will not tell her anything he plans to do in his struggle against the vampire and that he will not allow her to kiss him. Why not?

Act III

1. A change has taken place in Lucy. How do her appearance and behavior show that she is now more in Dracula's power? What shows that there is still hope for her?

2. Van Helsing, Harker and Seward corner Dracula and try to prevent his escape from the library of the sanitarium. What power do they have over him?

3. Final destruction of the vampire takes place when the three men track him to his lair. Where do they find him? How do they dispose of him?

Thinking It Through

"Dracula" is more than a melodrama of horror and suspense. The writers show the forces of good battling the forces of evil and ultimately overcoming them. Throughout the play we see the human yearning for salvation from the power of polluted spirits.

1. How does Renfield, although half-crazed and under Dracula's control, rescue Lucy?

2. Lucy, already in Dracula's power, struggles to save herself and Harker from eternal damnation. How?

3. The forces of evil, represented by Dracula, take the life's blood of their victims. How do the forces of good, represented by Van Helsing, Dr. Seward and Harker, try to give life back to their victims? What life-giving activities have been performed before the play opens and continue throughout?

4. The triumph of goodness is complete when Lucy asks the men to destroy Dracula "with pity in your hearts, not rage and vengeance." What should their feeling be? In what spirit must they approach their task? Why?

Building Vocabulary

The following sentences are based on the play. Decide which of the words following the sentences best fits each blank. Write your answers on a separate sheet of paper.

1. The action of the play takes place in Dr. Seward's _____ , a place generally more restful than it is during the events of this drama.

2. The building is very old, dating back to _____ times, its wooden, paneled walls decorated with hanging _____ .

3. Dr. Van Helsing has an alert manner and sharp, _____ speech, always to the point.

4. Professor Van Helsing turns to the power of religion rather than to the forces of the _____ to subdue Dracula.

5. Dracula conceals his _____ with great _____ .

6. Dracula stares at the cross with _____ .

7. Van Helsing's investigations win him a position that _____
will recognize.

8. The promise of insects to eat is enough to _____ Renfield to
work for Dracula.

occult	cunning	loathing	posterity
lair	medieval	sanitarium	tapestries
wolfsbane	incisive	entice	

Writing Projects

1. Many movies and TV programs are designed to create terror. Some do
this by relying on the supernatural, others use so-called "monsters" (like
Godzilla), and still others show creatures from a more advanced space
civilization taking over our own. All play on our helplessness to fight the
specific evil.

Write a **report** on such a film that you may have recently seen. Start by
describing the subject in a general way. Then explain briefly what happens
in the story. Third, name specific things and incidents that add to the terror. And, finally, discuss how effective the film was (tell how it made you
feel). (*For help with this assignment see Writing Manual, p. 202.*)

2. Although "Dracula" has some disturbing scenes, on the whole it is an absorbing, exciting drama that shows the forces of good ultimately winning
out over those of evil.

Write a **letter** to your school librarian recommending that he or she buy
copies of the play for student reading. Offer two reasons and cite specific
incidents in the play that support your argument. (*For help with this
assignment see Writing Manual, p. 210.*)

Questions for Final Review

1. Props in a play are very important. They may further the plot, help clarify the theme or give greater insight into character. What is the significance of these props:
   (a) a bird cage   in "Trifles"
   (b) a flashlight   in "Heat Lightning"
   (c) the cross   in "Dracula"
   (d) a mirror   in "The Dogs of War"

2. References to characters who never appear onstage help to prepare the audience for the threat that awaits a character in two of the plays you have read. How does Mina's death in "Dracula" serve this purpose? Why is it important that the first owner of the monkey's paw wished for death?

3. Playwrights often call upon the forces of nature to emphasize the mood of a play. How do the following natural acts serve this purpose:
   (a) the storm in "Heat Lightning"
   (b) the wind near the cemetery in "The Monkey's Paw"
   (c) the blazing desert heat in "I Shot an Arrow"

4. In some of the plays you have read, love is a force capable of overcoming evil. How does the power of love express itself in "Dracula"? In "The Dogs of War"?

5. Challenging situations bring out courage or cowardice in people. It may be a physical, a psychological or even a moral courage or weakness. Describe the situation that calls for courage in "Flight into Danger," "I Shot an Arrow," "The Dogs of War" and "Dracula." Which characters meet the challenge? Which fail? How does their behavior affect the outcome of the play?

6. The presence of evil or terror is sometimes emphasized by the innocence of the setting in which it occurs. Contrast the setting and the events in "Dracula," "The Dogs of War," "The Monkey's Paw" and "Trifles."

Vocabulary Review

1. The vocabulary questions at the end of each of the plays helped you understand meaning through *context*—the way in which the words were used in sentences.

   Another help to word understanding is recognizing *word parts*. If you can recognize the *prefix, root* or *suffix* in unfamiliar words, you may be able to work out the meaning of the word.

   (a) *Prefixes* are placed in front of words. Here are some Latin prefixes frequently used in English words:

Prefix	Meaning
ad-	to, toward
im-, in-, ir-, il-	not
mal-	bad
non-	not
post-	after, afterward
pro-	forward
re-	back, again
trans-	across

   (b) *Roots* contain the basic meaning of the word. These are frequently used Latin roots:

Root	Meaning
cide	kill
cred	believe
fac, fact	work, do, function
finit	finish, end
ject	throw
port	carry
rex, regis	king
sanitas	health
scrib, script	write
strat	stretch out, cover
volo	wish, free will

   Following is a list of words from the plays you have read. Apply the meanings of roots and prefixes to analyze the structure and work out the meanings of each word.

infinity	malfunction	project
incredible	nondescript	prostrate
involuntary	posterity	regicide
	sanitarium	

Can you analyze and define these common words?

transport	illegal	suicide
transcribe	factory	report
reject	finite	

(c) A word part added to the end of a root word is called a *suffix*. A suffix can both add to the word's meaning and change its use so that it can do a different job in the sentence.

Suffix	*Meaning*	*Part of Speech Formed*
-able, -ible	able to be, capable of	adjective
-ly	in the manner of	adverb
-ous, -ive, -ful	full of, characterized by	adjective
-sion, -tion	act of, state of	noun
-some	like, tending to, characterized by	adjective

What is the meaning of each of the following words? How is the meaning extended or changed by the suffix? Use each word in a sentence related to a character or an incident in one of the plays you have read.

awesome	sanitation	cessation
feebly	perilous	credible
viciously	pensive	solicitous

2. *Synonyms* are words with similar meanings. *Antonyms* are words that have opposite meanings. In comparing and contrasting characters, situations or settings, synonyms and antonyms are useful in bringing out similarities and differences. Each of the adjectives listed below is followed by a series of words, one of which is similar in meaning and one opposite. Find the synonym and antonym for each of the listed words.

covert	aboveboard, awesome, secret, piercing
drab	dull, feeble, strident, colorful
placid	disturbed, careful, hateful, calm
puny	involuntary, feeble, powerful, credible

crafty	extravagant, tedious, straightforward, cunning
facetious	abashed, solemn, sensible, joking
strident	harsh-sounding, talkative, melodious, shy
wary	trusting, wonderful, cautious, astute

Glossary

ACTION: a series of related incidents forming the plot of a play.

ANTAGONIST: the person who clashes with the main character (protagonist).

BUSINESS: gestures and actions left to the discretion of the individual actor or director such as opening a drawer, writing a letter, taking a drink.

CHARACTERIZATION: the creation and convincing representation through action and speech of characters in a play.

CLIMAX: the highest point of a dramatic action and the major turning point in the story.

CLOSE-UP: a camera shot taken at close range.

COMEDY: drama designed to entertain the audience, usually having a happy ending.

COMPLICATION: a detail, incident or situation introduced into a play that extends the action, heightens the suspense, and prolongs the struggle.

CONFLICT: the struggle between opposing factors, whether these be people, forces or ideas. **external conflict:** the struggle between the important character and an outside force. **internal conflict:** the struggle that occurs within the heart and mind of an important character.

CUT TO: in television, a fast switch from one scene to another.

DIALOGUE: conversation between characters.

DISSOLVE: in television, the gradual fading out of one picture and simultaneous fading in of another.

EXPOSITION: the opening action and dialogue which tells the audience who the characters are, where they are, what important events preceded the opening of the play, and what the situation is at the present time.

FADE-IN: the gradual appearance of the picture on the television screen, or the gradual increase in sound.

FADE-OUT: the gradual fading of the picture until the television screen is darkened, or the gradual decrease in sound until nothing can be heard.

FALLING ACTION: the action following the climax of a play. During this final section, sometimes referred to as *resolution* or *dénouement*, the conflict is resolved and the play is brought to an end.

FORESHADOWING: the important clues in a play that prepare the reader or audience for the events that are to come.

IRONY: an outcome of events contrary to what was, or might have been, expected. **dramatic irony:** a form of irony in which the audience knows something about which the character in the play is unaware. This irony occurs when the character says something that means more to the audience than to anyone in the play.

MELODRAMA: a play characterized by exaggerated sentiment, violence and passion. The emphasis is not on characterization or ideas, but on the creation of a sensational effect.

MONOLOGUE: a long speech said by a single actor.

NARRATOR: the actor who tells the story, speaking directly to the reader or audience. In television drama, the narrator is frequently a voice heard offstage as the action proceeds.

PANTOMIME: action carried out solely through significant movement and gesture, without speech.

PLOT: the series of incidents or episodes that make up the entire action of the play.

PROPS: (short for **properties**) objects used and handled by actors in the play, such as weapons, mirrors, household objects, religious items.

PROTAGONIST: the main character in a drama, the one most reponsible for bringing the conflict to an end.

RESOLUTION: the working out of a conflict in a play; the concluding action.

RISING ACTION: the series of events which intensify the conflict and lead to the climax.

SET: the constructed environment of a play within which the action takes place.

SETTING: the time and place of the story. In a stage or television play, the setting is indicated by the author in introductory stage directions. Sometimes it is related by the narrator's voice heard offscreen.

SOLILOQUY: the lines spoken by a character to him- or herself through which thoughts and feelings are revealed.

STAGE DIRECTIONS: the instructions in the script to directors, actors and technicians. These are usually italicized and in parentheses.

STAGE DIVISIONS:

UPSTAGE: toward the back wall of the stage.

DOWNSTAGE: toward the audience.

STAGE LEFT: to the actor's left as he or she faces the audience.

STAGE RIGHT: to the actor's right.

CENTER: the middle of the playing area.

OFFSTAGE: behind the setting; out of sight.

ONSTAGE: in the playing area; in view of the audience.

SUSPENSE: that quality in a literary work that makes the reader or audience uncertain or tense about what is to come next.

THEME: the idea, the view of life or human behavior dramatized through the characters and action of the play.

Writing Manual

Narrative

For Writing Projects:
#1, p. 13 ("Heat Lightning")
#2, p. 59 ("Flight into Danger")
#1, p. 96 ("The Dogs of War")
#1, p. 138 ("The Monkey's Paw")
#2, p. 138 ("The Monkey's Paw")
#1, p. 194 ("Dracula")

Each of these assignments has to do with *writing narrative*, or simply "telling a story." The events of a story are told in the order in which they happen (**chronological order**). They are linked together with **transitions**—single words like *later, before, next, then, during*, and groups of words like *at that instant, in a few days, not long afterwards*. These transitions act as signposts to keep the reader aware of the passage of time. They play an important part in a narrative.

Equally important are strong **action words** and vivid **descriptive words**. Look at the following narrative passage about a pearl diver's fight with an octopus:

At that instant I felt something touch me lightly on the arm. Instinct and underwater training saved my life. Quick as a flash, before I had the least notion of what it was, I whirled about, grabbing the razor sharp knife from my belt sheath, and slashed three or four times with a full sweep of my arms in the direction of this touch. By luck I severed two of the lassoing arms that were gripping me; in another instant the octopus would have had my two arms pinioned and I should have been helpless.

As I slashed and felt the blade cut through a mass of soft flesh, an arm took hold of me around the ankle. Then a second arm clutched the other ankle. A vicious jerk at my legs almost upset me.

Each time I tried to cut my ankles free, the creature jerked me so violently that I seemed to be a little boy pulled about at will by a strong man; it was with greatest difficulty that I kept my footing. The helmet and breastplate banged against my head and chest with punishing force. One jerk dashed me against a rock and left me breathless. The force of the beast was terrific and produced a deathly sense of fear. Also, the cold intelligence with which he appeared to anticipate my actions, and checkmate my every attempt, had a deep effect on nervous resistance.

It was life or death. Body and mind were working as if they had no relation to each other; one was straining, struggling, fighting against these violent, shattering tugs, trying to cut, to stab, to free myself; the other, somewhere, was carefully weighing chances, considering the elements of the situation, attempting to decide whether I dared to give the danger signal.

The author describes a tense, life-threatening encounter from which he miraculously escaped. The action is quick, almost frantic; it grips the reader. Notice how verbs like *whirled, slashed, clutched* and adjectives like *razor-sharp, vicious, shattering* add to the feeling of violent action and heighten the mood of the frantic encounter. See, too, how the transitions from action to action (*at that instant, quick as a flash, each time*) point up the rapid sequence of events.

Whether you are writing a plot summary, a new version of a story, a letter, a diary entry, a report, or any other kind of narrative, it is important to keep these ideas in mind.

Description

For Writing Projects
#1 p. 77 ("I Shot an Arrow")
#2 p. 115 ("Trifles")

How do you describe a place so clearly that your reader actually sees it? How can you reproduce in words a noisy party, a quiet cabin by the lake, a brightly decorated gym or the marching band at half-time? You can do all this if you pay careful attention to three things: **(1) adequate details (2) a strong, single impression (3) space transitions**.

Adequate details: To help your reader see, hear, smell and feel the place you are describing, you must provide specific details. Never settle for the easy generalization. Instead, support the generalization with concrete detail. Contrast the generalization and the specifics in the following examples.

(a) *Generalization:* Her locker was a mess.
   Specific details: Her locker was crammed with a dirty gym suit, three library books, a raincoat, a poster for art class, a pair of sneakers with no laces and a half-eaten baloney sandwich.

204 👈 _____ Writing Manual

(b) *Generalization:* The house looked deserted.
   Specific details: The empty house stared at us from a weed-choked lawn, its windows broken, its front door ajar, its porch steps twisted like a lopsided grin.

Strong single impression: When you have chosen a place to describe, make a list of all sight, sound, even smell and touch details that you can remember. Then look over your list. What single strong feeling does your list create? Put this feeling in a word or phrase. If some of your details do not support this generalization, cross them out. Everything in your description should contribute to the dominant feeling you have chosen.

Read the following paragraph taken from Bram Stoker's *Dracula*, the novel on which the play in your text is based. In this paragraph, the narrator describes his approach to Dracula's castle. One sentence, not present in the original, has been added. See if you can find the sentence which does not belong.

When I could see again, the driver was climbing into the caleche [carriage], and the wolves had disappeared. This was all so strange and uncanny that a dreadful fear came upon me, and I was afraid to speak or move. There was something restful in the darkness that made me feel sleepy and at peace with the world. The time seemed interminable as we swept on our way, now almost in complete darkness, for the rolling clouds obscured the moon. We kept on ascending, with occasional periods of quick descent, but in the main always ascending. Suddenly, I became conscious of the fact that the driver was in the act of pulling up the horses in the courtyard of a vast ruined castle, from whose tall black windows came no ray of light, and whose broken battlements showed a jagged line against the moonlit sky.

The paragraph creates a sense of mystery. Words like *strange, uncanny, ruined castle, broken battlements, jagged line* reinforce this feeling. Even at first reading it is clear that the third sentence breaks the mood created by the rest of the paragraph. Words like *restful, sleepy* and *at peace* intrude on the weird, strange atmosphere of the original description.

Space transitions: Unlike a photograph, your paragraph cannot give the reader all the details of a scene in one quick view. Instead, you must pan, as a movie camera does, from one section of the place you are describing to another. This movement should be orderly and logical, not haphazard. You might start at the front of a room, for instance, and move slowly to the back, or start at one side and cross to the other. Transitions like *in front of, behind,* *above, beneath* and *across from* help to show your reader the physical relationship of the different parts of your description. Like the time transitions, these space transitions keep your reader from getting lost.

Exposition—Developing a Paragraph with Reasons

For Writing Project:
#2, p. 96 ("The Dogs of War")

A good way to prove a point (or get people to accept a certain view, as in this assignment) is to find strong reasons to support it. Your reasons must be separate and distinct from one another: if they blend together, you have only one reason. To be most effective, you should present your reasons in the order of importance, putting the strongest reason last, and expanding each reason with supporting details.

The following paragraph gives reasons for the importance of the quarterback in football. Note the careful structure of the paragraph—the **topic sentence**, two **reasons** (each developed with specifics), and the **concluding sentence**.

> The job of the quarterback is the most demanding one on a football team. The quarterback is responsible for the offensive moves of his team. He is the strategist who decides what plays will best counter the defensive tactics of the opposition. In this sense, he is like a field general commanding the troops. In addition to these mental demands, he must be a superb athlete. He must pass accurately, hand-off precisely and face the charging lineman fearlessly. He must even be ready to run with the ball himself if a play misfires. It's no wonder that coaches think of the quarterback as the sparkplug of the team.

Note that the two reasons (the quarterback must think out the team strategy; the quarterback must be a superb athlete) are connected by the transition words *in addition*. Moreover, the reasons are presented in order of importance, and each is supported with explanatory details.

The sentence-by-sentence structure of the eight-sentence paragraph, then, looks like this:

Topic sentence

Reason One (responsibility for offensive moves)
    First detail (decision to counter defensive tactics)
    Second detail (behavior is like a general's)

Reason Two (athletic ability)
    First detail (ability to pass, hand-off, face lineman)
    Second detail (readiness to run with ball)

Concluding sentence

Make an outline similar to this one for Anton's speech to his people. Naturally, the number of supporting details you have under each reason will depend on the reason itself.

Exposition—Developing a Paragraph with Factual Details

For Writing Project:
#1, p. 115 ("Trifles")

This assignment requires that you support a statement with factual details. The following paragraph shows the destructive effect of hurricanes by presenting facts about the damage they cause. After reading the paragraph, note the factual details that develop it.

> A hurricane is one of nature's most damaging storms. Gale-force winds cause electrical outages, create dangerous flying debris and even collapse buildings. Part of the hurricane damage may come from the tornadoes that often accompany such a storm. In addition, high tides and storm surges send waves of twenty feet or more crashing over the land. Heavy rainfall, an ever-present part of the storm, causes flooding in low-lying areas and landslides in hilly country. Weather forecasters have learned how to track hurricanes and to warn residents in their path. But they have not yet learned how to prevent these devastating storms.

Note these points.

- The author begins with a **general statement** characterizing the effects of hurricanes.
- The generalization is followed by noting **facts** about the storm and the specific type of damage caused (*winds cause electrical outages, flying debris and collapsed buildings; high tides send waves over the land; heavy rains cause flooding and landslides*).
- Two of the sentences are joined with the **transition** words *in addition*.
- The paragraph concludes with a **comment** about the advances in forecasting hurricanes and the failure in preventing them.

Exposition—Developing a Paragraph with Contrasts

For Writing Project:
#2, p. 77 ("I Shot an Arrow")

One good way to present the particular qualities of a person, place or thing is to **contrast** it with something else. A playwright may contrast two characters in order to make their individual qualities stand out. It is through this contrast that we see them clearly as people. In "I Shot an Arrow," the contrast between Donlin and Corey helps to highlight the strength of one and the weakness of the other.

Writing contrast requires careful planning and logical development. Here is an example of a passage that develops one writer's view of the difference between cats and dogs.

> Although both are good pets, cats and dogs differ in the demands they make on an owner and the companionship they offer. Cats are easier to care for than dogs. They housebreak easily, they don't require daily walking, and they are usually quite content to be left alone for several hours at a time. Dogs, on the other hand, must be carefully house-broken, a process that can be difficult and time-consuming. In addition, they must be walked daily. Finally, if left alone for a long period of time, they may break training or become deliberately destructive.
>
> When it comes to companionship, however, cats do not provide the same warmth and responsiveness that dogs do. Cats are essentially in-dependent creatures. Return home after an absence of several hours and your cat *may* rub against your leg or jump into your lap and purr. On the other hand, it may simply ignore you. The dog, by contrast, seems total-ly dependent upon its master. It will greet you after a lengthy separation with noisy, wagging, irrepressible delight. Some people like the indepen-dent aloofness of the cat; others are charmed by the dog's constant show of affection.

The passage opens with a **topic sentence** presenting the two major areas the author will contrast (cats as pets; dogs as pets). Then comes two **general points of difference**.

The first point (the animal's demands on its owner) is divided into three **specific sub-points** (housebreaking; walking; breaking training). The second general point (companionship), meanwhile, is not divided into sub-points, but is supported by **illustrative examples** (cat may rub up against you or not; dog will always show affection).

Transitions are used throughout. Contrasting ideas are introduced by word-groups like *on the other hand, however* and *by contrast*. Other transitions (*in addition, finally*) come before additional examples.

Notice that the order in which the two contrasted ideas are presented in the topic sentence (cats first, dogs second) is maintained throughout the passage. An outline for the whole passage would look like this:

I. First point of difference
   A. Cat
      Dog
   B. Cat
      Dog
   C. Cat
      Dog
II. Second point of difference
      Cat
      Dog

As you can see, the writer has organized these paragraphs by points of difference. Suppose the writer had chosen to organize another way, giving all the information about cats first and then all the information about dogs. Then the paragraphs would look like this:

I. Cats
   A. First point of difference
      1.
      2.
      3.
   B. Second point of difference
II. Dogs
   A. First point of difference
      1.
      2.
      3.
   B. Second point of difference

You will find it helpful to use one of these two organizational plans in writing your paragraph(s) on Donlin and Corey. Don't forget: establish an order of names in your topic sentence (Donlin-Corey or Corey-Donlin), and then stick with it.

Dialogue

For Writing Projects:
#2, p. 13 ("Heat Lightning")
#1, p. 58 ("Flight into Danger")

Talk is an important part of life. We all talk constantly—to friends, family, strangers, sometimes even to ourselves. Our days are filled with *dialogue*.

Dialogue is the backbone of drama. Playwrights use it to reveal character, to show emotion, to establish a situation, to advance a plot, to create a mood and to build suspense.

The ability to write good dialogue is one of the most important skills a writer can have. No one is born with it; an ear for dialogue has to be developed. Here are some suggestions to help you learn this art.

1. Listen to the talk of people around you. Become aware of the **dynamics** of dialogue. Listen to a small group of friends or the family at the dinner table. Do people finish all their sentences? Do they interrupt one another? Do they really listen to one another and respond or do some people keep harping on a single point, regardless of what others say? Does the conversation have a tempo and movement? See if it doesn't rise to peaks of intensity and then diminish. Watch for changes from slow and leisurely talk to a fast-paced exchange.

2. Observe how **emotion** affects what people say and the way they say it. Listen to people in an argument. How do they show anger? How do others show joy? Sorrow? Fear? Listen to the talk of very old people and children. How do they sound? Become aware of the way speech can show character. Listen to the talk of friends and relatives. What little **oddities** of speech do you hear? Any mispronunciations? Favorite expressions?

3. Study the dialogue of professional writers. Dialogue in a play differs from actual speech, of course. In a play the writer makes every word count. There is no idle talk filling the gaps between important conversation. Every bit of dialogue is designed to **show character, advance plot** or **create a mood**.

In "Heat Lightning," the author uses dialogue to show the thoughts and emotions of his two characters, to intensify the relationship between them and to create a feeling of suspense. Before beginning either of the assignments on dialogue, turn back to "Heat Lightning." Starting with the first line of the play (p. 3) and going only as far as the stage direction on p. 6, *She moves toward the door up Left,* study the dialogue. Pay close attention to these things:

- The number of unfinished sentences and interruptions.
- The importance of each word and line (there is no "dead wood").
- The way in which character is shown through dialogue (the Girl's contradictions, for example, show that she is nervous and unsure).
- The fact that the dialogue, like actual conversation, has tempo (pace) and movement (it reaches a height of intensity when the Man coaxes the Girl into admitting that she could identify the flashlight).
- The way that the dialogue advances the plot (by the end of this passage we know the Man is planning to do away with the Girl).

Business Letter

For Writing Project:
#2, p. 194 ("Dracula")

Following is a sample business letter preceded by an **outline**. The form of the letter is standard. It always includes these five parts: a **heading,** an **inside address,** a **salutation**, the **body** (actual text) of the letter, and a **complimentary close**.

Outline

I. HEADING
   A. Writer's address (no
      abbreviations—2 lines)
   B. Date

II. INSIDE ADDRESS
   Name and address as they are
   to appear on the envelope—3
   lines (sometimes 4)

III. SALUTATION
   A. The name of a specific person
       preceded by "Dear"; use "Dear
       Sir or Madam" if only the name
       of the company is known
   B. Follow the name of the person
       or company with a colon (:)

IV. BODY OF LETTER

V. COMPLIMENTARY CLOSE
   A. Two words followed by
       a comma; capitalize only
       the first word (e.g.,
       Yours truly," "Yours
       sincerely")
   B. Your name

Letter

236 Ocean Spray Road
Daytona Beach, Florida   32014
October 3, 198_

Department of Programing
WFTV
P.O. Box 999
Orlando, Florida   32802

Dear Sir or Madam:

   My friends and I often watch the Wednesday night movie on your station. Many of the films you show are ones that came out when we were too
young to go to the movies, or even before we were born. It is good to be able
to see some of the classics that our older relatives still talk about.

   Now I have a request for a particular film. My English class has just fin-
ished reading *The Good Earth* and I would really like to see the movie based
on this book. It came out in the thirties, quite a bit before my time, but I have

heard about it from several older people, and if all they say about it is true, it is a great film.

I think this movie would, like the book, appeal to a general audience. People are very interested in China, and Pearl Buck's novel deals with an important period in Chinese history. It shows what life was like at the turn of the century for a poor farmer living through famine, flood and the battles of local war lords. It shows the low position of women at the time, something today's woman will find unbelievable. It also shows the beginning of the Chinese Revolution and the social changes coming about. All this makes the book very educational.

In addition to being as educational as the book, the movie is probably very exciting to watch. My family tells me that Louise Rainer was a fine actress and Paul Muni was certainly a famous star. Their acting and the very dramatic episodes of the book must combine to make a great film. People who have seen it talk about one scene in particular — the coming of the locusts. I spoke to people who saw the movie more than thirty years ago and they still remember that scene.

I hope you can schedule *The Good Earth* for one of your Wednesday night movies. I can't guarantee a huge audience, but I can promise you an enthusiastic one.

Sincerely yours,

Cathleen Engels

Since this particular assignment asks you to provide *reasons* why your librarian should order copies of the play, you might want to look at "Developing a Paragraph with Reasons" (p. 205) before starting to write. Notice that in the sample letter you just read the writer gives 2 good reasons why the program should be run (it is educational; it is probably exciting).